RELIGION AND SCIENCE AS FORMS OF LIFE

RELIGION AND SCIENCE AS FORMS OF LIFE

ANTHROPOLOGICAL INSIGHTS INTO REASON AND UNREASON

Edited by

Carles Salazar and Joan Bestard

berghahn

NEW YORK · OXFORD

www.berghahnbooks.com

Published in 2015 by
Berghahn Books
www.berghahnbooks.com

Library of Congress Cataloging-in-Publication Data

Religion and science as forms of life : anthropological insights into reason and unreason / edited by Carles Salazar and Joan Bestard.
    pages cm
Includes bibliographical references.
ISBN 978-1-78238-488-5 (hardback : alk. paper) – ISBN 978-1-78238-
489-2 (ebook)
1. Ethnology–Religious aspects. 2. Religion and science. 3. Faith and
reason. I. Salazar, Carles, editor of compilation. II. Bestard-Camps,
Joan, editor of compilation.
BL256.R438 2015
201'.65–dc23

                                                                    2014029067

British Library Cataloguing in Publication Data
A catalogue record for this book is available from the British Library

Printed on acid-free paper.

ISBN: 978-1-78238-488-5 hardback
ISBN: 978-1-78238-489-2 ebook

Contents

§§

Introduction

Science, Religion and Forms of Life

Carles Salazar

> We come to an island and we find beliefs there, and certain beliefs we are inclined to call religious ... Entirely different connections would make them into religious beliefs, and there can easily be imagined transitions where we wouldn't know for our life whether to call them religious beliefs or scientific beliefs.
> —Ludwig Wittgenstein, *Lectures and Conversations on Aesthetics, Psychology and Religious Belief*

Science and religion are modes of thought, ways of knowing or forms of life that have been pervasive in Western cultural formations for the last three to four centuries. As theories about the world and human life, they have often engendered conflicting viewpoints redolent of acrimonious social and cultural struggles. However, all theories and systems of truth are, simultaneously, the product of human endeavours, creations of the human mind in particular social and cultural contexts. The purpose of this book is to reflect upon the relationships, possible articulations and/or contradictions between religion and science as quintessentially human phenomena. Our goal is not to come up with another sociology, psychology or anthropology of religion and science, but to cross (question?) disciplinary boundaries in the analysis of an indisputably complex issue. Even though the majority of the contributors to this volume are anthropologists, we take a rather literalistic approach to the meaning of our discipline, which we define simply as the 'study of the human'. The common denominator of all the contributions consists, precisely, of seeing science and religion as human phenomena, as the products of socially and culturally situated, biologically evolved human minds. Thus, a first and the main boundary we wish to cross is that between naturalistic

1

and humanistic or social-scientific approaches. Admittedly, there is still a long way to go to achieve an integrated science of culture. However, dialogue between different viewpoints and disciplinary traditions is a necessary step towards that laudable (in our opinion) aim. Secondly, there are somewhat more mundane academic niches that we also wish to bring together, specifically those of anthropologists (with their different areas of specialization), sociologists, philosophers and religious scholars, theoretical workers and 'fieldworkers', all of whom have participated in this project.

Our hypothesis is that the study of the relationships between science and religion is about to enter a new phase, because those relationships are bound to change in our contemporary world, that of the so-called 'knowledge societies'. We believe that scientific knowledge has become increasingly relevant in the day-to-day life of many populations, beyond the institutional public spaces where it has traditionally developed. We wish to identify the possible tensions that this new development of scientific knowledge is likely to produce as regards religious beliefs, modes of thinking that have historically been hegemonic in both public spaces and individual consciousness. Thus, our purpose is to flesh out such reflection with theoretical and ethnographic research on different manifestations of scientific and religious cultures in the contemporary world. Our starting point is viewing science and religion as 'forms of life'. What exactly does that mean? Do we consider them fully commensurate systems of thought? Do we believe in science in the same way as we believe in religion?

The Anthropology of Belief

Here, I would like to make explicit some of the concepts that underlie the arguments put forward by the contributors to this volume. While I am sure that not all of them would agree with my particular interpretation of their theoretical toolkit, this is certainly a way of bringing their manifold arguments and approaches closer together. Let me start with the concepts of form of life and belief. A form of life is not a doctrine, not a theory of the world, but a form of engaging with the world (see Pina-Cabral, this volume), a form of 'dwelling' in that world (Ingold 2000). Let us suppose that science and religion can be seen from this perspective. To engage with the world, an organism does not need to have a theory, but it certainly needs to entertain some beliefs concerning that world (Salazar 2014). What, then, is a belief?

Belief is one of the most controversial concepts in the social sciences, especially in anthropology (Needham 1972; Ruel 1982; Good 1993; Kirsch 2004; Robbins 2007: 14–16; Lindquist and Coleman 2008; Carlisle and

Simon 2012; cf. Sperber 1996: 86–97; Saler 2001; Lanman 2008). Sometimes the alleged inappropriateness of the concept of belief is said to have its origins in the contrast with knowledge. 'We' (scientists, Westerners) have knowledge, 'they' (lay people, 'primitives') have beliefs (Good 1993: 14–24). This is just a matter of perspective. Whatever is knowledge to one person can be seen as belief by someone else. The attribution of knowledge does not entail the distinction between mental state and external reality. A person who knows that it is raining cannot be wrong, so there should be a perfect correspondence between their mental state and the external reality related thereto, otherwise the person does not really know what is going on. The attribution of belief, in contrast, is unthinkable without that distinction. A person who believes it is raining can be right or wrong. Thus, everything points to belief being, first and foremost, something that happens in people's minds, a mental state or representation, potentially different from events in the external world. Is this really the case though?

Are beliefs really mental states? Where do we store them? How do we elicit them? Can they be downloaded as if they were computer programs? Or are they just dispositions to behave in a certain way? In a celebrated essay, Rodney Needham argued that the state of believing in something has no external appearance: 'Where, then, do we get the notion of belief from? From the verb "believe" and its inflected forms, in everyday English usage. Statements of belief are the only evidence for the phenomenon; but the phenomenon itself appears to be no more than the custom of making such statements' (Needham 1972: 108; cf. Saler 2001). Beliefs are mental states attributed to an agent, but they should not be confused with thoughts. We can safely say that people sitting in a train believe it will take them to a particular destination. What is important, however, is that they do not have to be thinking about it for that attribution of belief to be true. So, where is that belief? It could be argued that it is, somehow, somewhere inside their minds, but what about their brains? Is the brain of someone who believes that the train will take them to a particular place in any way different from that of someone who does not entertain such a belief?

We like to think that we need brains to have beliefs, but, interestingly, this does not seem to be either a sufficient or necessary condition for the state of believing to occur. By itself, a brain does not believe in anything. As the philosopher Peter Hacker has argued, 'If someone believes something to be so, then he is either right or wrong; but his being in such-and-such neural state cannot be either right or wrong' (Hacker 2007: 252; see also Bennett and Hacker 2003: 431–45). Additionally, belief can perhaps be properly attributed to brainless entities, such as computers (Dennett 1989: 287–300). If brainless entities can have beliefs, belief originates not so much in any inherent quality of the believing entity but in attribution. What we should therefore try to find out is what conditions make the attribution of belief plausible. Furthermore, if belief originates in attribution, the key component of belief is not brain activity but interaction. At some stage in the belief–attribution chain there certainly has to be a brain, or something that works like a brain. On that basis, we might also talk about interaction between brains, and perhaps some brainless entities, as the fundamental condition for belief attribution.

If interaction turns out to be a key component of the concept of be-lief, the analysis of belief must then be the analysis of a form of interaction rather than a set of propositions, which is what the analysis of a theory or a doctrine involves (see Coleman, Pina-Cabral, Sørensen, this volume). We can see how closely related the concepts of belief and form of life happen to be when we look at belief from this perspective. The interaction we are talking about is part of the way of engaging with the world which defines a particular form of life. This is a fundamental common denominator of the contributions to this volume. We can study interactions in all sorts of differ-ent ways, ethnographically or otherwise, but viewing beliefs as interactions places all such different approaches to the study of belief on a similar level, as if they were all aimed at answering the same or very similar questions. Let us now be a bit more specific as regards the concept of belief itself. What about religious beliefs? In what way do they differ from the general kind of belief we have just considered?

A common position in anthropology, echoed in Good's sceptical stance concerning the opposition between belief and knowledge, is to argue that there is no such thing as religious beliefs as a valid cross-cultural category because we cannot have a cross-cultural concept of religion. 'My argument is that there cannot be a universal definition of religion, not only because its constituent elements and relationships are historically specific, but because that definition is itself the historical product of discursive processes' (Asad 1993: 29). The alleged anthropological uselessness of the concept of religion is a laudable position (upheld by some contributors to this volume) that, in-terestingly, has been defended equally well on the basis of very theoretically distinct approaches (see Boyer 2010). However, if religion happens to be cross-culturally inapplicable due to its historical specificity, the same would apply to the majority of social-scientific concepts (Saler 2000: x).[1]

A more pragmatic attitude would be to try to see how, despite the his-torical specificity of our concept of religion (or of any concept for that mat-ter), certain of its arbitrarily chosen characteristics can be said to have, with all due qualifications, universal or nearly universal validity. Suppose that among those characteristics we decide to include belief in the existence of supernatural agents with whom humans quite often (though not always) interact in various forms. Again, the universality of the natural/supernatural distinction has not gone unchallenged (Taylor 2007: 780–81, n.19). Admittedly, there are substantial cultural components in the definition of any supernatural (or natural) entity. This does not necessarily entail the impossibility of a cross-cultural concept of the supernatural, however. Let us try to spell this out.

It can be cogently argued that humans all over the world must entertain some notion of what ordinary reality looks like, that is, the reality humans encounter while going about their daily business of survival and reproduction. We can approach this somewhat fuzzy notion of ordinary reality as an instantiation of our intuitive ontologies (Boyer 1996) or as the genuine product of what Schutz skilfully described as our 'natural attitude' (Schutz 1945: 552–53). True, ordinary reality is likely to vary notably in different environments inhabited by humans. At a certain, very basic level though, those differences will tend to be minimal. All humans, whatever the environment they happen to live in, must draw very elementary distinctions between living and non-living things, between humans and non-humans, between kin and non-kin, friends and foes, dead and alive, prey and predator, past, present and future, and so on. There is no need to postulate any innate or 'hard-wired' predisposition to entertain such notions (cf. Boyer 2001: 112–13). Our natural attitude results from interaction between our poorly specified cognitive equipment and the sort of general environment humans have been living in for much of their evolutionary history.[2]

So, if there is such a thing as a natural attitude and an ordinary reality, we could define the sort of world that results from major violations of the main tenets of that natural reality, violations of our ontological intuitions, as constituting some form of 'extraordinary' or 'supernatural' reality. Familiar instances of such violations would be inanimate objects that behave as if they were human agents, beings who exist but are invisible, who are alive and do not die, who can simultaneously be in different places, and who wield all sorts of superhuman powers, such as knowing our deepest thoughts at all times, resurrecting the dead, and so forth. Let us set aside the matter of what kind of violations they are, bearing in mind that not just any violation would do to properly constitute that supernatural reality. Boyer (1994, 2001) and others have done substantial research on this issue, so there is no need to repeat it here. There is, however, a slightly different question I wish to raise. What does believing in that supernatural reality entail? What could the difference be, if there is any, between beliefs of this type – let us call them religious beliefs – and the rest of our beliefs, beliefs in our ordinary reality? Some would be tempted to argue that believing in such supernatural agents is merely an illusion, for those beings do not really exist. Ordinary human minds produce illusions of this kind in the same way as a schizophrenic mind produces all sorts of hallucinatory sensations. The question is: Why? Why do normal human minds, which do not suffer from any apparent dysfunction, organic or otherwise, make us entertain such patently false beliefs?

Within the cognitive science of religion, there are two main paradigms that attempt to provide an answer to that question: adaptationism and non-adaptationism. Adaptationists propose that these illusionary beliefs, no matter how false they happen to be, fulfilled an adaptive role in ancestral environments, in such a way that those who held them managed to have more children than those who did not, and were thus able to pass on their belief-prone genes to subsequent generations more successfully than the others (see Blume, this volume). Non-adaptationists, in contrast, consider that religious beliefs are a mere by-product of the human mind, and did not fulfil any adaptive role in human evolutionary history. On that basis, the human mind would produce religious beliefs in the same way as a car engine makes noise, even though it has not been specifically designed for that purpose (see McCauley, this volume).[3] Both perspectives certainly provide solid arguments to try to account for the existence of these somewhat strange illusions that we call religious beliefs. Our problem, however, is with the very concept of illusion. Are religious beliefs really 'illusory'? Note that it is not the metaphysical question of the actual existence of God or gods that we are raising now, but the more mundane (though no less important) issue of the nature of so-called mental illusions. Are we correct in equating religious beliefs with the hallucinations of a schizophrenic?

In his seminal work on the sociology of religion, Emile Durkheim made the following observation:

> It is inadmissible that systems of ideas like religions, which have held so considerable a place in history, and to which, in all times, men have come to receive the energy which they must have to live, should be made up of a tissue of illusions ... How could a vain fantasy have been able to fashion the human consciousness so strongly and so durably? (Durkheim 1915: 68–69)

Durkheim was right to question the alleged illusory nature of religious beliefs, although perhaps for the wrong reasons (Salazar n.d.). Our minds can create all sorts of illusions – that is, false beliefs – which may very well persist either because they fulfil some kind of adaptive function – what McKay and Dennett call 'positive illusions' (McKay and Dennett 2009: 505–7) – or merely because they are not hopelessly maladaptive. Consider our common-sense notions of space and time as absolute values. Ever since Einstein, we know that they are not absolute values, that the only such value is the speed of light. However, in the ordinary life of the majority of humans, including that of physicists, it would be utterly useless, and extremely cumbersome, to take Einstein's theory of relativity as our foundational belief concerning the nature of space and time. Our common-sense belief in the absolute values of space and time is thus a 'useful', probably adaptive illusion. Durkheim was mistaken, then, in thinking that mere illusions cannot fashion human consciousness strongly and durably. Is that also true in the case of religious beliefs though?

Science and Religion as Modes of Believing

Anthropologists should be well placed to deal with this question, since only a proper ethnography of belief can tell us exactly what religious belief, or any belief for that matter, is all about. Unfortunately, mainstream anthropology has historically tackled this subject matter from the wrong angle, so to speak. At one extreme, we have those who deny that there is such a thing as religious beliefs, because there is no such thing as religion as a cross-cultural phenomenon to begin with. We have already seen that, setting nominalistic controversies aside, this is a scientifically unproductive and misleading approach. At the other extreme, we have the apparently opposite perspective, which nonetheless ends up formulating a very similar argument. To put it bluntly, 'everything' is religion in so-called primitive societies, according to this view. The intellectual genealogy of this approach can be traced back to Lucien Lévy-Bruhl and his infamous theory of 'pre-logical' mentality (Lévy-Bruhl 1926). Savages' minds are so different from ours, argued Lévy-Bruhl, that they do not even think in logical terms as we do. Lévy-Bruhl was not even referring to complex logical reasoning, but to very elementary rules of Aristotelian logic, such as the principle of identity and that of non-contradiction, which savages supposedly did not follow, instead being submerged in a 'mystical' world wherein invisible and imperceptible forces were seen as the efficient cause of everything that happened (ibid.: 35–45). Although outstanding figures in the history of anthropology subsequently questioned, with very sound arguments, the existence of this pre-logical mentality (e.g. Evans-Pritchard 1934), and the majority of post-Malinowskian anthropologists (and eventually Lévy-Bruhl himself) rejected the crude evolutionist line of reasoning of framing the sequence from pre-logical to logical, the notion that religious or quasi-religious thinking is all-pervasive outside the secularized West, specifically among peasant and tribal peoples, has been prominent in modern anthropology. Whereas we draw a sharp distinction between the religious and the non-religious, the immanent and the transcendent, the natural and the supernatural, they do not. For them (whoever 'they' happen to be), religion is practically everything and everywhere.[4]

Somewhat paradoxically perhaps, the alleged over-religiosity of the subjects of anthropological enquiry has prevented many anthropologists from exploring the real nature of religious beliefs with good ethnographic insight. Two points should be emphasized at this stage. Firstly, religious beliefs are different from ordinary beliefs. They are beliefs in an invisible, extraordinary reality that, by definition, is poles apart from the world as experienced in everyday life. Secondly, as Durkheim pointed out, religious beliefs cannot be seen as mere 'illusions', although not for the reasons he put forward. We know that illusory perceptions of reality are and have been quite common among ordinary subjects (that is, those who do not suffer from any mental disorder). However, religious beliefs the world over are not merely beliefs in the existence of something (see Inglis, this volume). Consider ordinary people's belief in the existence of black holes. They have not seen them, nor do they understand much of the evidence of their existence. They simply take statements concerning their existence at face value because of the prestige and authority our culture attributes to science. Suppose that scientists were one day to discover that there is no such thing as black holes. Black holes would turn out to be a sort of scientific illusion that had eventually been dispelled and, consequently, popular belief therein would be a senseless belief. That is clearly not the case with religious beliefs, however. Whatever else the concept of religion is supposed to include, religion is certainly not a way of discovering some form of 'truth' about reality (see Rossano 2010: 21–24). This does not mean that there is not an empirical component in the constitution of religious beliefs, as there would otherwise be no such thing as religious experience. Religious beliefs are a complex, culturally determined amalgam of different components, empirical and non-empirical, factive and normative (see Kwon, this volume).[5]

Let us now move on to the question of whether science can be an object of belief in the same way as or a similar way to religion. The first thing we should bear in mind is that comparing science and religion entails comparing totally asymmetrical cultural formations. Religion could be confidently defined as a human quasi-universal. All human societies have or have had some form of religion, even though not all humans can be said to have religious beliefs. Science, in contrast, is a historical oddity. According to McCauley, one of the contributors to this volume (see also McCauley 2011: 90), even with a liberal conception of science, we can only find continuous scientific activity in very limited cases, namely some ancient cultures, including the Chinese, the Babylonians, the Egyptians and the Mayans, the Ancient

Greeks, some segments of Muslim societies and the Chinese up to the Middle Ages, and the Europeans from the sixteenth century onwards. That is no more than a tiny fraction of human history, and an even tinier fraction of human societies. McCauley has cogently demonstrated that the reasons for the comparative scarcity of science in human history have to do with its exorbitant cognitive costs. It takes great effort to produce and assimilate scientific knowledge, both on the part of the societies wherein that knowledge thrives and on that of the individuals who wish to pursue a scientific career. It is true that science is effective, the most effective form of knowledge ever created by humans. However, it appears to be so costly in cognitive terms simply because natural selection did not provide humans with a brain attuned to the production and assimilation of scientific knowledge. Science is, above all, a form of accumulated knowledge. A single scientist is actually a contradiction in terms, since no matter how brilliant a particular scientist happens to be, they could never have existed without the help of innumerable other scientists (teachers, colleagues and so forth) who, in turn, find themselves in the same situation. Thus, there would have been no selective advantage for any of our ancestors had they been born with an unusually scientifically minded brain. So, we need a complex society with complex institutions, capable of producing enough wealth to buy a few individuals out of everyday productive tasks so that they can devote themselves to the disinterested study of the laws of nature or something along those lines, and with sophisticated means of transmitting and accumulating knowledge, such as literacy. This is not the kind of society humans have lived in for most of their evolutionary history.

None of these requirements apply for religion to exist. I am not suggesting that religion merely grows, almost 'spontaneously', in human minds, with minimal external input, in the same way as language or sexual desire does, for instance. As has been argued from different theoretical standpoints, religious and magical ideas need special cultural mechanisms, such as ritual (see Sørensen, this volume), to ensure their communicability and believability. I am simply saying that whatever (cultural) environment is needed for religion to exist and thrive (see Salazar 2010: 52–53), it is very different from that required for the production of scientific knowledge. Furthermore, note that we are referring to popular religion (which is nowadays normally defined as 'vernacular' or 'lived' religion), not the religion of religious specialists and theologians, which can be almost as cognitively and socially costly as science itself. This, the so-called 'theological incorrectness' of popular religious beliefs (Slone 2004) is an important point, one that several scholars who advocate a cognitive approach to the study of religion have emphasized, and it is worth repeating here. It is such theologically incorrect religious beliefs that provide the sharpest contrast to science. They are quasi-universal and probably as old as *Homo sapiens*, if not older. Whence the first abysmal difference between science and religion, which justifies the idea that comparing them entails comparing asymmetric cultural formations. Another such idea is specifically related to the question of 'belief'. What does 'believe in science' actually mean? Can we believe in science in the same way as we believe in God or gods? Again, we are not concerned with beliefs upheld by scientists themselves, which would be somehow equivalent to the beliefs of theologians, but with popular beliefs (see Jenkins, this volume). The interesting thing about popular scientific beliefs is not so much what ordinary people might think about a given scientific statement or discovery, but the relevance of those beliefs in such people's lives.

At first glance, religious and scientific beliefs share many characteristics (see Sansi-Roca, this volume). To start with, people tend to believe in scientific and religious propositions without fully understanding them. We simply take them to be true on the basis of trust, or what Sperber defined as the 'argument of authority' (Sperber 1985: 84). However, this apparent similarity, as real as it is, hides a far more important difference. Popular belief in science seems to be mainly concerned with some form of 'truth', in the purely Aristotelian sense of correspondence between a statement and the state of affairs to which it refers. Consider, for instance, beliefs in a particular kind of scientific knowledge, such as modern genetics, and the relevance those beliefs have for the constitution of kinship relations (Finkler 2000; Konrad 2003; Carsten 2004; Pálsson 2007). What impels people to search for the form of scientific knowledge that accounts for their genetic connections is the desire to find out the 'truth' about their biological relations, whatever further purpose this truth might have, be it discovering whether they may suffer from a hereditary disease or simply finding out about their origins and so on (see Salazar 2009). An example taken from Carsten's ethnography of kinship relations in modern Britain illustrates this quite clearly. A woman whose birth father did not recognize his paternity was able to prove he was lying thanks to a DNA test performed on a half-brother on her father's side. When asked, it was evident that her aim in obtaining this genetic knowledge was simply to find out who her real father was. She just wanted to 'stop the lies' and 'waft the results under his nose'. In other words, she wanted to 'establish the truth' (Carsten 2004: 103–4, 151).

Arguably, this search for truth is probably as old as mankind. That is not what brings science into existence, however, but merely what makes it attractive and useful to non-scientists. In all likelihood, the aforementioned woman did not understand much of what goes on in genetic testing, but that did not affect her belief in science, as it was based, as we have already seen, on the argument of authority.[6] No matter how meagre or perhaps even flawed her knowledge of modern genetics may be though, it is fairly unlikely that her belief in the truth of genetic testing had anything to do with some sort of supernatural power, as in the case, for instance, of the famous poison oracles used in Zande magic (Evans-Pritchard 1976). Scientific propositions might look quite mysterious to non-scientists, quantum mechanics and relativity theory being obvious examples. However, that mystery originates in ignorance, and in the fact that propositions of the kind in question normally violate our ontological intuitions quite substantially. Such violations are different from those we find in religious representations. The mystery that stems from scientific violations of our ontological intuitions can be dispelled with proper education, as it has no other cause than mere ignorance. The mystery that surrounds religious representations, by contrast, has nothing to do with ignorance. Religious representations are inherently mysterious, both to ordinary folks and to religious specialists. Given their mystifying attributes, it is a moot point why they have been so successful throughout history, as already indicated. We have seen some of the answers to this question provided by the mainstream cognitive science of religion, such as adaptive value, by-product and so on. To my mind, none of them is fully satisfactory (see Salazar 2007, 2010), though this is not the issue I want to address in this introduction.

Forms of Life

Our concern is to look at the interactions between scientific and religious beliefs as 'forms of life', by which I mean, as I have already suggested, that we are not interested in looking at science and religion as theories. That is the way in which they and their interactions are normally dealt with. They are seen as theories, formulated by specialists about the world, about life, perhaps about everything. As such, they can be regarded as utterly incompatible (Dawkins 2006; Rosenberg 2012), or as having different degrees of compatibility and incompatibility (Gould 1999; McGrath 2011; Plantinga 2011). Our purpose is to consider science and religion from a different viewpoint, as fully fledged socio-cultural systems likely to colonize ordinary people's minds and impinge upon their lives in various ways. I subscribe to the Wittgensteinian concept of form of life as equivalent to a worldview, although not only as a way of thinking but also as a way of acting, behaving and living.[7] Anthropologists know only too well that all beliefs occur in a context; a 'trivial truth', according to Knight and Astuti (2008: S151). What they tend to ignore, however, is that this context is not simply a cultural construction but a complex network (I am struggling to find the right word here), a web of cultural and non-cultural determinants in interaction with each other.

Our hypothesis is that science and religion, as forms of life, are likely to come into more contact and interact with each other in contemporary societies, particularly (but not exclusively) Western societies, due to the growing relevance of scientific knowledge in ordinary people's lives (see Jenkins, Melhuus, this volume). I should add an important caveat. We are talking about the growing relevance of scientific knowledge as knowledge and not as a mere technology. As a tool for acting upon the world and producing certain effects, and which is the direct or indirect result of some form of scientific research, technology has been relevant to people's lives since the industrial revolution at least.[8] Nonetheless, our use of technology, no matter how sophisticated that technology happens to be, rarely impinges on our way of thinking, or only does so in a rather marginal way. It is true that technology can change our lives in the far from trivial sense of improving our living standards and so forth. Consider the case of biomedicine. Nowadays, practically all humans have had the chance to enjoy, to different extents, the enormous improvements in their health brought about by biomedicine. However, the degree to which the huge amount of scientific research that underlies modern biomedicine impinges upon its users' ways of thinking, in the sense of making them more familiar with the intricacies of scientific knowledge, is certainly very small. People 'believe' in biomedicine because they rely on its efficacy or because of the argument of authority. Whatever the case, it is not because they have become more scientifically minded (see Coma, this volume). I believe that the case of biomedicine can be extended to the other scientifically produced technologies that have been shaping the lives of ordinary citizens for quite a long time. The point we wish to make in our hypothesis is, precisely, that this state of affairs has begun to change in the so-called knowledge societies. Here, scientific knowledge, and not only scientific technology, is penetrating ordinary people's life-worlds (see Melhuus, this volume).

Let us again consider the scientific knowledge of our genome. When a particular kind of scientific research can tell an individual, such as the woman referred to before, who her 'real' father is, that scientific research is changing the way that woman thinks about her relations (cf. Strathern 1999: 65–85). This example involves only one form of scientific knowledge, that of human genetics. What about other forms of scientific knowledge? Are they becoming similarly relevant to ordinary people's lives? It is unclear how the relevance of scientific knowledge will affect other modes of thought that have been shaping ordinary people's ways of life since time immemorial. We think this is definitely a topic worth exploring.

Structure and Contents of the Volume

The object of this book is to rethink the concepts of religiosity, rationality and secularization in our contemporary world on the basis of specific pieces of research, theoretical and empirical alike, that take the situated human being as their starting point. The book is divided into three sections: 'Cognition', 'Beyond Science' and 'Meaning Systems'. The chapters included in the first section all deal with the nature of scientific knowledge, religious knowledge and the relationships between the two from a cognitive and evolutionary perspective, encompassing their natural or unnatural foundations (McCauley), the adaptive or maladaptive property of science and religion (Blume) and the persistence of religious and/or magic thought in the era of scientific knowledge (Sørensen). The contributors to the 'Beyond Science' section take a different approach. In all the chapters of this section, science seems to transcend itself while interacting with other belief systems. The subject matter examined consists of moral or extra-scientific uses of science (Jenkins), scientific creationism in the UK (Coleman), debates concerning the nature of the human embryo in Norway (Melhuus), the mutually constitutive character of science and religion in Brazil (Sansi-Roca) and notions about illness among Catholic charismatics in Barcelona (Coma). Finally, in the section entitled 'Meaning Systems', we find chapters that, in one way or another, take the so-called problem of meaning as their starting point. They look at the contextual nature of so-called superstitions (Pina-Cabral), religion and science in everyday life in contemporary Ireland (Inglis) and scientific and religious understandings of war-induced trauma in the US and Vietnam (Kwon). This division is somewhat arbitrary, since several chapters would fit equally well in more than one section. It is no more than a heuristic device that should help the reader locate particular chapters in a particular context.

The alleged naturalness of religious ideas and the supposed unnaturalness of science constitute the core argument of McCauley's chapter. Ever since the beginning of the Enlightenment, those who espouse any version of so-called secularization theory have been announcing the demise of religion, specifically its aspects that more blatantly contradict scientific discoveries. Nonetheless, even the most superficial observer cannot deny the resilience of religious symbolic-cultural systems in the face of scientific development. What could be the reason for this rather puzzling phenomenon? McCauley's point is that evolution made human maturationally natural cognition particularly vulnerable to the influence of religious messages, in the same way as it made our bodies susceptible to colonization by viruses and bacteria. In contrast, nothing in the human mind/brain facilitates the accommodation of scientific knowledge. Little cultural input is needed for religion to spread, while science can only be assimilated thanks to arduous cultural instruction. It is no wonder that science is such an intellectual oddity in human cultural history, in contrast to religion's ubiquity. Consequently, instead of science replacing religious ontologies, as classical secularization theories would have us believe, it is rather science itself that turns out to be the most cognitively vulnerable partner.

In a similar fashion, but perhaps with a more optimistic outlook as far as the future of science is concerned, the concept of epistemological pluralism is defended in Blume's contribution. He argues, in a non-relativistic manner, for the validity of different forms of knowledge, namely scientific, non-scientific and, in particular, religious knowledge. Picasso's painting *Guernica* provides us with a form of knowledge about the horrors of the Spanish Civil War which cannot be matched by any scientifically informed account. Perhaps religions the world over fulfil a comparable function. However, the efficacy of religious knowledge is not reflected in its empirical value but in its functional utility in promoting adaptive behaviour. Religious believers do not bring more empirical arguments to the science/religion controversy, Blume provocatively contends, but more children. We might thus be in a sort of evolutionary transitional stage as far as the biological basis of religiosity is concerned. If religious people are spreading their genes more successfully than the non-religious, atheistic or agnostic genotypes might become extinct at some time in the not too distant future.

Sørensen's chapter raises the issue of why magic persists in many contemporary societies, despite modernization and rationalization. Rational choice models of human behaviour have predicted the demise of magical thinking due to its vulnerability to being falsified by modern technology. Modernity will not get away with magic though, Sørensen asserts, in so far as modernity creates more rather than less uncertainties. Hence, magic might help us come to terms with the insecurities of the modern world. However, Sørensen's goal is to look not only at the functions fulfilled by magic (such as helping people cope with such uncertainty, as Malinowski had already argued in a different context), but also at what makes magical rituals believable for those who otherwise master 'technological' rationality. His answer is that ritualization prevents magical action from being assimilated into the rational cause–effect association, as if ritual interfered with our capacity for making logical inferences.

The connections, articulations and contradictions between science and religion in particular contexts are dealt with in the contributions of Jenkins, Coleman, Melhuus, Sansi-Roca and Coma. Scientific thinking can be mysteriously recast as a form of life that brings it into very close proximity to religion and magic in functional terms, as Jenkins argues in his contribution. His main concern is with the moral employment of science, how discoveries of science are recaptured by common sense and put to work in moral descriptions of the world. Science certainly breaks with common-sense categories, but then common sense might reuse science for its own ends, so to speak. Science can break with common sense because scientists form moral communities, the last pre-modern moral communities in existence, interestingly and somewhat paradoxically. Again, matters of life and death, as well as the afterlife, turn out to be particularly relevant in this context. An interesting illustration of Jenkins's thesis is provided by the way in which nineteenth-century 'scientific' spiritualism made use of scientific methodologies and discoveries, such as Newtonian physics, to explore the alleged materiality of ghosts. Another example of the moral or extra-scientific employment of science can be taken from the other end of the spectrum, so to speak, in Richard Dawkins's work against religion, a clear instance of 'thinking with science' in order to engage in particular moral crusades that have, or should have, nothing to do with scientific thinking strictly speaking.

Coleman's analysis of everyday creationism in the United Kingdom further develops the comparison between scientific and religious modes of thought. In creationism, we can once again, although perhaps rather unexpectedly in this particular case, see a clear instance of a belief system that cannot be approached as a theory about the world and its origins, but rather as a Foucauldian technology of the self, Coleman contends. In contrast to the intellectualist production of creationism as public discourse versus another public discourse – that is, scientific discourse – as implied by a proposition-based conception of belief, Coleman's research portrays creationism as an embodied and embedded form of knowledge. The evangelical Christians with whom Coleman has carried out fieldwork are reluctant to produce a 'creationist discourse' as a sort of autonomous body of knowledge separate from congregational life, from religious life itself. Hence the apparent paradox that Coleman came across at the beginning of his research, namely that creationist beliefs are conspicuously absent from creationists' ways of thinking. Torn apart from the rest of religious life, creationism becomes a caricature of itself, a 'situated ignorance', as implied in Dawkins's performative disclosure of creationist discourse.

Melhuus puts forward a similar argument in her analysis of the moral status of the embryo. On the one hand, the embryo can be seen as an object of scientific scrutiny, in the same way as any other biological entity, with the particularity, perhaps, of its regenerative potential. Hence, the value ascribed to the embryo as a biological substance originates in the possibility of generating totipotent cells with which degenerative diseases might be cured. On the other hand though, it is also a moral entity, a hybrid substance of sorts, on the verge of becoming a human being. This is what Melhuus defines as its reproductive potential. The problem is that, no matter how much we invoke science, or scientifically based moral arguments, such as the so-called 'twinning argument', we can never be sure of how such a moral status should be ascertained. It could be argued that the embryo looks very much like a 'creation', as humans are created 'in the image of God'. A creationist claim, or conception, does not have to refer to the Genesis story in a literalist way, but can be regarded as an argument that defends the human identity or quality of a 'bunch of cells', because they are seen as a value, not a mere fact.

Sansi's analysis of candomblé and the religions of Brazil looks at the issue of the mutually constitutive nature of science and religion. An interesting blend of 'scientific' and 'religious' approaches can be seen in spiritualism, where, as in the case of a previous chapter of this volume, science is put to work for the purposes of a religious cult, and, eventually, in candomblé itself, where the very scientists (psychologists and anthropologists) who study it become its practitioners. Sansi's notion of 'multiplicity' to define spirit possession in Brazil refers to the fact that such possession can be found in Afro-Brazilian religions and supposedly 'scientific' religions, such as spiritualism (of European origin), and perhaps even in Catholicism. This miscegenation of epistemologies can only be envisioned if we take science and religion as historical formations of a particular society – the notion of 'forms of life' referred to in the title of this volume – without either of them becoming a privileged standpoint from which to observe and analyse the other.

Finally, from a different point of view, the articulations between science and religion are brought to the fore in Coma's analysis of Catholic charismatic healing. There is an interesting paradox in the way scientific knowledge impinges on ordinary people's lives. Scientific world-views are cognitively costly, whereas the practical results of those world-views, what we normally define as 'technology', are ubiquitous. Nowhere is this contradiction more apparent than in the case of biomedicine. We all enjoy biomedicine's applications, even though we hardly understand how they come about. Interestingly, the very opposite seems to be the case where some religious beliefs are concerned. Here, it is overall world-views that agree with our intuitions (God is good, evil will be defeated and so forth), whereas the particular technologies that turn those general beliefs into practical results, such as miraculous healings, are harder to figure out. An intriguing complementarity between biomedical technologies and religious world-views manifests itself in the minds of the group of Catholic charismatics Coma has been studying.

The problem of magic's believability is also tackled in Pina-Cabral's chapter, although from a different point of view to that of Sørensen, specifically that of the complexity of belief and the need to contextualize belief so that it is not understood in a 'propositional way', as a theory about the world, but as a form of engagement with the world. Not all beliefs are held in the same state of mind. We can adopt an ironic stance on belief, or treat it recursively, playfully, symbolically; we behave 'as if', but we do not really ... Beliefs make sense when they are interconnected with other beliefs, which is what the author calls 'retentivity', rather than with the things that underlie them, or 'ostensivity'. Pina-Cabral reclaims 'superstition' as situated belief, the sort of fuzzy logic that helps us get on with our lives, in contrast to scientific rationality (we do not live 'scientific lives' in the same way as we have a 'religious life'). Superstition is defined as the 'proneness of human beings anywhere to constitute their informal worlds in terms of the mutuality of personhood, polythetic thinking and the retentiveness of belief'.

Seeing belief as a situated form of knowledge leads us directly to the problem of meaning, in this case Meaning with a capital 'm', referring to how humans manage to turn their often chaotic experience of the world into a meaningful whole. Together with Pina-Cabral's chapter, the contributions of Inglis and Kwon take the issue of meaning as their central concern. Inglis's chapter approaches this contentious subject by postulating a close association between magic and religious beliefs in contemporary Ireland with a Kantian 'practical reason'. Religion and magic have to do with bonding and communication rather than with the search for some form of naked 'truth'. Hence, in popular belief, science, magic and religion do not necessarily contradict each other and there seems to be room for all of them. Furthermore, again in popular belief, no clear-cut boundaries can be identified between those modes of thought, for they seem to sit 'inside' rather than beside each other, Inglis contends. Interestingly, people who openly deny believing quite often act as if they do believe, as if their bodily movements occur for their own reasons, separately from what goes on in their mind. That is further proof of the embodied nature of belief, as seen in previous chapters.

Life and death are two sides of the same coin of human experience. Thus, the meaning of life and the meaning of death always appear inextricably linked. This is clearly demonstrated in Kwon's ethnography of trauma in the US and Vietnam following the Vietnam/American War, and beliefs in the afterlife in Vietnam in relation to the vagaries of Vietnamese political history. Kwon pits scientific approaches to the study of post-traumatic stress disorder against socio-historical interpretations that turn them into fundamental categories of understanding, to paraphrase Durkheim's jargon, fragments of collective consciousness that help people cope with and make sense of terrible tragedies, such as mass deaths in wars. Whatever the intuitive or counter-intuitive foundations of such beliefs may be, their moral repercussions are constitutive. Making sense of life and death lies at the core of what it is to be human. Kwon ends his chapter with the provocative assertion that in the particular case of trauma brought about by the Vietnam/American War, it is the modern clinical tradition that turns out to be parochial in its application, whereas traditional Vietnamese religious views (interestingly, more concerned with the troubles of the dead than those of the living) appear more attuned to universally shared concerns with and concern for human suffering.

As stated at the beginning of this introduction, our purpose is to cross boundaries, build bridges and draw connections between different theoretical and disciplinary views of the same phenomena. Science and religion are multifaceted cultural formations that have been analysed from very different, sometimes contradictory perspectives. This volume is innovative in that it not only brings together some of these differing approaches, but also establishes a fruitful conversation between them. While a dialogue with an intelligent opponent may not necessarily change our views, it normally leaves us feeling more insightful and enlightened. That is how we hope the reader will feel after a thorough examination of this volume.

Acknowledgements

Financial support was provided by the Agència de Gestió d'Ajuts Universitaris i de Recerca (2010ARCS54), the Ministerio de Ciencia e Innovación (CSO2009-08093), the University of Lleida and the University of Barcelona. We would also like to thank three readers for their constructive comments on an earlier draft.

Notes

1. Compare anthropologists' endless discussions concerning the universal validity of the concept of kinship after Schneider's critique (Schneider 1984).
2. Note that 'poorly specified' does not necessarily refer to 'general purpose' cognitive tools. It merely alludes to the need for environmental (both natural

and cultural, as far as humans are concerned) input to turn any genetic instruction into concrete behaviour.

3. See Salazar (2010) for a critical overview of the two approaches in question.

4. 'The superstitious man, and frequently also the religious man, believes in a twofold order of reality, the one visible, palpable, and subordinate to the essential laws of motion; the other invisible, intangible, "spiritual", forming a mystic sphere which encompasses the first. But the primitive's mentality does not recognize two distinct worlds in contact with each other, and more or less interpenetrating. To him there is but one. Every reality, like every influence, is mystic, and consequently every perception is also mystic' (Lévy-Bruhl 1926: 68).

5. 'If the question arises as to the existence of a god or God, it plays an entirely different role to that of the existence of any person or object I ever heard of. One said, had to say, that one believed in the existence, and if one did not believe, this was regarded as something bad. Normally if I did not believe in the existence of something no one would think there was anything wrong in this' (Wittgenstein 1996: 59).

6. The fact that humans have the capacity to process cultural representations that are not fully understood might have had an adaptive value in human evolution. Thanks to this capacity, humans could acquire complex items of cultural knowledge at a very low cognitive cost. Imagine we had to fully understand the process of production of every item of cultural knowledge we make use of (computers, medicines, planes, etc.). The obvious drawback is that this very same capacity makes us vulnerable to all sorts of harmful or 'maladaptive' cultural information (see Richerson and Boyd 2005).

7. Compare Coleman's 'technologies of the self' (Coleman, this volume).

8. I mean 'scientifically based technology', since technology originating from ordinary knowledge of the environment has been with us, much like religion, since the very beginnings of our species (see McCauley 2011: 88–100).

References

Asad, T. 1993. *Formations of the Secular: Christianity, Islam, Modernity*. Stanford: Stanford University Press.

Bennett, M.R., and P.M.S. Hacker. 2003. *Philosophical Foundations of Neuroscience*. Oxford: Blackwell.

Boyer, P. 1994. *The Naturalness of Religious Ideas*. Berkeley: University of California Press.

——. 1996. 'What Makes Anthropomorphism Natural? Intuitive Ontology and Cultural Representations', *Journal of the Royal Anthropological Institute* 2(1): 83–97.

——. 2001. *Religion Explained*. New York: Basic Books.

——. 2010. *The Fracture of an Illusion: Science and the Dissolution of Religion*. Göttingen: Vandenhoek and Ruprecht.

Carlisle, S., and G. Simon. 2012. 'Believing Selves: Negotiating Social and Psychological Experiences of Belief', *Ethos* 40(3): 221–36.

Carsten, J. 2004. *After Kinship*. Cambridge: Cambridge University Press.

Dawkins, R. 2006. *The God Delusion*. New York: Mariner Books.

Dennett, D. 1989. *The Intentional Stance*. Cambridge, MA: MIT Press.

Durkheim, E. 1915. *The Elementary Forms of the Religious Life*. London: Allen and Unwin.

Evans-Pritchard, E.E. 1934. 'Lévy-Bruhl's Theory of Primitive Mentality', *Bulletin of the Faculty of Arts of the University of Cairo* 2(1): 1–36.

———. 1976 [1937]. *Witchcraft, Oracles and Magic among the Azande*, abr. edn. Oxford: Oxford University Press.

Finkler, K. 2000. *Experiencing the New Genetics: Family and Kinship on the Medical Frontier*. Philadelphia: University of Pennsylvania Press.

Good, B. 1993. *Medicine, Rationality and Experience: An Anthropological Perspective*. Cambridge: Cambridge University Press.

Gould, S.J. 1999. *Rock of the Ages: Science and Religion in the Fullness of Life*. New York: Ballantine.

Hacker, P.M.S. 2007. *Human Nature: The Categorial Framework*. Oxford: Blackwell.

Ingold, T. 2000. *The Perception of the Environment: Essays on Livelihood, Dwelling and Skill*. London: Routledge.

Kirsch, T.G. 2004. 'Restating the Will to Believe: Religious Pluralism, Anti-syncretism, and the Problem of Belief', *American Anthropologist* 106(4): 699–709.

Knight, N., and R. Astuti. 2008. 'Some Problems with Property Ascription', *Journal of the Royal Anthropological Institute* 14, Issue Supplement s1: S142–S158.

Konrad, M. 2003. 'From Secrets of Life to the Life of Secrets: Tracing Genetic Knowledge as Genealogical Ethics in Biomedical Britain', *Journal of the Royal Anthropological Institute* 9: 339–58.

Lanman, J.A. 2008. 'In Defence of "Belief"', *Issues in Ethnology and Anthropology* 3(3): 49–62.

Lévy-Bruhl, L. 1926. *How Natives Think*. London: Allen and Unwin.

Lindquist, G., and S. Coleman. 2008. 'Introduction: Against Belief?' *Social Analysis* 52(1): 1–18.

McCauley, R.N. 2011. *Why Religion Is Natural and Science Is Not*. New York: Oxford University Press.

McGrath, A. 2011. *Surprised by Meaning: Science, Faith, and How We Make Sense of Things*. Louisville, KY: Westminster John Knox Press.

McKay, R.T., and D.C. Dennett. 2009. 'The Evolution of Misbelief', *Behavioral and Brain Sciences* 32: 493–561.

Needham, R. 1972. *Belief, Language, and Experience*. Chicago: University of Chicago Press.

Pálsson, G. 2007. *Anthropology and the New Genetics*. Cambridge: Cambridge University Press.

Plantinga, A. 2011. *Where the Conflict Really Lies: Science, Religion, and Naturalism*. Oxford: Oxford University Press.

Richerson, P.J., and R. Boyd. 2005. *Not by Genes Alone: How Culture Transformed Human Evolution.* Chicago: University of Chicago Press.

Robbins, J. 2007. 'Continuity Thinking and the Problem of Christian Culture: Belief, Time, and the Anthropology of Christianity', *Current Anthropology* 48(1): 5–38.

Rosenberg, A. 2012. *Philosophy of Science: A Contemporary Introduction.* New York: Routledge.

Rossano, M. 2010. *Supernatural Selection: How Religion Evolved.* Oxford: Oxford University Press.

Ruel, M. 1982. 'Christians as Believers', in J. Davis (ed.), *Religious Organization and Religious Experience.* London: Academic Press, pp.9–31.

Salazar, C. 2007. 'Cause and Meaning in the Anthropology of Religion', *Quaderns de l'Institut Català d'Antropologia* 23: 15–35. Available at: www.raco.cat/index.php/QuadernsICA/article/view/136820/231598.

———. 2009. 'Are Genes Good to Think With?' in J. Edwards and C. Salazar (eds), *European Kinship in the Age of Biotechnology.* Oxford: Berghahn, pp.177–96.

———. 2010. 'Anthropology and the Cognitive Science of Religion: A Critical Assessment', *Religion and Society* 1: 44–56.

———. 2014. 'Understanding Belief: Some Qualitative Evidence', *Journal of Empirical Theology* 27(2): 199–213.

———. n.d. 'Religious Symbolism and the Human Mind: Rethinking Durkheim's *Elementary Forms of Religious Life*', *Method and Theory in the Study of Religion.*

Saler, B. 2000. *Conceptualizing Religion: Immanent Anthropologists, Transcendent Natives, and Unbounded Categories.* New York: Berghahn.

———. 2001. 'On What We May Believe about Beliefs', in J. Andersen (ed.), *Religion in Mind: Cognitive Perspectives on Religious Belief, Ritual, and Experience.* Cambridge: Cambridge University Press, pp.47–69.

Schneider, D. 1984. *A Critique of the Study of Kinship.* Ann Arbor: University of Michigan Press.

Schutz, A. 1945. 'On Multiple Realities', *Philosophy and Phenomenological Research* 5(4): 533–76.

Slone, L.S. 2004. *Theological Incorrectness: Why Religious People Believe What They Shouldn't.* Oxford: Oxford University Press.

Sperber, D. 1985. 'Anthropology and Psychology: Towards an Epidemiology of Representations', *Man* 20(1): 73–89.

———. 1996. *Explaining Culture: A Naturalistic Approach.* Oxford: Blackwell.

Strathern, M. 1999. *Property, Substance and Effect: Anthropological Essays on Power and Things.* London: Athlone Press.

Taylor, C. 2007. *A Secular Age.* Cambridge, MA: Belknap Press.

Wittgenstein, L. 1996. *Lectures and Conversations on Aesthetics, Psychology and Religious Belief.* Oxford: Blackwell.

Part I

❦❦

Cognition

Chapter One

Maturationally Natural Cognition Impedes Professional Science and Facilitates Popular Religion

Robert N. McCauley

Both defenders and opponents have portrayed religion in a slow but inexorable intellectual retreat as science has relentlessly gained epistemic authority and cultural prestige. Since the Europeans' rediscovery of ancient science in the Middle Ages, many have attempted to forestall that retreat by squaring religious beliefs and doctrines with the theories and findings of the sciences. During this secular age, religion faces not only intellectual but social reversals too (Talmont-Kaminski 2013). In northern Europe, the state provides citizens with many of life's basic requirements (education, health care, mass-transportation and so on), and the churches are empty.

For a variety of reasons, however, obituaries for religion in the Western world are premature and probably ill-advised, as are hymns to the inescapable ascendancy and triumph of science. The reasons I explore are primarily cognitive. From the standpoint of their cognitive foundations, we have good reasons to expect that religious ideas and beliefs will reliably erupt and persist in human populations and possess an appeal that science's elaborate procedures and esoteric theories will never match. Humans' cognitive predilections largely obstruct scientific thought and interfere with scientific reasoning and understanding.

I devote the first section to distinguishing maturationally natural cognition from another version of fast cognitive processing, and from slower, reflective cognitive processing that plays a prominent role in conscious mental life. The second section examines how maturationally natural cognition mostly impedes humans' attempts to learn and do science. Scientific representations are radically discontinuous with our maturationally natural conceptions of the world and require types of cognitive processing that are foreign to maturationally natural patterns of thought. In the third section, I show how, by contrast, religions engage humans' maturationally natural cognitive susceptibilities. Religious representations cue various maturationally natural cognitive processes and their concomitant default inferences. This makes religious ideas and practices appealing and insures their easy acquisition. Finally, I examine some consequences of this comparison. I suggest that threats to the persistence of religion that science allegedly poses are exaggerated, and that it is the continued flourishing of science that will likely prove the more difficult to sustain.

Maturationally Natural Cognition

Dual-processing theories of cognition have prevailed in cognitive science for more than thirty years (Schneider and Shiffrin 1977; Shiffrin and Schneider 1977). Occasional dissenters (e.g. Keren and Schul 2009) have noted the vagueness of proposed criteria for distinguishing cognitive systems, mixed and inconclusive evidence for their support, and the availability of alternative conceptions that might accommodate those findings. However, most researchers continue to favour dual-process views (Evans and Frankish 2009; Kahneman 2011).

Dual-process theories contrast two forms of human mental life, exhibiting constellations of contrasting properties. Slow reflective thinking is conscious, deliberate, explicit, conjectural and easier to formulate linguistically. Mentally talking to ourselves involves this slow reflective processing. Proponents maintain that slow reflection is usefully distinguished from the tremendous amount of intuitive cognition that occurs, which is fast, (mostly) unconscious, automatic, implicit, presumptive and comparatively difficult to formulate linguistically. With this intuitive mode of thinking we seem to know things instantly, and it is in this light that I have referred to such thought as 'cognitively natural' (McCauley 2000). A few relevant cues are sufficient to ignite such processing. Much of it is so natural that we are unaware how or why we know these things. For example, we routinely leap to conclusions about individuals' emotional states on the basis of their facial expressions, tones of voice or bodily comportment, and we do so with little, if any, explicit awareness of what informed our inferential leaps. This is carried out on-line in the basements of human minds. Whether it concerns recognition of emotions, comprehension of utterances or attribution of mental states to others, on-line intuitive cognition addresses problems of perception, cognition and action immediately and unquestioningly.

Slow, conscious reflection is pursued upstairs. Slow reflection does not concern automatic mental operations, and to the extent that it is considered and laborious, it takes place off-line. Because of this, and because thinking this way often builds on explicit instruction, I refer to this as 'unnatural' cognition (ibid.). Slow reflection is thoroughly cultural in its forms. It is what occupies lawyers when they prepare briefs: they formulate arguments carefully and consciously, and explicitly ponder how claims are best put to insure proper understanding and appropriate rhetoric.

The remainder of this section concentrates on fast intuition, because this kind of human cognition itself needs sub-dividing. Fast intuition, whether it concerns perception, cognition or action, comes in two forms.

Practised Naturalness

A familiar English idiom describes capacities as becoming 'second nature'. Some perception, thought and action become second nature to us after extensive experience in some domain, often supplemented by considerable teaching. Following a great deal of practice in some area, our perception, cognition and action progressively shift from being conscious, laboured and deliberate to unconscious, easy and automatic. With considerable practice or experience in some domain, unnatural cognition can come to mimic natural cognition. It becomes second nature (McCauley 2013). Depending upon the complexity of the domains, this transition might take years, as in acquiring a skill. Whether recognizing a tartan, calculating logarithms or swinging a golf club, tasks that were once challenging begin to feel natural by virtue of frequent and extended exposure. We develop expertise in those domains.

Experts have ready intuitions about what they master. Expertise need not involve the esoteric. Sometimes, experts are rare (such as in high-energy physics), but expertise can be quite widespread (for example, dealing with a city's subway system). Perception, thought and action[1] that have become second nature enjoy what might be called a 'practised naturalness' (McCauley 2011). Human beings attain practised naturalness in different domains, and what they obtain is a function of their culture and time period. Learning how to ride a bicycle is widespread in cultures where bicycles are available, but no one possessed this skill in the ancient world.

Maturational Naturalness

Talk of second nature implicitly presumes forms of cognition that are 'first nature' – that is, forms that are comparably unconscious, easy and automatic, but which require little experience and no tutelage. Prominent discussions of such systems have underscored their innateness, their modularity, or both (Fodor 1983). Since both features are controversial (e.g. Barrett and Kurzban 2006), and since neither is necessary for characterizing such maturationally natural systems, I focus on other facets of these systems, remaining agnostic about their putative innateness and modular status (whatever each of those attributions mean).

The temptation to stress innateness arises, in part, from the fundamentality of the problems for human survival such systems address. Whether it is perceptual recognition of objects in the environment, cognitive discrimination of syntactic distinctions or action responses to environmental contaminants, maturationally natural cognition addresses basic problems human beings must handle to get by in the world. Many maturationally natural systems (concerning perception and locomotion, for example) seem intimately connected to the evolution not only of our species but of others as well. No one invented maturationally natural capacities – unlike the technologies with which humans can achieve practised naturalness.

Most maturationally natural capacities appear early and are active by the time humans reach school age. This is why 'school age' is fairly uniform across cultures. By six years of age, humans can typically recognize agents, hypothesize plausibly about their mental states, control their own locomotion, produce and comprehend everyday language and so on. Maturationally natural capacities are also functioning before we realize they are. Humans do not recall learning to walk or talk or read minds, as opposed to learning to ride a bicycle or to read and write. The emergence of maturationally natural capacities constitutes what we take to be normal development.

Their emergence also does not hang on any culturally distinctive support. Unquestionably, culture infiltrates and tunes maturationally natural systems. The same infants in a Mandarin-speaking community who learn to speak Mandarin are no less able to learn to speak Catalan, if they had been raised among Catalan speakers. The development of such capacities does not depend upon direct teaching or explicit instruction. Nor does it turn on artefacts or the careful preparation of learning environments. No one needs to teach a normal child the language in which it is immersed. It will learn that language on its own.

Not only does establishing maturationally natural capacities not rely on culturally distinctive inputs, it may, in some cases, not rely on any distinctively cultural inputs. What appears to be a spontaneous emergence of a collective sign language among students at a Nicaraguan school for the deaf suggests that such capacities may emerge from basic features of human social interaction (Senghas et al. 2004; Coppola and Newport 2005).

Endless debates have swirled around maturationally natural capacities' origins. The relative specificity of the learning principles informing their development remains controversial. Few, however, dispute the fact that such cognitive systems constitute domain-specific capacities by the time they are operating. What school-age children think about biological kinds and their inferences about them apply to that domain only. The underlying principles cannot be generalized to language any more than the principles of a language can be applied to biological kinds.

Most of the time, the operations of maturationally natural systems are automatic and fast. That comports with the claim that these systems concern fundamental matters concerning survival. In some situations it is imprudent to insist on the highest standards of evidence. If preliminary indications suggest that a dangerous predator is nearby, fleeing, rather than striving for corroboration, is generally the better course. Consequently, satisfying a few diagnostic cues, their occasional fallibility notwithstanding, is enough to trigger our maturationally natural dispositions. These systems leap to conclusions woefully underdetermined by the available evidence. Participants cannot help interpreting some kinds of movement of dots on a screen as motions of animate agents, pursuing or fleeing from one another (Michotte 1963). This penchant for acting on relevant but slight evidence renders us susceptible to illusions, when some stimulus mimics cues sufficient to activate one of our maturationally natural systems. Humans' daily experiences with movie screens and televisions are obvious illustrations. Typically, we cannot help ourselves from reacting according to these systems' dictates.

As noted, focusing on maturationally natural systems escapes the burden of proof for modularity and innateness. Evolutionary psychologists have argued that humans possess dozens of innate, modularized capacities (Buss 2005). If any cognitive systems are innate or modular in the senses that Fodor or the evolutionary psychologists have advanced, they would qualify as maturationally natural systems. For more than fifty years, language has been the leading candidate, although promising accounts eschew strong modular claims on its behalf (e.g. Christiansen and Chater 1999). Other putative cognitive modules that would qualify as maturationally natural systems include the basic physics of solid objects (Spelke et al. 1992), contamination avoidance (Rozin et al. 1995), face recognition (Duchaine and Nakayama 2006) and theory of mind (Baron-Cohen 1995).

The Place of Maturationally Natural Cognition in Science

Maturationally natural cognition obstructs and intrudes upon scientific thought and, thereby, impedes scientific progress. By contrast, it undergirds popular religious thought and facilitates religion.

Radically Counter-intuitive Scientific Representations

The sciences advance, usually sooner rather than later, representations that are radically unlike the deliverances of our maturationally natural cognitive systems. The sciences reliably traffic in radically counter-intuitive representations that imply that the world is not as our maturationally natural systems suggest. The world, in short, is not as it appears. Radically counter-intuitive representations improve upon our maturationally natural conceptions of things, and show why they work when they do.

The theories and concepts of the sciences reorder and recategorize things by presenting new, unobvious regularities based, in psychology and social science no less than in physical science, on mechanisms and forces that are not perceptually manifest (McCauley 1986). The sciences offer more penetrating explanations than our maturationally natural folk physics, folk biology and folk psychology. Scientific theories do not just make sense of the familiar world; they also have implications for how things work in unfamiliar environments. This gives scientific claims theoretical depth. They must be extended to circumstances either inexplicable before, inaccessible before or, often, unknown before. Scientists devise technologies to access those exotic environments. The experimental investigation of theories' implications in unexplored settings constitutes a major means for testing them against the world and extending knowledge.

Such endeavours inevitably result in representations that diverge drastically from our common-sense conceptions of the world. Consider one of the first ground-breaking discoveries of modern science, viz. that the earth moves. We are all Copernicans. Yet we retain the language of pre-Copernican conceptions, almost no one ever looks at the sky within a Copernican framework, and when we do, it can be startlingly disconcerting (Churchland 1979, 2012).

General science education and some familiarity with basic practices of modern medicine make it more difficult to imagine how radically counter-intuitive the germ theory of disease once was. That theory's counter-intuitiveness earlier in history explains why it took more than 150 years from inventing microscopy and the discovery of micro-organisms for scientists to consider the possibility that some might play an important role in infectious diseases. To people of that time, such microscopic creatures did not seem remotely equal to the effects such diseases produce in macroscopic organisms. More recently, new sciences of the human mind/brain have unearthed phenomena that overturn some of our most basic folk psychological assumptions. These include a variety of what seem conceptually impossible pathologies, such as blindness denial (Churchland 1983).

Probably the single most influential feature of science contributing to religion's inexorable intellectual retreat is how modern scientific progress has marked an advancing restriction on domains in which appeals to agent causality are no longer deemed legitimate. In non-scientific cultures, everything can be agents capable of acting, including heavenly bodies, the seas, the wind, mountains and more. Maturing physical sciences have discredited and supplanted agentive explanations of wondrous celestial events, such as comets and supernovae, and wondrous geological events such as earthquakes, volcanoes and tsunamis. The combination of Darwin's theory of evolution and the subsequent rise of cellular and molecular biology eliminated any need for appeals to agent causality in the biological realm. Vitalism, the notion that vital spirits were responsible for life, was moribund in biological science by the early twentieth century. Over the last fifty years, the cognitive and brain sciences have begun to weaken the grip of appeals to conscious mental operations even within ourselves as satisfactory explanations of much human conduct.

Difficulties Associated with Cognitive Processing in Science

Most, though not all, of the cognitive processes on which the sciences depend are as unnatural as their radically counter-intuitive representations. Humans have no problem cooking up hypotheses, and, when facing upended expectations, toddlers and pre-school children seek evidence in exploratory play and carry out explanatory reasoning (Legare et al. 2010; Legare 2012). But science involves more than mere sensitivity to evidence. It requires recognizing, collecting, generating, analysing and assessing relevant empirical evidence for the purpose of testing and criticizing theories. Those processes demand forms of thought and types of practice that humans, including scientists, find difficult to learn and master.

That difficulty is a function of these intellectual tasks' cognitive unnaturalness. The necessary skills do not rely on standard cognitive equipment. An extended education in mathematics and science gives scientists plenty of practice with these culturally invented cognitive tools, but any naturalness their use assumes is thoroughly practised. Scientists have the same maturationally natural penchants of mind that other humans do, and the cognitive processes associated with the half of science concerned with criticizing theories are not abetted by any maturationally natural dispositions. Their deliverances can interfere with scientists' judgement, reasoning and memory, just as they can with anyone else's.

The cognitive science of science has uncovered many barriers to grasping scientific claims and doing good science. Maturationally natural dispositions reliably intrude in the domains that they address. Since they operate automatically, neither explicit, reflective knowledge nor even long histories of practice undo their operations or influence, especially in unfamiliar settings. Most constitute obstacles to learning and doing science.

Michael McCloskey and his colleagues (Caramazza et al. 1981; McCloskey 1983; McCloskey et al. 1983) showed that most naive participants rely on their folk physics when making judgements about the motions of objects. Surprisingly, they also showed that roughly one quarter of participants who had successfully completed a course in basic mechanics also reverted to their pre-Galilean folk intuitions when queried about objects' motions. Maturationally natural folk physics intruded and swamped reflectively acquired physical knowledge, leading participants to ignore such basic physical principles as inertia. Recently, Deborah Kelemen and her colleagues (Kelemen et al. 2012) have shown that even professional scientists are vulnerable to similar lapses in other areas when demands on cognitive processing are extreme, for example, when handling tasks under acute time pressure. Their instantaneous maturationally natural deliverances prevail.

A variety of research over the past forty years has shown that even well-trained participants perform poorly on experimental tasks investigating their command of the deductive and probabilistic inferences science routinely involves. Dozens of studies show that our intuitions about probabilities violate normative principles (Kahneman et al. 1982; Gilovich et al. 2002). Participants ignore base-rate information, sample sizes and regression to the mean. They employ maturationally natural heuristics, such as representativeness, which holds that 'like goes with like' (Gilovich 1991: 136). Operating with this heuristic can lead to the neglect of elementary rules of probabilistic inference, as when judgements of similarity are based on considerations that do not track objective probabilities. Tversky and Kahneman hold that this and other such heuristics inform our 'natural assessments' of probabilities (Tversky and Kahneman 2002: 20).

Although these heuristics apply across domains, they satisfy the features outlined earlier for maturationally natural systems. They operate unconsciously, automatically and intuitively. Their verdicts occur instantly.

For most everyday problems, they do well enough; however, they are biased and, as many studies demonstrate, fallible. Their decrees are inadequate in the exotic environments scientists seek or create in their experiments. Consequently, they are utterly inadequate for scientific purposes. The research shows that lay persons are not the only people susceptible to those heuristics' operations. Tversky and Kahneman found 'no effect of statistical sophistication' (ibid.: 20) in how participants performed in assessing probabilities of conjunctions and their conjuncts. More than 80 per cent of their 'highly sophisticated respondents' followed dictates of the representativeness heuristic rather than normative probability theory. In other studies, monetary rewards for correct answers failed to improve performance (Camerer and Hogarth 1999). This illustrates Tversky and Kahneman's claim that even once apprised of the correct answer and the reasoning for it, the incorrect answer the heuristic promotes still feels right.

The history of research on conditional deductive inference is longer and no more encouraging. Peter Wason (1966) provided striking evidence that 70 to 80 per cent of participants were either susceptible to one or both fallacies connected with the simplest form of hypothetical inference, or impervious to the validity of *modus tollens* inferences, or manifested all three of these problems. The Wason four-card selection task is one of the most frequently examined designs in modern experimental psychology. For decades researchers have been searching for the features of the task that are responsible for producing such consistently dismal findings. Leda Cosmides discovered that formulating the Wason selection task in terms of social contracts unfailingly boosted participants' performance (Cosmides and Tooby 2005).[2] Crucially, though, hypothetical reasoning in science rarely concerns social contracts. The findings about the Wason selection task suggest that conditional inference about the implications of scientific theories is a skill most humans cannot typically execute correctly, yet it is a key capacity in the recognition, generation, analysis and assessment of empirical evidence.

Scientists are perfectly normal human beings cognitively. That is also true about their social psychology. Scientists have the same susceptibilities to self-interest and motivated perception as others. In science this can result in a confirmation bias for preferred theories and viewpoints. Coalitional loyalties and outright fraud can mar scientific proceedings (Gratzer 2000).

One of the consequences of humans' penchant for such fallacies and frailties is that scientific rationality is best understood as the outcome of the operations of scientific communities, rather than of individual scientists. Science compensates for the cognitive and character weaknesses of individual scientists through institutional arrangements aimed at insuring that everyone's work is checked by, if not everyone else, then at least parties with competing views. Scientific institutions (journals, university departments, professional societies and so on) insist on the public availability of scientific work, including apparatus, designs and findings. The scientific community seeks the replication of experimental results, and demands it if they are credibly disputed. These measures are designed to increase the probabilities that the collective outcome of scientific activity in the long run improves upon individuals' efforts in the short run.

The Place of Maturationally Natural Cognition in Religion

The goal of the previous section was to convey how our maturationally natural predilections of mind impede science. By contrast, the objective of this section is to highlight how many of those same capacities abet religion. My second parallel thesis is that popular religion largely depends on ordinary variations in the operations of various domain-specific, maturationally natural, cognitive mechanisms.

Although some individuals are not religious, religion arises in every human culture. Unlike professional science, which is comparatively rare in human history, religion is culturally universal. Religious ideas and practices invariably erupt in human populations across a wide array of physical and cultural settings. Maturationally natural dispositions of mind spur recurring patterns in the stories, beliefs, practices and artefacts of popular religion.

A side-bar: this contrasts not only with the radically counter-intuitive representations and cultivated cognitive processing science involves. It also diverges from the often substantially counter-intuitive representations and sophisticated forms of inference that extended theological reflection involves. Theological reflection is more like the intellectual work of professional science than the cognition that informs popular religion. Theology, like science but unlike popular religion, is not ubiquitous in human societies. Both theology and science turn on the invention of literacy and the development of centres of learning devoted to concentrated reflection on ideas that sharply diverge from humans' maturationally natural deliverances. Assertions about how one god can be three persons are no less counter-intuitive than claims about multiple personality disorder. In literate religions in large-scale societies, theologians and religious leaders formulate, teach and police radically counter-intuitive doctrines that participants learn and affirm. Still, such training probably has no more influence in on-line cognition and inference about religious matters than McCloskey's research suggests scientific training has on people's inferences about basic mechanics.[3] Theological and scientific educations both aspire to substantive commitments and reflective habits of mind that attain a practised naturalness capable of operating beside and independently of humans' maturationally natural presumptions. Still, whether proposals are theological or scientific, maturationally natural systems' intrusions are probably impossible to expunge. End of side-bar.

Compared with science and theology, popular religion relies on assumptions that are more common, materials that are more familiar and judgements and inferences that are more intuitive. The ideas and patterns of thought popular religion engages are naturally appealing to human minds. The items of popular religion inherit their forms by engaging various maturationally natural penchants of mind that are in place as the consequence of considerations that have nothing to do either with one another or with religion.

Modestly Counter-intuitive Religious Representations

The most conspicuous cognitive products of popular religion encompass only 'modestly' counter-intuitive representations of special sorts of agents, 'at most'. Those representations arise on the basis of 'normal' variations in the operations of garden variety, domain-specific, maturationally natural cognitive equipment. Let me expand on the character of the products of religious cognition by taking up these points.

Why do the products of popular religion count as only 'modestly' counter-intuitive representations? Because, as Pascal Boyer (2000, 2001) has argued, they contain limited violations of maturationally natural intuitions in just a few familiar domains. Boyer holds that popular religious representations are constrained on two fronts. First, they concern humans' intuitions in but three maturationally natural ontological domains: intuitive physics, intuitive biology and intuitive psychology. Both developmental (e.g. Karmiloff-Smith 1992) and cross-cultural evidence (e.g. Atran et al. 2002; Callaghan et al. 2005) substantiate the recurrence of these domain-specific systems in human minds. Second, Boyer underscores that violations come in only two varieties: transfers and breaches.

Transfers involve the application of properties and principles from one of these three ontological domains to items that are not usually counted as eligible instances of that domain. Talk about living mountains transfers the properties of an organism to a physical entity that is not an organism. Representations of snakes that talk transfer the sophisticated psychological capacities underlying language use in conversation to organisms incapable of such exchanges.

Breaches arise when a representation violates some default assumption connected with intuitive physics, intuitive biology or intuitive psychology. Representations of persons who can walk through walls contravene the principle of intuitive physics that holds that two physical things cannot occupy the same space at the same time. Conceptions of humans born from molluscs violate the principle of species essentialism in folk biology, which entails that organisms descend from organisms of the same kind. Representations of gods who can read our every thought violate the folk psychological assumption that our thoughts are our own.

Boyer argues that religious representations are quite modestly counter-intuitive – indeed, typically minimally counter-intuitive in that customarily these representations encompass no more than one transfer or one breach. The snake who talks to Adam and Eve is loquacious (with the requisite psychological sophistication) but reptilian in all other respects. Jesus transforms water into wine, but he and the other wedding guests drink it normally; if they drink enough, it might have intoxicating effects; if they spill it, it might stain their clothes, because it is otherwise just like wines produced the standard way.

Religions' modestly counter-intuitive representations possess significant advantages in the marketplace of ideas. Because they violate maturationally natural expectations about the world, they grab our attention. Experimental evidence (Barrett and Nyhof 2001), including cross-cultural research (Boyer and Ramble 2001), suggests that minimally counter-intuitive representations, in particular, are also more memorable, at a variety of retention intervals, than are representations of everyday items (a plaid couch), representations of curious items that do not violate maturationally natural ontological assumptions (a chocolate couch), and representations of items that violate multiple ontological assumptions (a couch that only remembers things that did not happen).[4] Minimally counter-intuitive representations' mnemonic advantage over less modestly counter-intuitive representations indicates that grabbing attention and memorability involve a trade-off. Representations with more violations may grab attention better, but are less likely to be recalled. Furthermore, a majority of Barrett and Nyhof's (2001) experimental participants exhibited a tendency at a three month retention interval to recall odd items (a bright pink newspaper blowing in the wind) as minimally counter-intuitive items (a bright pink newspaper that runs).

Minimally counter-intuitive representations constitute an attractor in the space of possible cognitive representations. They approximate a cognitive sweet spot. They attract attention, and the items they represent are easier to remember under most circumstances than other sorts of things. Crucially, though, the advantages of quite modestly counter-intuitive representations also enlist a bevy of default inferences, which provide a considerable body of information about the items in question cost free.

This is why I claimed that popular religion wields modestly counterintuitive representations 'at most'. Plentiful violations of maturationally natural assumptions quickly mark out which inferences hold; however, modestly counter-intuitive representations that involve one or two violations at most (such as a burning bush that is not consumed by the fire and that talks) are mostly not counter-intuitive. Knowing that something is an intentional agent, even if it can read minds, allows inferences that it has goals, desires, preferences and beliefs, that it finds some attitudes and behaviours offensive, and that it is disinclined to help anyone who displays them.

Although transfers in religious narratives usually implicate only one property explicitly (recall that garrulous serpent), they presume the importation of all of the default inferences associated with the domain of the transferred item. Any talking snake also schemes, tempts, acts and enjoys the status of an intentional agent with mental representations. Breaches work differently. They are specific, violating but a single default assumption. Religious representations that rely on a breach preserve all of that domain's default assumptions, save the one that is breached. The Jesus who violates our physical intuitions by walking on water still weighs more than twenty pounds, uses energy to walk and reflects light.

Why are the variations in the operation of this everyday cognitive equipment 'normal'? They count as normal because they arise in many other contexts. The modestly counter-intuitive representations in which religions traffic appear in everything from folk tales, fantasy and fiction to commercials, comic books and cartoons. Possessing maturationally natural capacities, especially theory of mind, outfits people to acquire religion in a way that is not true about science.

Maturationally Natural Cognitive Processing Facilitates Religion

Religions' most noticeable cognitive representations are those of agents manifesting counter-intuitive properties. Such representations' abilities to cue theory of mind and, more generally, humans' intuitive psychology occasion religious people's inferences about all sorts of religious matters. I will return to these in the second half of this sub-section. Humans' intuitive physics, biology and psychology, however, do not exhaust the maturationally natural capacities that religions cash in on. Religions can instigate cognitive processing by engaging other maturationally natural propensities. Two brief examples must suffice.

First, religions frequently elicit group loyalty by profiting from humans' inclination to aid kin. Reflection on kin selection and inclusive fitness, in particular, preceded and inspired evolutionary psychologists' theories and research over the past two decades. W.D. Hamilton's formal modelling of organisms' genetic interests pointed to the genetic advantages, under a variety of circumstances, of favouring kin, sometimes even distant kin and at considerable cost to oneself (Hamilton 1963, 1964, 1970). Evolutionary psychologists have hypothesized that human psychology is sensitive, though not necessarily consciously sensitive, to relevant information about kin, and have carried out empirical studies that support that hypothesis (Kurland and Gaulin 2005). Automatic, unconscious sensitivities and biases in the treatment of conspecifics bear the earmarks of maturationally natural aptitudes.

Many religions cue fictive kin. People often address one another with familial titles: priests are 'fathers', nuns are 'sisters'. Freud (1961) headlined what is, perhaps, the most obvious illustration: father gods. A religion's followers are the father-god's children. As siblings – 'brothers and sisters in Christ', for example – they become candidates for aid and support. Religions are not the only human arrangements that take advantage of this proclivity. People often use the titles and modes of address associated with kinship to reinforce affiliations with allies and friends.

Second, various cognitive scientists of religion (Hinde 1999; Boyer 2001) have argued that the standard view of the connection between religion and morality has things backwards. They maintain that people are inclined to moral conduct not because the gods command it; rather, the gods characteristically command such conduct as a means of capitalizing on evolved intuitions that incline us towards such conduct. Those intuitions concern such matters as the care of the young and vulnerable, the distribution of resources, reciprocity, respect for social hierarchies, purity with regard to a host of features concerned with humans' bodies, and the treatment of in-group members (Haidt and Bjorklund 2008).

Religions activate theory of mind in myriad ways. I will briefly describe three. Even in literate cultures, religious representations and beliefs are primarily transmitted through myths and stories. Such narratives carry significant cognitive advantages in comparison to science's experimental papers and review articles! Agents' actions drive narratives. Most human minds readily understand a world of agents interacting with one another and their environments.[5] Ordinarily, agents act rationally; thus, their reasons for action can serve in a framework for explaining those actions. A series of events connected through agent causality is endowed with instant plausibility and striking mnemonic advantages, by comparison to a comparable string of events connected mechanically (Piatelli-Palmerini 1994; Gregory 2009). An elementary principle of probability theory is that the probability of a series of events is the product of the various individual events' probabilities. It follows that even an extended series of probable events will itself be highly improbable. Yet when the threads of agents' intentions, reasons and actions stitch events together, humans not only find the series plausible, but often regard the outcome as inevitable. Because maturationally natural assumptions about how agents work, which myths and stories trigger, are so basic, narratives' consumers are typically oblivious to how those assumptions' entitle the representations of the gods that populate them.

Agents can act on the material world, but their social interactions with one another provoke the most sophisticated inferences about minds and the relations between the agents who possess them. Myths and stories make the gods and their actions plausible. Their plausibility, their counter-intuitive properties and their interests in human conduct render them particularly alluring candidates for social interaction. Rituals are salient vehicles for carrying out individual and collective transactions with these agents (Sørensen 2007). Tom Lawson and I (Lawson and McCauley 1990; McCauley and Lawson 2002) have argued that religious rituals engage maturationally natural cognitive machinery in human minds devoted to distinguishing agents from other things in the world and actions from other events. Rituals cue their representations as actions, which provoke spontaneous inferences about what is transpiring.

Rituals also incorporate a variety of features that have salutary cognitive effects for perpetuating religions and their ritual systems. These features include rituals' rigid adherence to scripts, their repetition and redundancy, their concentration on hazard precautions of various kinds, and their focus on low level features of action (Boyer and Liénard 2006; Liénard and Boyer 2006). These features tend to obscure two things: first, that little, if anything, of instrumental significance has occurred; second, that how what has occurred achieves anything remains unexplained. Boyer and Liénard hold that demands for attention to low-level features of action in rituals leads to inattention to rituals' putative goals ('goal-demotion'), to overloading memory, to the prevention of automaticity and to the suppression of thought (Nielbo and Sørensen 2011). Moment-by-moment on-line demands in rituals discourage the development of either reflective distance or practised naturalness (Boyer and Liénard 2006).

Stewart Guthrie (1993) advances the most developed version of an anthropomorphic theory of religion in our time. Guthrie highlights our maturationally natural perceptual inclinations to detect human forms and faces based on fragmentary evidence. He too accentuates the hypersensitivity of such systems and their susceptibility to illusions. Subsequent experimental evidence (e.g. Bateson et al. 2006) corroborates Guthrie's hypothesis about the importance of humans' perceptual sensitivities to the presence of other humans. Although he notes that, 'what matters is not so much the physical appearance of gods as their behaviour', Guthrie stresses that anthropomorphism results from 'an unconscious perceptual strategy' (Guthrie 1993: 193, 200). Religious icons most directly exploit this perceptual strategy.

Justin Barrett spotlights a psychological anthropomorphism, for which engaging theory of mind is at least as prominent as engaging the perceptual strategy that Guthrie underscores. In a study that tested participants' cognitive representations and inferences (and that included no perceptual component beyond reading texts), Barrett and Frank Keil (1996) furnished evidence that people reliably revert to their intuitive representations of agents in their on-line cognitive processing. After priming participants' consciously affirmed, explicit religious representations, Barrett and Keil had their participants read passages describing humans interacting with God. Crucially, the passages' contents were fully consistent with the participants' previously articulated, theologically correct pronouncements. Nevertheless, when participants tackled a free-recall task immediately thereafter, they automatically transformed the passages' contents to conform to their maturationally natural intuitive assumptions about how normal agents and their minds work. In their on-line recall, participants no longer thought about their theologically correct representations of God. Instead, they conceived of God as rather like Superman. In their on-line cognitive processing, religious participants presume that the gods are basically like us, regardless of what they say when they consciously reflect on their (theologically correct) religious representations.

This intrusion of maturationally natural assumptions in on-line religious thought is comparable to the intrusion of folk physical assumptions in on-line physical thinking in McCloskey's work. In both cases, maturationally natural intuitions swamp the radically counter-intuitive representations of theology and science (respectively) that participants acquired on the basis of painstaking formal education. Maturationally natural proclivities of mind subvert the enforcement of theologically correct doctrines and reinforce popular religious conceptions.

Some Consequences of Comparing the Cognitive Foundations of Science and Religion

Examining the cognitive bases of professional science and popular religion yields at least three consequences bearing on those enterprises' fates as knowledge communities. Compared to contemporary discussions of such matters, all three consequences examine less-travelled paths.

First, science poses no significant challenge to the persistence of religion. Recent attacks on religion (Harris 2004; Dawkins 2006; Hitchens 2007), based, in part, on extolling science, are unlikely to prove successful. This is not to say that no logical conflicts exist but only that people are not typically argued out of positions that they did not adopt on the basis of argument in the first place. Religion may meet with more or less popularity, as cultural and material conditions vary (Talmont-Kaminski 2013), but our maturationally natural penchants insure that religious ideas and representations will constantly surface in populations of human minds. Nothing that science or that any other intellectual endeavour generates will make religion go away. Neither the scientific enterprise, nor any particular scientific finding, nor antireligious polemics will undo the appeal of religious representations. Every human culture has had its ghosts and gods. Human minds generally find religious representations ideas that are good to think.

This is all contrary to the ironic confluence of opinion between many religious people and many critics of religion. Both hold that science threatens the survival of religion. In doing so, both simultaneously underestimate the appeal of religion, the ease of its acquisition and the difficulty of learning, mastering and producing science. They also misjudge the ingenuity of theologians. No revolutionary scientific accomplishment has surpassed theologians' abilities after a time to accommodate it.

Second, religion relies on institutional support far less than science. Impressive religious gatherings, edifices, practices and arrangements notwithstanding, religion has much less need of institutional structures than appearances suggest. Religion, after all, has prehistoric roots and is no less prominent in hunter-gatherer societies than in large-scale societies. The contemporary prominence of religions of the book, which clearly depend upon literacy, publications and schools, should not impede appreciating that those accoutrements are unnecessary for either the eruption or continuation of religion. Obviously, extravagant institutional trappings are not sufficient for religion either. Critics and participants note the Church of England's steady decrease in participation and religiosity, regardless of its institutional status. That religiosity and religions arise and endure when they are directly suppressed, by governments or other religions, is further testimony to the peripheral role of institutions in religions' invention and prolongation.

Institutions, by contrast, are indispensable for the perpetuation of science. Since scientific rationality relies on scientific communities, science is inherently institutional. An extensive educational and research infrastructure bolsters professional science. Science is almost exclusively pursued under the auspices of the most imposing institutions in human history, viz., governments, militaries, universities, corporations, research institutes, foundations and hospitals.

Institutions pursuing scientific education and research are the most conspicuous illustrations, but professional societies, scientific meetings, publication outlets and processes for distributing scarce resources, and for safeguarding scientific integrity, are vital and logistically complicated. Science does not rely on unregimented scepticism. Founding the Royal Society in England and the Royal Academy in France in the 1660s was pivotal to the consolidation and continuation of early modern science. Each formulated and enforced evidential standards, supported research projects and sponsored regular scientific meetings to demonstrate and test apparatuses and findings. Both also produced and disseminated scientific publications (Jardine 2000). Maintaining such institutions is the price of serious, ongoing scrutiny of explanatory proposals.

Third, professional science's dependence on such institutions points to the first salient reason why, contemporary appearances to the contrary notwithstanding, it is science's persistence, not that of religion, that is fragile over the long term. Sustaining scientific institutions is both costly and complex (Stephan 2012). The outlays for educating scientists are substantial. Mere entry to most fields requires nearly two decades of schooling and apprenticeship. The costs of scientific research are unrelenting. Progress commonly hangs on developing sophisticated technologies that enable scientists to observe, simulate or produce the exotic circumstances necessary to explore theories' implications.

Maintaining journals, professional societies, national academies and the like are expensive too, but authenticating and safeguarding the scientific process is, in some ways, an even greater challenge. The institutions of modern science foster conditions that routinely produce knowledge that is uncongenial to the institutions – governments, corporations, armies and so forth – which provide the money that science needs. Science's survival turns on the collective success of political, military, commercial and philanthropic institutions from which it must, simultaneously, preserve its independence. Funders' intrusions reducing science's critical distance from such institutions are inimical to its epistemic authority.

Financing an educational system sufficient to train a steady supply of new scientists and underwriting the institutional arrangements of modern science pose formidable economic and political challenges, even for the wealthiest societies. In the face of competing legitimate needs and the sheer limits on resources, let alone the pervasive temptations of political expediency, sustaining major scientific enterprises needs ample doses of both intellectual and political courage.

Science is also fragile because it traffics in difficult ideas and forms of thought. Early on, the sciences abandoned the deliverances of our maturationally natural cognitive capacities. Science constantly discloses principles by which the world operates that we find unintuitive, abstruse and difficult to learn, recall and employ. In many domains that is because our maturationally natural perceptions and conceptions intrude. Some ideas have natural disadvantages cognitively. If humans find religious ideas good to think, the opposite is true about most scientific ideas. This is the price of their radical counter-intuitiveness.

Religious ideas naturally inspire inferential leaps. Inferential leaps in science, by contrast, only occur after years of formal training and the mastery of large bodies of scientific knowledge. Most humans take years to acquire the inferential abilities, particularly in mathematics, that most sciences demand, and research indicates that, once learned, whatever practised naturalness they develop notably depends upon the familiarity of problems, materials and contexts.

Religion's exploitation of maturationally natural cognitive dispositions, its recurrence across cultures and its comparative independence of elaborate institutions suggest it is here to stay. Professional science's position is nearly the opposite on these counts. Its cognitive unnaturalness, its rarity in human history and its overwhelmingly social and institutional character all point to its fragility.

Acknowledgements

I wish to thank Tamara Beck, Matthew Homan and Carles Salazar for their helpful comments.

Notes

1. Instead of employing the triumvirate of 'perception, cognition and action', I will use 'cognition' only hereafter. It will stand for all three, unless indicated otherwise either directly or in context.
2. Controversy has raged about Cosmides and Tooby's hypothesis for explaining their findings (Buller 2005; Richardson 2007), but those findings have stood.

3. Research in the cognitive science of religion suggests that the inculcation of doctrines may be even more vulnerable to erosion in the face of maturationally natural intrusions – more on this anon.

4. This thesis has inspired considerable experimental work (Gonce et al. 2006; Norenzayan et al. 2006; Tweney et al. 2006; Upal et al. 2007). See Barrett (2008) for an overview of this research.

5. For a discussion of exceptions to this generalization, see Baron-Cohen (1995, 2003).

References

Atran, S., D. Medin and N. Ross. 2002. 'Thinking about Biology: Modular Constraints on Categorization and Reasoning in the Everyday Life of Americans, Maya and Scientists', *Mind and Society* 3(6): 31–63.

Baron-Cohen, S. 1995. *Mindblindness: An Essay on Autism and Theory of Mind.* Cambridge, MA: MIT Press.

———. 2003. *The Essential Difference: Male and Female Brains and the Truth about Autism.* New York: Basic Books.

Barrett, H.C., and R. Kurzban. 2006. 'Modularity in Cognition: Framing the Debate', *Psychological Review* 113(3): 628–47.

Barrett, J. 2008. 'Coding and Quantifying Counter-intuitiveness in Religious Concepts: Theoretical and Methodological Reflections', *Method and Theory in the Study of Religion* 20(4): 308–38.

Barrett, J., and F. Keil. 1996. 'Conceptualizing a Non-natural Entity: Anthropomorphism in God Concepts', *Cognitive Psychology* 31(3): 219–47.

Barrett, J.L., and M.A. Nyhof. 2001. 'Spreading Non-natural Concepts: The Role of Intuitive Conceptual Structures in Memory and Transmission of Cultural Materials', *Journal of Cognition and Culture* 1(1): 69–100.

Bateson, M., D. Nettle and G. Roberts. 2006. 'Cues of Being Watched Enhance Co-operation in a Real-world Setting', *Biology Letters* 2(3): 412–14.

Boyer, P. 2000. 'Functional Origins of Religious Concepts: Ontological and Strategic Selection in Evolved Minds', *Journal of the Royal Anthropological Institute* 6(2): 195–214.

———. 2001. *Religion Explained: The Evolutionary Origins of Religious Thought.* New York: Basic Books.

Boyer, P., and P. Liénard. 2006. 'Why Ritualized Behavior? Precaution Systems and Action Parsing in Developmental, Pathological, and Cultural Rituals', *Behavioral and Brain Sciences* 29(6): 1–56.

Boyer, P., and C. Ramble. 2001. 'Cognitive Templates for Religious Concepts: Cross-cultural Evidence for Recall of Counter-intuitive Representations', *Cognitive Science* 25(4): 535–64.

Buller, D.J. 2005. *Adapting Minds: Evolutionary Psychology and the Persistent Quest for Human Nature.* Cambridge, MA: MIT Press.

Buss, D. (ed.) 2005. *The Handbook of Evolutionary Psychology*. New York: Wiley.

Callaghan, T., et al. 2005. 'Synchrony in the Onset of Mental-state Reasoning', *Psychological Science* 16(5): 378–84.

Camerer, C.F., and R.M. Hogarth. 1999. 'The Effects of Financial Incentives in Experiments: A Review and Capital–Labor Production Framework', *Journal of Risk and Uncertainty* 19(1–3): 7–42.

Caramazza, A., M. McCloskey and B. Green. 1981. 'Naive Beliefs in "Sophisticated" Subjects: Misconceptions about Trajectories of Objects', *Cognition* 9(2): 117–24.

Christiansen, M.H. and N. Chater. 1999. 'Connectionist Natural Language Processing: The State of the Art'. *Cognitive Science* 23(4): 417–37.

Churchland, P.M. 1979. *Scientific Realism and the Plasticity of Mind*. Cambridge: Cambridge University Press.

——. 2012. *Plato's Camera: How the Physical Brain Captures a Landscape of Abstract Universals*. Cambridge, MA: MIT Press.

Churchland, P.S. 1983. 'Consciousness: The Transmutation of a Concept', *Pacific Philosophical Quarterly* 64(1): 80–93.

Coppola, M., and E.L. Newport. 2005. 'Grammatical Subjects in Home Sign: Abstract Linguistic Structure in Adult Primary Gesture Systems without Linguistic Input', *Proceedings of the National Academy of Sciences* 102(52): 19249–53.

Cosmides, L., and J. Tooby. 2005. 'Neurocognitive Adaptations Designed for Social Exchange', in D. Buss (ed.), *The Handbook of Evolutionary Psychology*. New York: Wiley, pp.584–627.

Dawkins, R. 2006. *The God Delusion*. Boston: Houghton Mifflin.

Duchaine, B. and K. Nakayama. 2006. 'Developmental Prosopagnosia: A Window to Content-specific Face Processing', *Current Opinion in Neurobiology* 16(2): 166–73.

Evans, J.S.B.T., and K. Frankish (eds). 2009. *In Two Minds: Dual Process and Beyond*. New York: Oxford University Press.

Fodor, J.A. 1983. *The Modularity of Mind*. Cambridge, MA: MIT Press.

Freud, S. 1961. *The Future of an Illusion*, trans. W.D. Robson-Scott, ed. J. Strachey. New York: Anchor.

Gilovich, T. 1991. *How We Know What Isn't So: The Fallibility of Human Reason in Everyday Life*. New York: Free Press.

Gilovich, T., D. Griffin and D. Kahneman. 2002. *Heuristics and Biases: The Psychology of Intuitive Judgment*. Cambridge: Cambridge University Press.

Gonce, L.O., et al. 2006. 'Role of Context in the Recall of Counter-intuitive Concepts', *Journal of Cognition and Culture* 6 (3/4): 521–47.

Gratzer, W. 2000. *The Undergrowth of Science: Delusion, Self-deception and Human Frailty*. Oxford: Oxford University Press.

Gregory, M.W. 2009. *Shaped by Stories: The Ethical Power of Narratives*. Notre Dame, IL: University of Notre Dame Press.

Guthrie, S. 1993. *Faces in the Clouds*. Oxford: Oxford University Press.

Haidt, J., and F. Bjorklund. 2008. 'Social Intuitionists Answer Six Questions about Moral Psychology', in W. Sinnott-Armstrong (ed.), *Moral Psychology: The Cognitive Science of Morality, Intuition and Diversity*. Cambridge, MA: MIT Press, pp.181–217.

Hamilton, W.D. 1963. 'The Evolution of Altruistic Behavior', *American Naturalist* 97(896): 354–56.

——. 1964. 'The Genetical Evolution of Social Behavior', *Journal of Theoretical Biology* 7(1): 1–52.

——. 1970. 'Selfish and Spiteful Behavior in an Evolutionary Model', *Nature* 228(5277): 1218–20.

Harris, S. 2004. *The End of Faith: Religion, Terror, and the Future of Reason*. New York: Norton.

Hinde, R. 1999. *Why Gods Persist*. New York: Routledge.

Hitchens, C. 2007. *God Is Not Great: How Religion Poisons Everything*. New York: Twelve.

Jardine, L. 2000. *Ingenious Pursuits: Building the Scientific Revolution*. London: Abacus.

Kahneman, D. 2011. *Thinking, Fast and Slow*. New York: Farrar, Straus and Giroux.

Kahneman, D., P. Slovic and A. Tversky (eds). 1982. *Judgment under Uncertainty: Heuristics and Biases*. Cambridge: Cambridge University Press.

Karmiloff-Smith, A. 1992. *Beyond Modularity: A Developmental Perspective on Cognitive Science*. Cambridge, MA: MIT Press.

Kelemen, D., J. Rottman and R. Seston. 2012. 'Professional Physical Scientists Display Tenacious Teleological Tendencies: Purpose-based Reasoning as a Cognitive Default', *Journal of Experimental Psychology: General* 142(4): 1074.

Keren, G., and Y. Schul. 2009. 'Two Is Not Always Better Than One: A Critical Evaluation of Two System Theories', *Perspectives on Psychological Science* 4(6): 533–50.

Kurland, J.A., and S.J. Gaulin. 2005. 'Cooperation and Conflict among Kin', in D. Buss (ed.), *The Handbook of Evolutionary Psychology*. New York: Wiley, pp.447–82.

Lawson, E.T., and R.N. McCauley. 1990. *Rethinking Religion: Connecting Cognition and Culture*. Cambridge: Cambridge University Press.

Legare, C.H. 2012. 'Exploring Explanation: Explaining Inconsistent Evidence Informs Exploratory, Hypothesis-testing Behavior in Young Children', *Child Development* 83(1): 173–85.

Legare, C.H., S.A. Gelman and H.M. Wellman. 2010. 'Inconsistency with Prior Knowledge Triggers Children's Causal Explanatory Reasoning', *Child Development* 81(1): 929–44.

Liénard, P., and P. Boyer. 2006. 'Why Cultural Rituals? A Cultural Selection Model of Ritualized Behaviour', *American Anthropologist* 108(4): 814–27.

McCauley, R.N. 1986. 'Truth, Epistemic Ideals and the Psychology of Categorization', in A. Fine and P. Machamer (eds.), *Philosophy of Science Association, 1986*, vol. 1. East Lansing, MI: Philosophy of Science Association, pp.198–207.

——. 2000. 'The Naturalness of Religion and the Unnaturalness of Science', in F. Keil and R. Wilson (eds.), *Explanation and Cognition*. Cambridge, MA: MIT Press, pp.61–85.

——. 2011. *Why Religion Is Natural and Science Is Not*. New York: Oxford University Press.

——. 2013. 'Why Science Is Exceptional and Religion Is Not: A Response to Commentators on *Why Religion Is Natural and Science Is Not*', *Religion, Brain and Behavior* 3(2): 165–82.

McCauley, R.N., and E.T. Lawson. 2002. *Bringing Ritual to Mind: Psychological Foundations of Cultural Forms*. Cambridge: Cambridge University Press.

McCloskey, M. 1983. 'Intuitive Physics', *Scientific American* 248(4): 122–30.

McCloskey, M., A. Washburn and L. Felch. 1983. 'Intuitive Physics: The Straight-down Belief and its Origin', *Journal of Experimental Psychology: Learning, Memory and Cognition* 9(4): 636–49.

Michotte, A. 1963. *The Perception of Causality*. Andover: Methuen.

Nielbo, K.L., and J. Sørensen. 2011. 'Spontaneous Processing of Functional and Nonfunctional Action Sequences', *Religion, Brain and Behavior* 1(1): 18–30.

Norenzayan, A., et al. 2006. 'Memory and Mystery: The Cultural Selection of Minimally Counter-intuitive Narratives', *Cognitive Science* 30(3): 531–53.

Piatelli-Palmarini, M. 1994. *Inevitable Illusions: How Mistakes of Reason Rule Our Minds*, trans. M. Piatelli-Palmarini and K. Botsford. New York: Wiley.

Richardson, R. 2007. *Evolutionary Psychology as Maladapted Psychology*. Cambridge, MA: MIT Press.

Rozin, P., et al. 1995. 'The Borders of the Self: Contamination Sensitivity and Potency of the Mouth, Other Apertures and Body Parts', *Journal of Research in Personality* 29(3): 318–40.

Schneider, W., and R.M. Shiffrin. 1977. 'Controlled and Automatic Human Information Processing, I: Detection, Search, and Attention', *Psychological Review* 84(1): 1–66.

Senghas, A., S. Kita and A. Özyürek. 2004. 'Children Creating Core Properties of Language: Evidence from an Emerging Sign Language in Nicaragua', *Science* 305(5691): 1779–82.

Shiffrin, R.M., and W. Schneider. 1977. 'Controlled and Automatic Human Information Processing, II: Perceptual Learning, Automatic Attending, and a General Theory', *Psychological Review* 84(2): 127–90.

Spelke, E.S., et al. 1992. 'Origins of Knowledge', *Psychological Review* 99(4): 605–32.

Sperber, D., F. Cara and V. Girotto. 1995. 'Relevance Theory Explains the Selection Task', *Cognition* 57(1): 31–95.

Stephan, P. 2012. *How Economics Shapes Science*. Cambridge, MA: Harvard University Press.

Sørensen, J. 2007. 'Acts that Work: A Cognitive Approach to Ritual Agency', *Method and Theory in the Study of Religion* 19(3/4): 281–300.

Talmont-Kaminski, K. 2013. *Religion as Magical Ideology: How the Supernatural Reflects Rationality*. Sheffield: Acumen/Equinox Publishing.

Tversky, A., and D. Kahneman. 2002. 'Extensional versus Intuitive Reasoning: The Conjunction Fallacy in Probability Judgment', in T. Gilovich, D. Griffin and D. Kahneman (eds), *Heuristics and Biases: The Psychology of Intuitive Judgment*. Cambridge: Cambridge University Press, pp.19–48.

Tweney, R.D., et al. 2006. 'The Creative Structuring of Counter-intuitive Worlds', *Journal of Cognition and Culture* 6(3/4): 483–98.

Upal, M.A., L. Owsianiecki, D.J. Slone and R. Tweney. 2007. 'Contextualizing Coun-
     ter-intuitiveness: How Context Affects Comprehension and Memorability of
     Counter-intuitive Concepts', *Cognitive Science* 31(1): 1–25.
Wason, P.C. 1966. 'Reasoning', in B.M. Foss (ed.), *New Horizons in Psychology*. Har-
     mondsworth: Penguin, pp.135–51.

Chapter Two

Scientific versus Religious 'Knowledge' in Evolutionary Perspective

Michael Blume

Throughout the twentieth century, evolutionary and religious explanations of life have mostly been discussed as conflicting and exclusive. Even those models that tried to separate these perspectives into non-overlapping magisteria indicated that religious lore would lose parts of its functionality. But over the last few years, new and interdisciplinary evolutionary studies of religiosity and religions have yielded empirical findings supporting a hypothesis first formulated by Friedrich August von Hayek in 1982: religious beliefs in super-empirical agents watching and motivating behaviour may be adaptive or even necessary for human life, although they seem to conflict with modern scientific knowledge. For example, religious demography has been able to explain a central factor in ongoing struggles between proponents of evolutionary theory and advocates of religious creation mythologies in the US, Israel and other countries: although evolutionists emphasizing empirical methodology tended to bring up far more scientific arguments, creationists believing in a God endorsing community and family life tended to bring up far more children. This holds empirically true even if other variables such as education, income or urbanization are controlled for. And the philosophical weight of these findings is indicated by a central assumption of evolutionary theories of cognition and evolutionary epistemology: all of our senses are assumed to have evolved by approximating aspects of reality, with 'better' information resulting in higher chances of survival and reproduction. Therefore, recent evolutionary and cognitive studies indicate the need to reassess our established perspectives on the functionality of scientific versus

49

religious 'knowledge', on the role of women in evolutionary history and on epistemological pluralism.

Evolutionary Studies of Religiosity and Religions

A century before evolutionary theory was formulated, David Hume presented a proto-evolutionary scenario of religious history in his eminent *Natural History of Religion* (1757). According to him, 'polytheism was the primary religion of man', rooted in human cognition inadvertently detecting agencies and forming theories of mind:

> There is an [*sic*] universal tendency among mankind to conceive all beings like themselves, and to transfer to every object, those qualities, with which they are familiarly acquainted, and of which they are intimately conscious. We find human faces in the moon, armies in the clouds; and by a natural propensity, if not corrected by experience and reflection, ascribe malice or good-will to every thing, that hurts or pleases us. (Hume 1757/2014: 7)

Hume further assumed a foundational role of women in the formation of religious groups: 'The leaders and examples of every kind of superstition, says Strabo, are the women. These excite the men to devotion and supplications, and the observance of religious days. It is rare to meet with one that lives apart from the females, and yet is addicted to such practices' (ibid.: 8). And in naming the functions of polytheist pantheons, Hume started with two goddesses and matters of reproduction. 'Accordingly, we find, that all idolaters, having separated the provinces of their deities, have recourse to that invisible agent, to whose authority they are immediately subjected, and whose province it is to superintend that course of actions, in which they are, at any time, engaged. Juno is invoked at marriages; Lucina at births' (ibid.: 5).

Charles Darwin was influenced by Hume's many works, including *The Natural History of Religion*. In his account of the evolution of religion in his *Descent of Man* (1871), he concurred with Hume on many points, such as the rejection of the still popular thesis of a primary monotheism ('Urmonotheismus'). Being a learned theologian, he also agreed in assuming cognitive processes were the source of early animist and (later) polytheist and finally monotheist conceptions of 'spiritual agencies' – contemporarily called supernatural or (more precisely) super-empirical agents.

Adding a social perspective to these cognitive processes, Darwin further assumed that the thus perceived monitoring might contribute to stabilizing and enhancing social and cooperative behaviour within groups, thereby increasing their chances in evolutionary competition. But then, Darwin referred to males and their purported tasks only, as he observed that

> It is almost necessary for him to avoid the disapprobation, whether reasonable or not, of his fellow men. Nor must he break through the fixed habits of his life, especially if these are supported by reason; for if he does, he will assuredly feel dissatisfaction. He must likewise avoid the reprobation of the one God or gods, in whom according to his knowledge or superstition he may believe; but in this case the additional fear of divine punishment often supervenes. (Darwin 1871: 89)

Following Malthusianism, which predicted un-stated, inherited means of massive reproduction in any human population 'surviving' competition, Darwin did not discuss reproductive advantage or female contributions in his evolutionary studies of religion. Instead, his male-centred assumptions can be directly linked to contemporary 'Gods of War' hypotheses, which assumed that religion primarily served to promote in-group cohesion in violent 'intra-group competition' (Johnson 2008).

After many trials and errors, contemporary evolutionary perspectives slowly returned to many terms and observations very close to those brought up by Darwin. Religiosity can indeed be defined as 'beliefs in super-empirical agents' such as ancestors, spirits, demons, angels, hidden space aliens, god or God. As with other biocultural traits, it seems to have emerged in evolutionary history by bringing together older, cognitive and emotive foundations into a new system of thoughts, beliefs and observable behaviour by promoting in-group cooperation (Wilson 2002; Voland and Schiefenhövel 2009; Frey 2010).

Although there have been assumptions about much earlier origins, the first widely acknowledged burials – emerging among *Homo sapiens* and *Homo neanderthalensis* – have been dated to about a hundred thousand years, while symbolic figurines and cave paintings have been around for at least forty thousand years. Recent findings of a complex temple site at Göbekli Tepe are refuelling debates whether religious behaviour may have brought about the formation of settled civilizations (Mann 2011).

But why did it take so long for many to accept the obvious argument already formulated by Darwin himself: that religiosity turns out to be an adaptive and successful trait of human evolution? The root of the assumed and popular 'conflict' between science(s) and religion(s) is a philosophical one. Many self-declared 'Darwinists' added an epistemological monism to their world-view that the learned theologian Darwin himself never endorsed: that there is only one kind of knowledge which is best accessed by empirical science(s).

As an example of scientism, Sam Harris argues that: 'The conflict between religion and science is inherent and (very nearly) zero-sum. The success of science often comes at the expense of religious dogma; the maintenance of religious dogma always comes at the expense of science' (Harris 2006: 1). But ranging from the Ancient Greeks right through great philosophers such as Immanuel Kant to contemporary evolutionary epistemology (Vollmer 2010), there has been the other possible assumption: that 'knowledge' is inherently multi-dimensional. Therefore, it is best explored by various means such as empirical science, arts and metaphysics, which are able to enrich, but not to replace, each other. For example, in his acknowledgement of evolutionary theory as 'more than a hypothesis', Pope John Paul II discerned 'various branches of knowledge'. In answering him, the eminent evolutionary biologist Stephen Jay Gould (a non-believer with a Jewish background) accepted the 'non-overlapping magisteria (NOMA)' of science(s) and religion(s) (Gould 1997).

Therefore, we might readily acknowledge that the famous painting *Guernica* by Pablo Picasso does not compete with an empirical photograph of the destroyed city, nor does it offer any peer-reviewed, scientific and statistical data about the bombs. But formed in the mould of a Christian triptych, the painting conveys a specific kind of partially emotional 'knowledge' about the terror and the losses caused by the Spanish civil war. It has prompted numerous human beings to remember the fate of Guernica and to rethink their stance on warfare ever since. We could argue that no scientific paper could have produced the same kind of 'knowledge' that Picasso's painting brought to the world.

In the same way we could ask whether religious myths such as God creating Adam and Eve may be offering 'symbolic truths' as a special, socially motivating and evolutionary successful kind of knowledge, as assumed for example by von Hayek (1988). After all, if Hume had been right in assuming that there is 'a universal tendency among mankind to conceive all beings like themselves, and to transfer to every object, those qualities, with which they are familiarly acquainted, and of which they are intimately conscious', this would imply that we are not functioning simply as calculating computers devising empirical hypotheses about our surroundings. Instead, we could be seen as evolved beings perceiving ourselves and the world we live in primarily in terms of social and meaningful relations. We might want to take notice that Michelangelo painted his image of God in the form of a human brain, possibly hinting at such an interactive, social constructivism, and preceding respective modern 'neurotheologies' by about five centuries (see Blume 2011).

We no longer have merely to speculate on these topics. After all, evolutionary theory offers us a way of empirically testing conflicting hypotheses of epistemological monism and epistemological pluralism. If religious myths constitute no more than an outdated or inferior kind of 'knowledge' as assumed by scientific monisms, its application to life should lower the average reproductive success of its adherents – that is, its evolutionary fitness. In contrast, if religious lore constitutes a magisteria or realm of knowledge beyond empirical science, it should, on average, go with higher numbers of offspring across subsequent generations.

The Reproductive Potentials of Religiosity

In a nearly forgotten lecture given by von Hayek in 1982, the evolutionary scientist noted that the first commandment given by God to the freshly created human pair is to 'be fruitful and multiply'. And he assumed that this myth could be one of many 'symbolic truths' functionally nurturing human life and culture in the course of its evolutionary history 'because' it reached beyond rational, scientific and immanent arguments (von Hayek 1982, 1988). After years of researching and probing this assumption, I no longer hesitate in acknowledging that von Hayek was right empirically: religious lore is even more adaptive than he or Darwin could have imagined. In fact, it may even be necessary for human culture(s) to survive the centuries.

As one of many examples, Dominik Enste tested the correlation of religious worship and the average number of children with data from waves of the World Value Surveys spanning eighty-two countries from all continents and world religions. The result was statistically solid across nations and cultures: regardless of denomination, the devout tended to have far more children among Christians, Muslims, Jews, Hindus, Buddhists and other religions. Those participants of the World Value Surveys who did not attend religious services were reported to have on average 1.65 children. Their contemporaries worshipping once a month averaged 2.01 kids. And those that went to a church, mosque, synagogue or temple more than once a week had the biggest families, with 2.5 children. Statistically highly significant, religiously affiliated humans reproduce (on average) more successfully than their secular peers (Enste 2007).

On closer scrutiny, the exploration not only of statistical correlations but also of qualitative case studies turned up numerous variants of non-reproductive religious traditions, such as the Christian Shakers. But then, only those communities survived to grow into world religions that endorsed marriage and large families. Of course, this does not imply that religion is the only demographic factor, but that it is an independent one.

Interestingly, the findings help us understand why scientific monists have not been able to defeat their fundamentalist adversaries: while non-religious evolutionists tend to bring up far more scientific arguments, religious creationists tend to bring up far more children. It is a surprising stalemate with a deep and informative, evolutionary irony. In fact, the far higher numbers of children among the religious recently became a central topic in sociology and politics. For example, ultra-Orthodox Jews (Haredim) in Israel formed a miniscule minority of about 1 per cent of the population at the formation of the state in 1948. However, they not only managed to retain their birth rate of more than six children per woman right until the 1980s, they managed to increase it to 7.6 children per woman in 1995, at the same time as the overall total fertility rate in Israel declined by 0.24 to barely above 2 children per woman. Doubling their numbers about every two decades, Haredim now form more than 10 per cent of the Israeli population and have become a major player in the Israeli parliament. And it is interesting to observe that specific religious traditions such as Orthodox Judaism have managed to retain extremely high fertility rates across subsequent generations, both with state support in Israel and outside it in the US (Berman 2009: 85–89; Kaufmann 2011).

Surveys comparing Muslim families in various countries that sent their children to religious schools (madrasas) to those that did not showed a respective fertility gap. Those families preferring madrasas had 0.67 more children on average in Indonesia than other Muslim families, 0.77 more children in the Indian provinces of Uttar Pradesh and Bihar, 0.58 more children in Bangladesh, 0.66 more children in Pakistan and 0.81 more children in the Cote d'Ivoire (Berman 2009: 92–94).

The Old Order Amish comprise another case, and one which I have had the opportunity of studying in detail. Although they hesitate to accept converts and are losing members in every generation, their numbers doubled during the twentieth century every fifteen to twenty years, rising from a meagre 5,000 people in 1900 to more than 200,000 adherents in 2005 (Blume 2010b). Other examples of religious traditions whose adherents have high fertility rates include Hutterites, Old Order Mennonites, Mormons, the Quiverfull movement and orthodox Muslims (e.g. Kraybill and Bowman 2002; Joyce 2009). Some of them actively avoid scientific education in order to secure their religious world-views, lifestyle and, ultimately, their evolutionary success.

In European societies with lower levels of religious and educational liberties, such as Switzerland (where the Amish originated, but had to flee), the demographic potentials of religiosity are visible, too. For example, we found that the religiously non-affiliated showed the lowest fertility rates in comparison to 'all' religious denominations differentiated by the Swiss Office of Statistics. In contrast, the Jewish as well as some smaller Christian denominations managed to combine higher percentages of academic education and membership of leading occupational classes with nearly double as many births than the non-religious (Blume 2009).

Finally, I would like to point out another finding with maybe far-reaching implications: in exploring the reproductive outcomes of diverse human populations, communities and traditions, we found a lot of religious variants that managed to retain high levels of fertility across many generations. In contrast, we did not find even a single example of a non-religious human group past or present that was able to maintain at least the replacement level of two children per woman for a century. Wherever the potential 'social glue' of religious traditions dissolved, family structures crumbled as well.

The Proximate Mechanisms Linking Religious 'Knowledge' and Evolutionary Fitness

Of course, the proximate mechanisms linking religious affiliation to evolutionary potentials are complex and diverse: At the individual level, (bio) cultural evolution selects for prolific religious commandments such as injunctions to marry early, to have many children and to regard them as a duty as well as a blessing from super-empirical agents. At the social level, commandments are selected for if they manage to bolster in-group cooperation such as long marriages, in-group loyalty and reciprocal charity. And at the institutional level, those religious traditions endorsing institutions of child-care such as kindergartens, schools, home-schooling networks or hospitals enjoy on average higher demographic and thus evolutionary success.

Actually, a range of diverse religious traditions established celibate roles, whose inhabitants do not form families of their own but are trying to support the survival and reproduction of their communities by service and example. In diverse configurations, such 'helpers at the nest' are found among many animal species. And it is interesting to see that, for example, the term 'nun' shares its etymological root with the family-supporting 'nanny'. In exploring the demographics of various Catholic countries, Berman et al. even went so far as to measure the reproductive impact of religious alloparenting in a special index: children per nun (Berman 2004).

If broken down to a single mechanism, the core, evolutionary potential of religiosity lies in its possibility of personal attachment by providing culturally 'tested' mythologies, rituals and symbols about 'watching' super-empirical agents and their behavioural expectations (Shariff et al.2009). We are not evolved to accept 'commandments' by non-living things, but instinctively ready to adjust our behaviour if we believe we are being observed and judged by relevant (if super-empirical) agents (Bering 2011).

For example, although evolutionary scholars agree on the central importance of differential reproductive success as the main indicator of evolutionary fitness, most would not accept this finding as a personal commandment to have many children, rightfully discovering that this would constitute an ontological fallacy. There is no direct way from the empirical and evolutionary 'is' to a binding 'ought'.

But if we believe we are seen, judged and maybe even loved and awaited by specific super-empirical agents, that is another situation. The ancestors might expect us to 'multiply' or to cooperate faithfully among our extended as-if kin, our 'brothers and sisters'. There is a motivational potential among religious beliefs that can be shaped into such diverse forms as extreme submission to cult leaders, to terrorism or even outright suicide – or into pro-social, life-supporting activities and dedicated communities and families. By (bio)cultural evolution, religious communities endorsing those rules helping them to prosper will do just that (cf. von Hayek 1988; Wilson 2002). The non-religious may be no less able to live moral and happy lives, but they seem to find (on average) fewer motivations, rules and institutions guiding them into cooperative groups and bigger families. Moral 'values' are not confined to religious people. But religious beliefs in super-empirical agents may endorse their impact by sanctioning them beyond rational deliberation.

Are There Biological Bases to 'Religiosity'?

In an attempt to avoid exploring religious traditions and their 'symbolic truths', a proponent of naturalistic reductionism could argue that the reproductive potential of religious traditions might be 'just cultural', and therefore without relevance to evolutionary biology and epistemology. But on closer scrutiny, this reductionist approach has long been overcome. For example, the human traits of preparing and cooking food are primarily transmitted 'just' by culture(s). Nevertheless, they have been proven to be enormously adaptive, hugely influencing human genes, brains and anatomy by providing larger amounts of easy and quickly digestible nutrients. In fact, cooking is one of many examples emphasizing the fact that it is not possible to understand human nature by excluding human culture – both are part of the same, intertwined evolutionary history (Wrangham 2010).

Concerning religiosity as a cognitive trait of the human brain, one would expect respective tendencies to be at least partially heritable by genes underlying neuronal architecture. In fact, a range of empirical twin studies concluded just that: religiosity turned out to constitute a polygenetic trait transmitted by many genes and neuronal structures with a medium to large heritability and individual variance just like many other human personality traits such as intelligence or musicality (Vance et al. 2010). Therefore, Kaufmann's (2011) rhetorical question – 'shall the religious inherit the earth?' – could be answered as follows: given contemporary genetic as well as demographic data, we should indeed expect further growth of religious inclinations in future generations (Rowthorn 2010).

The evolutionary process has not stopped and it seems to favour those capacities of our brains constructing multidimensional perspectives of reality and meaning. What is more, whereas an epistemological monism would turn out as gender-blind, the reproductive potentials brought about by the formation of religious networks and groups indicate an indispensable role of both sexes in the evolutionary process.

Religiosity Evolving by Enhancing Social Cognition and Cooperative Breeding

In the light of these evolutionary findings, Hume's hypotheses about female members of religious groups trying to 'excite' men into joining them resonate strongly with evolutionary scenarios of 'cooperative breeding' (CB). In evolutionary biology, CB is assumed to almost exclusively begin among females (such as in many social insects and mammals) and to potentially expand to include fathers and other males (such as in primates and, most profoundly, in humans). As Burkart, Hrdy and van Schait put it:

> In many non-human primates and mammals in general, cooperative breeding is accompanied by psychological changes leading to greater prosociality, which directly enhance performance in social cognition. Here we propose that these cognitive consequences of cooperative breeding could become more pervasive in the human lineage because the psychological changes were added to an ape-level cognitive system capable of understanding simple mental states, albeit mainly in competitive contexts. Once more prosocial motivations were added, these cognitive abilities could also be used for cooperative purposes, including a willingness to share mental states, thereby enabling the emergence of shared intentionality. (Burkart et al. 2009: 175)

Whereas it is safe to assume that our capacities to do modern science emerged on our evolved bases of rational cognition (for example deducing non-personal laws of gravitation), we are now able to see that religiosity grew out of our inherited social cognition – for example, deducing another person's state of mind – further strengthening them via reproductive success. A range of behavioural and brain-scanning studies exploring the neurological correlates to religious activities support this perspective.

Nina Azari, Petra Stoerig and colleagues have explored the brain activities of participants reading Psalm 23, and compared a group of devout (German) Christians with one of declared atheists. Among the believers, they found distinctive patterns in the frontoparietal lobes indicating processing of perceived, social interactions with God, a super-empirical agent purportedly hearing and an¬swering prayers. The non–believers, however, did not show these respective brain activities (Azari et al. 2001). Jesse Bering, meanwhile, was able to observe changes in the behaviour of children towards rule-observance if they had been told that they were observed by a nice but invisible 'Princess Alice' in contrast to a control group purportedly not observed (Bering and Johnson 2006). Ara Norenzayan and Azim Shariff have found higher levels of pro-social behaviour among participants in a game if they had been unconsciously primed by concepts of a (watching) God (Norenzayan and Shariff 2007). Finally, Shihui Han (2009) has presented a comparison of neurocognitive processes of the self by participants who saw pictures of religious and political personalities. Han found distinctive differences of self-processing patterns among groups of participating (Chinese) Christians and seculars.

All of these – and many more – studies point to the complex immersion of human brains and cognitions in their biographies, and social and cultural surroundings. Rational cognition is important in itself, but it forms only an aspect of the multi-dimensional processes by which we are constructing ourselves, our world-views and behaviour. Being a species depending on social life to flourish, our perceptions evolved to be fundamentally social too. Both science and (human) breeding turn out to be cooperative projects, but the latter is clearly the indispensable foundation of the first. Sciences and religions are addressing different magisteria or realms of human experience (McCauley 2011).

Conclusions

I would like to end by formulating three main hypotheses based on recent findings among evolutionary studies of religiosity and religions.

First, religiosity evolved on the basis of social cognition to become a successful evolutionary trait. By motivating believers, the trait shows the potential and tendency to raise cooperative and thereby reproductive potentials across generations. Of course, this does not prove the existence of super-empirical agents, but neither does it prove the opposite. It is possible to interpret these evolutionary findings in the frame of an 'adaptive illusion' (see Bering 2011). However, it is also possible to see it as a strong indication that successful religious traditions are bringing forth specific knowledge approaching a fundamentally personal and social reality through the ongoing evolution of religiosity and religions (see Dowd 2009).

Second, the role of women in the evolution of religiosity and religions has been greatly underestimated. Recent empirical findings, as well as the symbolically rich artwork depicting female 'Venus figurines' throughout long time spans and expanded regions of Stone Age humanity, all seem to indicate that religiosity did not evolve as a means to augment cooperative killing, but to support cooperative breeding. As forcefully described by Sarah Blaffer Hrdy (2009), the role of women and child-care has been greatly underestimated in evolutionary studies of humanity. Unfortunately, the same holds true in still-prevalent perspectives on the evolutionary history and present of religiosity and religious traditions (cf. Slone 2008; Blume 2009). Purported gender neutrality quite often disguised simple neglect of female contributions to our shared, evolutionary history.

Third, epistemological monism is refuted empirically. Sciences, arts and religions offer different kinds of knowledge(s). Both scientific and religious radicals got it wrong: Religious mythologies are not primarily outdated, scientific hypotheses. They are symbolic narratives motivating believers by social and communal attachment to perceived, super-empirical agents. Religious traditions such as the Old Order Amish or Hutterites manage to flourish by abstaining from scientific knowledge that they call 'worldly wisdom'. In contrast, we do not know of any human community past or present that has been able to survive demographically with the narratives offered by empirical science(s) alone. Rationality may be indispensable in itself, but it is not enough in a species depending on social relations, love and cooperative breeding of increasingly expensive children.

Evolution shaped us to be epistemological pluralists capable of valuable discoveries in all the 'various branches of knowledge' of rationalistic science(s), symbolic art(s) and social religion(s). Instead of wasting more years with fruitless strife among anti-theists and religious fundamentalists, we should proceed our quest to understand the multi-dimensionality of 'knowledge' with readiness for dialogue and open-minded curiosity.

References

Azari, N., P. Stoerig et al. 2001. 'Neural Correlates of Religious Experience', *European Journal of Neuroscience* 13: 1649–52.

Bering, J. 2011. *The God Instinct*. London: Nicholas Brealey.

Bering, J., and D. Johnson. 2006. 'Hand of God, Mind of Man', *Evolutionary Psychology* 4: 219–33.

Berman, E. 2004. 'From Empty Pews to Empty Cradles: Fertility Decline among European Catholics', unpublished paper. Retrieved 20 August 2012 from: econ. ucsd.edu

———. 2009. *Radical, Religious and Violent*. Cambridge, MA: MIT Press.

Blume, M. 2009. 'The Reproductive Benefits of Religious Affiliation', in E. Voland, and W. Schievenhövel (eds), *The Biological Evolution of Religious Mind and Behavior*. New York: Springer, pp.117–27.

———. 2010a. 'Charles Darwin über die Evolution von Religiosität und Religionen', in M. Delgado, O. Krüger and G. Vergauwn (eds), *Das Prinzip Evolution: Darwin und die Folgen für Religionstheorie und Philosophie*. Munich: Kohlhammer, pp.193–204.

———. 2010b. 'Von Hayek and the Amish Fertility: How Religious Communities Manage to Be Fruitful and Multiply. A Case Study', in U. Frey (ed.), *The Nature of God: Evolution and Religion*. Marburg: Tectum, pp.157–74.

———. 2011. 'God in the Brain: How Much can "Neurotheology" Explain?' in P. Becker and U. Diewald (eds), *Zukunftsperspektiven im theologisch-naturwissenschaftlichen Dialog*. Göttingen: Vandenhoeck and Ruprecht, pp.306–14.

Burkart, J.M., S. Hrdy and C. Van Schaik. 2009. 'Cooperative Breeding and Human Cognitive Evolution', *Evolutionary Anthropology* 18(5): 175–86.

Darwin, C. 1871/2012. *The Descent of Man, and Selection in Relation to Sex*. London. Online Reprint by Project Gutenberg 2012.

Dowd, M. 2009. *Thank God for Evolution: How the Marriage of Science and Religion Will Transform Your Life and Our World*. New York: Plume.

Enste, D. 2007. 'Kinder – Auch eine Frage der Überzeugung', *iwd* 2007(13): 3.

Frey, U. (ed.). 2010. *The Nature of God – Evolution and Religion*, Marburg: Tectum.

Gould, S.J. 1997. 'Nonoverlapping Magisteria (NOMA)', *Natural History* 106(3): 16–22.

Han, S. 2009. 'Religious Belief and Neurocognitive Processes of the Self', in E. Voland and W. Schievenhövel (eds), *The Biological Evolution of Religious Mind and Behavior*. New York: Springer, pp.195–204.

Harris, S. 2006. 'Science Must Destroy Religion', *Huffington Post*, 2 January 2006. Retrieved 20 August 2012 from: www.huffingtonpost.com.

Hrdy, S.B. 2009. *Mothers and Others: The Evolutionary Origins of Mutual Understanding*. Cambridge, MA: Harvard University Press.

Hume, D. 1757/2014: *The Natural History of Religion*. London 1757 / Universidade de Sao Paulo 2014. Available at: http://stoa.usp.br/briannaloch/files/2564/16389/ The+Natural+History+of+Religion+-+David+Hume.pdf

Johnson, D. 2008. 'Gods of War: The Adaptive Logic of Religious Conflict', in J. Bulbulia and R. Sosis (eds), *The Evolution of Religion: Studies, Theories and Critiques.* Santa Margarita, CA: Collins Foundation Press, pp.111–17.

Joyce, K. 2009. *Quiverfull: Inside the Christian Patriarchy Movement.* Boston: Beacon Press.

Kaufmann, E. 2011. *Shall the Religious Inherit the Earth? Demography and Politics in the Twenty-first Century.* London: Profile Books.

Kraybill, D.B., and C.D. Bowman. 2002. *On the Backroad to Heaven: Old Order Hutterites, Mennonites, Amish and Brethren.* Baltimore: Johns Hopkins University Press.

McCauley, R. 2011. *Why Religion is Natural and Science Is Not.* New York: Oxford University Press.

Mann, C. 2011. 'The Birth of Religion: The World's First Temple', *National Geographic* 219(6): 34–59.

Norenzayan, A., and A. Shariff. 2007. 'God Is Watching You: Priming God Concepts Increases Prosocial Behavior in an Anonymous Economic Game', *Psychological Science* 18: 803–80.

Rowthorn, R. 2010. 'Religion, Fertility and Genes: A Dual Inheritance Model', *Proceedings of the Royal Society* B 278: 2519–27.

Shariff, A., A. Norenzayan and J. Henrich. 2009. 'The Birth of High Gods. How the Cultural Evolution of Supernatural Policing Influenced the Emergence of Complex, Cooperative Human Societies, Paving the Way for Civilization', in M. Schaller and A. Norenzayan (eds), *Evolution, Culture, and the Human Mind.* London: Psychology Press, pp.119–36.

Slone, J. 2008. 'The Attraction of Religion: A Sexual Selectionist Account', in J. Bulbulia and R. Sosis (eds), *The Evolution of Religion: Studies, Theories and Critiques.* Santa Margarita, CA: Collins Foundation Press, pp.181–88.

Vance, T., H. Maes and K. Kendler. 2010. 'Genetic and Environmental Influences on Multiple Dimensions of Religiosity: A Twin Study', *Journal of Nervous and Mental Disease* 198(10): 755–61.

Voland, E., and W. Schiefenhövel (eds). 2009. *The Biological Evolution of Religious Mind and Behavior.* New York: Springer.

Vollmer, G. 2010. 'Menschliches Erkennen in evolutionärer Sicht', in J. Oehler (ed.), *Der Mensch: Evolution, Natur und Kultur.* Heidelberg: Springer, pp.141–54.

Von Hayek, F.A. 1982. 'Die überschätzte Vernunft', in W. Kerber (ed.), *Die Anmaßung von Wissen.* Tübingen: Mohr, pp.76–101.

———. 1988. *The Fatal Conceit.* Chicago: University of Chicago Press.

Wilson, D.S. 2002. *Darwin's Cathedral: Evolution, Religion, and the Nature of Society.* Chicago: University of Chicago Press.

Wrangham, R. 2010. *Catching Fire: How Cooking Made Us Human.* New York: Basic Books.

Chapter Three

Magic and Ritual in an Age of Science

Jesper Sørensen

Several theories have prophesized the end of 'religion' and 'magic' as scientific progress expands the human ability to control its environment. Thus, secularization hypotheses claim that religion in general should decline under modernity, even if some aspects might remain as basic identity markers in a globalized world. In contrast, other theories argue that modernization would not influence religion as it is based on non-falsifiable claims, whereas magic, addressing particular pragmatic concerns, should decline as a result of increasing technological control. In this chapter it shall be argued that modernity brings new pragmatic dangers not easily fixed by technology; that perceived dangers elicit ritual behaviour; that magic is therefore not a thing of the past but a behavioural response grounded in universal cognitive capacities; and that focusing on cognition and concrete behaviour enable us to ground the relation between 'magic', 'religion' and 'science' in an institutional and contextual framework.

Religion, Magic, Secularization and Modernity

Despite numerous attempts to provide a general theory, it remains a persistent question why religious and magical beliefs and practices persevere in Europe and America despite more than one hundred years of modernization. Why has the growth in explanatory and technical mastery of the surrounding environment supplied by science not resulted in a corresponding decline in beliefs and behaviour in more or less open conflict with these insights? Why has the enlightenment ideal of a world without so-called irrational beliefs not come true? These questions are, of course, not new, and numerous scholars have addressed them over the last three to four decades. Most relate the question directly to theories of secularization that outline different ways in which 'religion', however conceived, would decline as a result of modernization, itself understood as some mixture of social, technological or epistemological change (Shiner 1967). Even if not dead, most secularization theories struggle when confronted with the seeming increase in or at least continuing importance of religion in world affairs. In fact, the apparent secularization of north-western Europe, and most particular Scandinavia, may be the 'oddball' in a world characterized by unremitting strong religious commitments.

So how do we address the relation between modernization, religion, magic and science? Discussions of these phenomena are, naturally, informed by what phenomena are included under the respective definitions (Beckford 2003). Thus, understanding secularization as operating on several distinct levels of social organization, a macro-social, global tendency of secularization can be defended even while recognizing that at lower levels, say individual membership of religious organizations, we do not necessarily find a corresponding tendency. Accordingly, distinct levels may develop in opposite directions resulting in a rather complex picture of sacralization and secularization as divergent tendencies at different organizational levels (Kühle 1999; Dobbelaire 2002). Even in Scandinavia, generally considered the vanguard of secularization, we find opposing tendencies. Despite low church attendance and declining self-proclaimed belief in the doctrines of the majority Christian religion, church membership is still very high (about 80 per cent in Denmark). At the same time, non-orthodox beliefs, for instance in reincarnation and ritual healing, are also widespread, a fact that adds to the muddy picture of the role, spread, depth and importance of religious beliefs and practices in the modern world (Ahlin 2010; Andersen and Lüchau 2011).

A more fruitful way of tackling the problem of the persistence of religion under modernity might be to distinguish not only levels of social organization, but also different types of practices and different types of belief. Theories of secularization depend on precise definitions of religion delineating what it is that is supposed to diminish, become privatized or be functionally separated. In short, the question is: What belongs to the domain of religion? Until quite recently, this lack of conceptual clarification has corresponded with rather few attempts to create precise models able to produce generalized propositions about the development of religion in the modern world (Sherkat and Ellison 1999). A notable exception is rational choice theory (RCT), in particular the theory of religion developed by Stark and Bainbridge (Stark and Bainbridge 1980, 1985, 1987; see also Stark 1999; Stark and Finke 2000). As they have explicitly formulated predictions about the role of magic in modernity, a critical examination of their position will be our point of departure before presenting an alternative model informed by findings in cognitive science.

Criticizing central assumptions of secularization theory, Stark and Bainbridge have proposed a demand-driven understanding of religion. Based on a behaviourist model of humans as rational actors seeking rewards, Stark and Bainbridge describe religion as subject to a market with demand and supply, and they argue that religion can be differentiated from magic based on the types of reward supplied. Both magic and religion are 'compensators' – that is, symbolic representations that promise future rewards ('I owe yous', or IOUs) in place of unavailable or hard to get rewards.[1] These rewards are distinct in both scope and generality, and thus function to delineate magic from religion. Whereas magic is directly linked to particular, concrete future outcomes of pragmatic actions (for example, a better harvest), the promises of religion are more general, encompassing and, usually, related to existential long-term rewards, such as eternal life.

Stark and Bainbridge further argue that this difference is important in a modern world characterized by cumulative scientific innovations and a constantly growing technological mastery of the surrounding environment. This development not only entails that the 'special compensators' of magic are under constant risk of being falsified due to their pragmatic embedding (the 'chant' did not ensure a good harvest, for example), magic is also pressed by a market that supplies technological fixes against negative outcomes previously conceived to be beyond human control (fertilizers and pesticides ensure a good harvest). In short, magic is constantly proven wrong, and the problems it is supposed to fix are increasingly solved by new technology. In contrast, the 'general compensators' of religion are more immune to social and technological change as their purported goals are neither easily falsified nor rendered superfluous by technology. Religions promise such things as eternal life and universal justice – all future rewards not easily falsified and, at least presently, way beyond the scope of technology. According to Stark and Bainbridge, the decline of religion in north-western Europe is therefore not a question of diminishing demand (e.g., people still crave immortality), but rather a product of a non-functional market – of state-supported institutional monopolies that need not stimulate popular demand in order to survive. Thus, even if a non-functioning market situation might temporarily quell religious participation, religion does not disappear as it is based on unceasing, universal demands. Ultimately, new organizations will emerge to fulfil demands that are not being met by church monopolies.

Stark and Bainbridge are well aware that magic – defined as a supernatural attempt to manipulate concrete, pragmatically defined outcomes – is still found in modern contexts. Thus, new so-called 'client cults' promise special compensators directed at particular problems, such as heightened states of consciousness or knowledge about the future. These are, however, not connected to broader social movements and they will thrive only as long as there is a demand for the reward supplied by the cult not presently met by technology or falsified by experience. Further, new religious movements tend to have strong magical components at their outset, but Stark and Bainbridge's model predicts that the vulnerability of magic functions as a selective mechanism: only groups that successfully transform special into general compensators will survive as viable religious organizations (Stark and Bainbridge 1980, 1985). Those that do not manage this transformation will vanish together with the specific compensators that are falsified or rendered superfluous due to technology.

Stark and Bainbridge thereby present a new take on the process of rationalization that Max Weber described as inherent in the development of religious organizations. They make a more sophisticated description of the differential development of religious and magical ideas and practices in a modern world dominated by science. The question remains, however, whether the most successful religions in a modern world are really those devoid of magic (cf. Inglis, this volume). It also remains a question whether the division of labour between religious organizations supplying general compensators and magical specialists supplying specific compensators really is as 'natural' as argued by Stark and Bainbridge. I shall return to these questions below, but first we need to critically address two basic assumptions in Stark and Bainbridge's model.[2]

Firstly, as mentioned above, Stark and Bainbridge's approach is based on RCT. RCT envisions humans as rational beings that make decisions in the (religious) market based on deliberate reflections and rational calculations in order to maximize expected utility. In short, humans invest resources (costs) in particular religious institutions because they expect an outcome (reward) in the form of a return that makes the investment worthwhile. This reward, the expected utility of the investment, is identical to the content of the explicit promises made by the institution (such as eternal life). By implication, people invest in religious practices because of an explicit representation of the future rewards promised by the institution, and they are able to calculate the utility based on adequate representations of the relation between costs and rewards.

Cognitive psychology, however, unanimously argues that this is not an adequate picture of human reasoning, and that the rational-actor model is a mirage of certain economic models (Jones 2005; Kahneman 2011). Human minds are not blank slates driven only by a general urge to maximize rewards. Human reasoning is informed by cognitive processes, which for the most part are both outside our conscious control (thus not deliberate), are structured by domain-specific constraints (evolved aspect) and are informed by cultural schemas (learned aspect). To the extent that human behaviour is directed towards the obtaining of universal rewards, these generally take the form of goals that are relevant, either in terms of adaptive fitness or, at a more proximate level, to the developmental environment of any particular individual. Thus, rather than being a general maximizing machine, human reasoning is ultimately constrained by evolved motivational structures, that is, by a mental architecture geared to process particular types of information. Further, it is directed towards a range of proximate goals informed by a particular socio-cultural environment.

Therefore, a capitalist, economic market with its abstract system of exchange based on symbolic compensators (money, the ultimate IOU) is not a very precise model of how humans reason in other situations. Actually, it does not even fit economic behaviour very well, but is more adequately described as a model of the behaviour of an ideal market participant. Over the last three decades, behavioural economists have shown that human economic reasoning is strongly biased by a number of heuristics (e.g. Tversky and Kahneman 1982), even when these work against the maximization of expected utility. To summarize, human psychology is more complex than the simple rational-actor model employed by Stark and Bainbridge. If we want to explain the role of religion and magic in the modern world, we must go beyond participants' understanding of the explicit claims found in religious and magical practices and unearth the implicit effects of underlying cognitive structures. In other words, we need to go beyond the intellectualist approach, where behaviour is driven by particular, explicit belief states, in order to show how particular beliefs and practices survive due to their direct impact on human cognitive processing.

Secondly, the more fractionated picture of the human mind argued by cognitive science is at odds with the broad analytical categories of 'religion' and 'magic' used by Stark and Bainbridge to reflect universal and unchanging demands. The human mind does not react to and process 'religion' or 'magic'. Rather, it processes particular types of information, and if we want to explain the causal story underlying this process – that is, what type of information appears to be conducive to the propagation of particular behaviours or beliefs – we need to fractionate religion and magic into its constituent parts as well (Boyer 1996; Sørensen 2007a). Among these parts are, of course, the explicit rewards promised. Being told that a particular practice will guarantee a better life in the world to come, or that a ritual will produce a better harvest, is likely to enhance propagation of these behaviours in a population. However, such representations are themselves built upon a number of premises: first, that a promise is believable within the recipients' frame of reference; second, that the authority expressing the promise is trustworthy and eligible to make the promise; and third, that the behaviour can be represented as somehow correlated to the desired reward, that is, that it is able to function as a compensator. Thus, the choice of compensator as well as the representation of its efficacy will be dependent on a number of cognitive processes not themselves determined by a representation of utility maximization.

Another line of criticism is based on findings in both ethnography and historiography that question the direct relation between explicit propositions about the meaning, reason or effect of a particular practice and the motivation underlying actual performance. Thus, when prompted by ethnographers to explain the reasons for the performance of particular rituals, informants quite often strongly disagree upon such reasons or they have no explicit representations except that such behaviour is customary and socially expected (e.g. Humphrey and Laidlaw 1994). And even in cases where (some) informants are able to explicitly state 'theologically correct', explicit reasons (Barrett 1999), we should be wary of concluding that these are the real motives underlying performance. These might as well be understood as post hoc explanations prompted by the question asked rather than being the initial motivating factor underlying behaviour. The human tendency to spontaneously understand actions as prompted by particular beliefs (such as 'you open your umbrella because you believe it rains') might seriously impede our ability to understand the proliferation and stabilization of actions, in which the relation between the motor sequence performed and its postulated effects are disputed, opaque or even non-existent (Boyer and Liénard 2006; Sørensen 2007b).

Moving from ethnography to history, the disentangling of observed behaviour from explicitly expressed doctrines might help explain an oft-noted historical finding: whereas some types of behaviour, notably ritual, tend to be extremely stable over long periods of time, the explicitly expressed reasons for performance might change dramatically. But why would behaviour remain stable if the reward it is thought to compensate for has changed? A traditional explanatory alternative to the intellectualist approach defended by Stark and Bainbridge reverses the causal sequence and argues the primacy of behaviour. Accordingly, religious behaviour should not be explained by reference to the explicit propositions said to motivate these. Rather, it is behaviour that prompts the production of these doctrinal explanations, and these might change to fit new social and cultural environments. Accordingly, successful religious institutions are those that rope in and connect behaviour, performed for other reasons, to particular types of propositions and organizational structures (Schjoedt et al. 2013). Organizations might promote such behaviour by means of techniques addressing particular motivational structures – such as fear, contamination, ostracism or submission (see Boyer and Liénard 2006) – but it is unlikely that a promise of reward in the far future is in itself a very efficient motivator. In fact, humans have a strong tendency to choose a small immediate reward rather than a larger future reward – a phenomenon known as the hyperbolic discounting bias (Green and Myerson 2004). Thus, religious organizations might stimulate or quell demands for their services (Bauman 1998), but they do so by affecting particular cognitive systems that, in turn, motivate human behaviour.

Where does this leave magic? Stark and Bainbridge's time-honoured claim that magical practices are directed towards particular outcomes seems intuitively correct. Even so, two problems remain. First, it is not a trivial matter to stipulate the dividing line between specific and general compensators. Whereas the end points of a continuum between magic and religion might be easy to pinpoint based on the ease of falsification (for example, saying a spell to win the lottery versus praying for eternal life), in other cases it is unclear if a practice should be classified as a specific or a general compensator. For instance, should such practices as a community praying to their god(s) for an abundant harvest be defined as a specific or a general compensator? It might seem like a clear case of a specific compensator as it addresses a particular problem (getting food), but the potentially dire consequences of failure (starvation and potentially death) points to much graver consequences that engage both existential concerns and the relation between the community and the god(s) prayed to. Thus special compensators might be important as they directly activate more basic assumptions about the world, generally described by Stark and Bainbridge as general compensators.[3] Further, religious organizations that disengage themselves and their religious practices from mundane human concerns are likely to become irrelevant to participants. In fact such a 'triviality effect' is likely to impose a more serious risk to continuous performance than that imposed by any particular compensator being falsified (Sørensen 2005a). Special and general compensators are thus more entwined than envisioned by Stark and Bainbridge.

This points to the second problem, namely Stark and Bainbridge's adoption of the Durkhemian dictum that there is no church of magic (Durkheim 1965). If we adopt the definition of magic as a specific compensator, Durkheim's position is negated by the fact that most successful religions contain large amount of rituals aimed at specific goals that are deemed relevant by participants (for an example, see Inglis, this volume). In their attempt to delineate religion and magic, Stark and Bainbridge seem too informed by theological, normative descriptions of what religious practices should be performed, rather than by the practices actually found within these. Most religious organizations in the world, including so-called world religions, endorse practices addressing matters of pressing human concern, such as business success, fertility, security, health, psychological well-being or luck in hunting, fishing and/or agriculture. Thus, they reflect and address the everyday concerns of their participants by means of ritual. But how, then, do they avoid the problem of falsification? Why do people not abandon their ritual practices when the harvest fails, when no game is tracked down or when health inevitably fails? Part of the answer is that ritual practices related to such concerns are not the sole efficient causal factor represented by participants. Activities, such as agriculture, are not done by magic alone, and a failed harvest might be explained by reference to other factors, such as a lack of technical skill, as the result of sabotage (by pests, for example) or as the workings of powerful malignant agents (Malinowski 1992). Rituals aimed at specific results are represented as taking part in a larger network of interrelated events, all believed to play some role in attaining a desired reward. They usually address only aspects of this network, and the possibilities of *post hoc* explanations of ritual failure are legion (e.g. Evans-Pritchard 1937). This is true for both freelance ritual experts selling their talents on the marketplace, and priests practising within an organized religion. The risk of falsification of too specific compensators – that is, compensators believed to be the exclusive cause of a reward – is not just a risk of organized religion but equally faces ritual specialists that attempt to uphold their clientele. In fact, the human aversion to the disconfirmation of cherished beliefs would make the danger of falsification much larger for the freelancer working outside the organizational and conceptual umbrella of a religious organization than for the priest protected by its representations of authority, loyalty, in-group favouritism and a more or less coherent conceptual framework (Sørensen 2004). Religious organizations thus provide special compensators with a degree of immunity against falsification.

Naturalizing Religion and Magic

A natural conclusion to the argument presented so far is that, if we are to elicit the causal mechanisms underlying religious and magical beliefs and practices in modernity, we need a more refined picture of the human mind than that presented by Stark and Bainbridge. Humans are not driven by a general reward-seeking mechanism, but by a host of domain-specific inference systems. Further, the motivations underlying religious and magical behaviour cannot be explained solely by reference to the explicitly stated goals of these actions and a general model of the maximization of utility. That being said, cognitive models of religion and magic have at least one important feature in common with that of Stark and Bainbridge: both envision contemporary religious organizations, ideas and practices to be the result of selective processes (Boyer 1994, 2001). The difference lies in what features are believed to produce this selection. Stark and Bainbridge defend a general market model driven by supply and explicit demands. In contrast, the model of magic and religion presented in this chapter suggests a more complex picture combining cognitive constraints, entrenched conceptual models and the emergence of status groups organizing social exchange.

We have already looked at some of the assumption concerning the underlying cognitive mechanisms: human minds and therefore our basic motivational structures are moulded by our evolutionary past; these are organized into distinct domains of cognitive processing; and successful cultural forms get at least part of their motivational force from latching on to these evolved domains. It is further a basic assumption that the study of religion is overwhelmingly the study of ideas and practices transmitted through communicative processes (Boyer 1994). Over the last two decades, this view has developed into a notion of 'representational epidemiology' (Boyer 1994, 2001; Sperber 1996; Atran 2002). The gist of the argument is that our cognitive system imposes selective constraints on what representations are faithfully transmitted. Human cognition thus functions as a selective mechanism allowing some representations to be communicated relatively unchanged, whereas other representations either die out or are systematically transformed into more optimal versions during the transmission process. In contrast to 'code theories' of communication that present communication as an act of a sender coding and a receiver decoding a message by means of a common system of signs, epidemiology argues that in every communicative situation much remains unsaid and that a substantial part of the meaning of any utterance is the product of cognitive inferences made by both sender and receiver. This entails that successful communication uses material media (such as sound) to deliberately evoke particular inferences in recipients, and that we, as scientists studying culture, must keep in mind this underdetermination of the material symbol when we study culture as communicative processes (Boyer 1994). Two processes are proposed to constrain the reconstructive process done by the recipient: one, the pragmatic situations in which the communication is received; and two, the domain-specific inferences that the communication gives rise to. Together these processes designate the cognitive relevance of the input, and function as selective constraints on the transmission of representations (Sperber 1996). In addition, widespread cultural models impose a third selective constraint on relevance (that is, a 'cultural immunology') as information that integrates better into existing models supplies more inferential potential (Sørensen 2004).

This model of transmission is in accordance with recent developments in cognitive neuroscience that understand cognitive processes in terms of prediction (Frith 2007). When engaging in communication, we use available cues both to predict the intention of the speaker and to assess whether this new knowledge should lead to a modification of our present model of our immediate environment. It also entails that our expectations, both implicit and explicit, play a significant role when we understand the world around us, including the signs produced by other people. Prediction as a cognitive process thus seems to be the key to understanding such diverse phenomena as on-line action perception (Zacks and Tversky 2001), the categorical perception of entities into kinds (Bar 2009), the construction of social stereotypes (Brubaker et al. 2004) and episodic memory (Schacter et al. 2008).

To summarize, the human cognitive system is geared to enhance the survival of the organism by allowing it to predict its environment. In evolutionary terms, some types of information are more important and relevant than others, and human cognition is biased towards obtaining such information. This poses constraints on the transmission of cultural information such as those found in religion and magic. Further, it entails that human cognition is flexible enough to learn patterns arising from a particular environment to enhance the knowledge base used to make predictions.

Our cognitive system can thus be understood as a learning device constrained by evolved biases that ensure that some types of information are acquired at the expense of others. But how is this relevant when trying to understand and explain the role of magic in a modern age of science? First, it will help us reach a basic understanding of the universal aspects of magic, an understanding that is logically prior to understanding how any of these might be distinct in any particular socio-cultural setting. Second, isolating particular cognitive mechanisms allows us to investigate how changing socio-cultural circumstances alter the informational environment of a cognizing subject, both in terms of available cues, type of knowledge expected and how it relates to social status groups.

A number of studies in the cognitive science of religion have focused on how human cognitive systems constrain the transmission of religious ideas.[4] Space does not permit a more thorough discussion, but on a general level, gods and other superhuman agents are understood as particularly relevant exchange partners as they combine attention-demanding violations of intuitive assumptions with privileged access to social knowledge (Boyer 2001). A more directly relevant strain of studies investigates how participation in or observation of ritual affects cognitive processing, including how rituals connect to central narratives and values in society (e.g. Lawson and McCauley 1990; Schjoedt et al. 2013), and why rituals are often believed to influence the outcome of pragmatic endeavours – that is, why magic persists (e.g. Vyse 1997; Sørensen 2007a, 2007b; Subbotsky 2010). It is a central assumption of these studies that ritual, as a type of action, is processed by the same cognitive systems engaged in ordinary action processing (Lawson and McCauley 1990). Further, it is observed that ritualized behaviour, in a systematic way, departs from canonical actions, and that these departures systematically affect cognitive processing (Rappaport 1979, 1999). The remainder of this chapter will address a host of related problems: What types of endeavours elicit ritual performance? How do rituals connect with other types of action? What makes ritual distinct? How do the peculiarities of ritual behaviour create particular effects, both in terms of the representation of pragmatic success as well as representations of responsibility and agency? Naturally, I can only present a rough outline of potential answers, but this will hopefully encourage further future research into how religious phenomena find expression under modernity.

Magic, Ritual and Dangerous Actions

Almost one hundred years ago, Bronislaw Malinowski observed that the inhabitants of the Trobriand Islands of the Massim region, off the east coast of Papua New Guinea, only performed magical rituals in conjunction with certain types of endeavours. Reacting to Lévy-Bruhl's (in)famous theory of primitive mentality (Lévy-Bruhl 1985), Malinowski argued that so-called primitive people, rather than stumbling around in a mystical fog, is guided by logical reasoning in most of their activities, and have in their possession a large number of technologies used to control the environment (Malinowski 1935, 1992). Malinowski was, in fact, quite impressed with the technical mastery allowing the Trobrianders to survive on a small coral atoll. Not only were they able to produce an agricultural surplus by growing yams with a very simple technology, they also built canoes capable of crossing the vast distances between the islands of the Massim region enabling them to take part in the traditional ceremonial exchange system known as the *kula*.

Malinowski focused on the basic skills needed to survive, how these depended on cultural learning (moving beyond individual learning by trial and error) and how transmission processes depended on the necessary construction of cumulative traditions of particular skills. This pragmatic focus led him to wonder about the potential functional role of social institutions such as myth, religion and magic. Malinowski argued that, whereas the primary functions of myth and religion are to legitimize tradition, ensure the transmission of knowledge and control potential disruptive aspects of inevitable life crises, magical rituals achieve their function in relation to pragmatic goals. Magical rituals are intertwined with, but never mistaken for, technical actions, and this observation led Malinowski to a simple question: Why would people with a rational mastery of their environment seek recourse to magical rituals?

In order to address this question, Malinowski first observed that not all technical endeavours are surrounded by magic. Whereas poison fishing in the lagoon has no accompanying magic, deep-sea fishing outside the coral reef is steeped in magic. Malinowski explained this by two variables: the agents' degree of technical control, and the potential danger and uncertainty involved. Lagoon fishing by poisoning is a rather simple and safe procedure with a quite certain result. In contrast, deep-sea fishing involves a number of potential dangers, and its result is dependent on factors outside the technical control of the fisherman. According to Malinowski, magic addresses the contingencies involved in pragmatic pursuits, and constitutes an attempt to control these aspects, especially if some element of danger is involved (Malinowski 1992). Second, Malinowski observed that this distinction not only differentiates types of pragmatic pursuits, but also different aspects of a pursuit. Most endeavours combine elements that are within the agents' technical control with those that are not, and magic is an attempt to control the latter by non-technical means. For instance, canoe building, agriculture and trade all involve a large number of features over which the Trobrianders have excellent technical mastery. In addition, however, they all involve a number of contingencies addressed by means of magical ritual.

Thus, Malinowski argued that the performance of magical ritual is prompted by the representation of risk and uncertainty about the outcome of some pragmatic endeavour. But what is its function? Malinowski pointed to three interrelated functions of magic: first, it presents an outlet for the emotional anxiety arising from the uncertainty; second, it gives the sense of some mastery over otherwise uncontrollable aspects of the action; and third, the preceding two functions effect a potential improvement of the action. To a certain extent, magic actually works, even if an observer's causal explanation for this effect naturally differs radically from any local explanation.

The point of this selective account of Malinowski's well-known theory of magic is to point out that the questions raised by Malinowski and his attempts to answer them are still relevant when addressing the role of magic under modernity. Malinowski pointed to fundamental features such as anxiety arising due to the human ability to represent potential outcomes of action; he attempted to answer why ritual performance should have an effect, and he related psychological processes to both social aspects (group cohesion) and technological development (level of pragmatic control). However, even if it fits well within a modern evolutionary and cognitive framework (Sørensen 2007c; Sosis and Handwerker 2011), it needs to be refined, developed and brought up to date on a number counts in order to produce testable hypotheses.[5]

Firstly, we need to address why only limited numbers of actions involving uncertainty elicit ritual behaviour. From an evolutionary perspective, one hypothesis would be that some actions are more likely to be connected with magical rituals, not only due to representations of risk and uncertainty, but also due to relative importance in terms of adaptive fitness.[6] It is a well-known observation that humans do not have sound judgments of what constitutes risk in a modern environment. For instance, traffic in general and cars in particular are among the greatest dangers encountered in people's immediate surroundings, but our behaviour seems to be much stronger affected when we are confronted with cues of dangerous animals or human aggressors (Barrett 2005; Duntley 2005). Extrapolating on this point, our judgment of importance might be significantly informed by cues that activate evolved cognitive predispositions, rather than rational assessment of the dangers prevalent in the modern environment. Magical rituals thus seem to cluster around a limited repertoire of pursuits and related goals: acquiring sufficient sustenance (food); ensuring procreation (love); avoiding predation (security); avoiding social ostracism (exchange); security when moving into unknown territory (protection); and protecting the body against attack and decay (health).

Secondly, we need to address the structure of risk and uncertainty. Whereas Malinowski described these in general terms, risk and uncertainty come in many forms, and we can analytically distinguish between different types in order to unearth when and how ritual actions are integrated with pragmatic endeavours. For instance, one type of uncertainty is structurally bifurcated. Either one wins the lottery or not, and getting heads when flipping a coin is an either/or, one-shot situation. This bifurcated uncertainty structure is most thoroughly investigated in relation to pathological gambling, where numerous studies have pointed to the tendency of gamblers to, more or less spontaneously, employ magical rituals in order to influence the outcome of stochastic (such as dice) or semi-stochastic games (for example, poker) (Bersabe and Arias 2000; Huber et al. 2010). Some human activities are also characterized by simple bifurcation structures: either one gets a job or not; either one marries a particular person or not. In many human activities, however, the outcome is not either/or but rather more-or-less, whether in terms of yield or functionality. Thus a second type of activity is characterized by a graded risk and uncertainty structure. One might experience better health than previously, receive a higher salary or feel more confident in the dating market. In all cases, the purpose of the ritual is to contribute in favour of the desired outcome, even though it is generally recognized that other factors also have a role to play. Thus, in both types of uncertainty, magical rituals can be understood as the sole determining factor or, more likely, as one among several potential factors that can steer the outcome in a specific direction. Magic is thus, more realistically, understood as taking part in networks of inter-related events all participating one way or another to bring about a desired result (Sørensen 2007a).

This points to the path-dependent structure of representations of risk and uncertainty. Numerous human endeavours, for instance agriculture or education, are extended over considerable time, and involve a number of hierarchically related actions all needed to bring about the desired result. Importantly, such hierarchical structures contain nodal points – that is, points represented as particularly important for the overall outcome the endeavour, such as a harvest or an exam – and magical rituals are likely to cluster around these points. For instance, Malinowski describes how Trobriand garden magic comprises a number of rituals that address particular points in the agricultural cycle (Malinowski 1935).

To summarize, we have isolated two variables in how humans represent the relation between action, goal and uncertainty: the relative importance of the themes involved (that is, its importance in terms of fitness consequences), and the representation of types of uncertainties involved. We can hypothesize that these two variables influence what type of activities are imbued with magical rituals, what form these rituals will take, and how they relate to the total structure of the activity – that is, to the network of actions underlying most pragmatic endeavours. This, however, does not explain why magical rituals can be represented as efficacious in the first place. How can people come to represent a behavioural modality – ritual – as having instrumental efficacy, even when it is clearly distinguished from ordinary functional action by the performers themselves?[7]

In a number of conceptual studies (Sørensen 2005a, 2007a, 2007b) and in a recent series of experimental studies (Nielbo and Sørensen 2011, 2013; Nielbo et al. 2013), we have investigated how ritual and ritualization influence human action perception. Based on studies of ordinary event perception (Zacks and Tversky 2001), we argue that human action processing consists of a two-layered system. Firstly, a bottom-up system that recognizes basic action gestalts, such as 'grabbing a cup' and 'lifting a cup', and integrates these into causally determined action sequences ('grapping' is prior to 'lifting'). The integration is constrained by a second, top-down system that supplies available action schemas informed by prior experiences, which enable a smooth integration of the individual action gestalt into sequences defined by their causal structure (such as 'drinking coffee'). This enables the cognitive system to predict the unfolding of an event, and thereby lowers the amount of cognitive resources spent in processing information, freeing these for other tasks (for example, 'having a conversation'). Whenever the perceived action gestalt does not fit into the present schema (such as when a new action commences), this produces an error signal that, in turn, elicits a cognitive search for another schema better able to integrate the information given by the senses. It is important to recognize that this integration process normally happens seamlessly and without any conscious effort, both when we perceive actions performed by others and when we perform the actions ourselves. It allows us to predict the actions of others, and it facilitates the automatic planning and execution of motor behaviour when we are ourselves the agents of actions.

In light of this model, the crucial question concerns how cognitive processing is affected by having ritual performance as its input. Addressing this question, of course, presumes the isolation of a number of relevant characteristics of ritual behaviour. Since the late 1970s, scholars have discussed the so-called 'obvious features of ritual action', focusing on features such as redundancy, repetition, causal opacity and intentional under-specification (Rappaport 1979, 1999; Staal 1979; Humphrey and Laidlaw 1994; Boyer and Liénard 2006). Relating these features to the model of ordinary action, we hypothesized that ritualization hinders the seamless integration of bottom-up action gestalts into top-down action schemas (Sørensen 2007b). In a series of experimental studies, we have shown that altering the causal coherence of an action structure led subjects to segment actions at a finer level, and resulted in less integration between higher and lower level action perception (Nielbo and Sørensen 2011, 2013; Nielbo et al. 2013). These studies support the interpretation that central features of ritualized actions have particular effects on basic action perception. Ritualization produces a higher error signal, as cognizing subjects constantly need to update their action schema in an attempt to integrate perceived movements into meaningful wholes. It must be emphasized that this seems to be the case even if subjects have been familiarized with the actions. Thus, at a basic perceptual level, prior cultural knowledge about ritual actions seems to have limited effect on cognitive processing. This might help explain a number of features about cultural rituals, such as the aforementioned tendency of perpetual permutations of ritual interpretation. The question remains whether or not cognitive processing can explain how rituals can be perceived as instrumental for the achievement of particular pragmatic goals.

We hypothesize that two processes might explain the production of representations of ritual efficacy. First, our model predicts that failure to integrate action gestalts into a causally coherent schema affects a redirection of attention to finely detailed, perceptual features of the action. When we experience a novel or unclear action, we search for information in the environment that will help us identify a relevant schema. In contrast to ordinary actions, where this process is fast and unproblematic, rituals are causally under-determined, and therefore other perceptible cues based on relations of similarity, contagion and spatial contiguity are highlighted. These associative principles of similarity and contagion were not only argued by Frazer to be modes of reasoning underlying magic (Frazer 1911), but are understood by modern ethology as a general cognitive strategy applied when the organism lacks causally relevant cues ('weak causal connections'; see Kummer 1995).

Second, as rituals have no immediate perceivable result, knowledge of success can only come from perception of correct or satisfactory performance. We therefore hypothesize that correct execution of the ritual, in itself, is likely to activate the dopaminergic reward system in the brain – a system whose activation is associated with positive emotional arousal. Positive emotional states, in turn, have been shown to significantly influence decisions to perform actions imbued with uncertainty by lowering attention to potential negative outcomes (Loewenstein and Lerner 2003). Gambling studies consistently point to the existence of cognitive phenomena such as the 'hot hand', presuming that certain outcomes come in streaks, even in games of pure chance; and the 'illusion of control', presuming that the successful outcome of one chance game is indicative of agentive control in subsequent chance games (Bersabe and Arias 2000; Huber et al. 2010). Performing a ritual action before commencing on activities involving risk and uncertainty is thus likely to heighten representations of future successful outcomes.

To summarize, representations of ritual efficacy are the likely product of how humans process ordinary actions. By tweaking this system through ritualization (such as by causal opacity and rigidity), the human cognitive system automatically searches for available perceptible cues that might help relate actions to their immediate pragmatic context. It also raises estimations of success in subsequent actions. Ritualized actions thus fit like a hand in a glove when humans have to navigate important situations involving varying degrees of uncertainty. It not only enhances representations of agentive control even in pure chance situations. It also redirects attention towards perceptible features of the ritual that connects it to the pragmatic context. Harming an enemy by means of a ritual might in itself enhance the agent's feeling of control and power, but adding an effigy and/or an indexical token of the target might strengthen representations of ritual efficacy considerably.

Magic under Modernity?

The relation between recurrent cues of potential danger, structural types of risk and uncertainty, and effects of ritualization might help explain why magic persists in modernity. At this point, it should be emphasized that, contrary to early ideological assumptions, modernity has not led to decreased representations of risk and uncertainty. In fact, increased social and technological complexity and improved access to information are correlated with heightened representations of risk and uncertainty (Beck 1986; Bauman 1998). Obviously, modernity introduces new types of risks. Hunger, predation, armed conflict and large epidemics have, if not disappeared, at least diminished significantly as a direct threat to most individuals in the Western world. Instead, unknown dangers lurk, from nanoparticles and gene-modified food to unemployment, social alienation, terrorism and climate change. The potential correlation between these new threat factors and ritualized behaviour needs to be investigated empirically by systematic sociological and anthropological studies. Anecdotal evidence indicates that numerous rituals are performed to prevent particular risks introduced by modern society, and surveys show that complementary and alternative medicine is a constantly growing industry (Eisenberg et al. 1998). One hypothesis would be that ritualized behaviour is more prevalent when modern risks take the form of evolutionary recurrent cues of danger. When gene-modified food is represented as pollution, unemployment as caused by predating capitalists and health problems as caused by the self's insufficient ability to cope with the surroundings, rituals are likely to thrive as a cognitive optimal response.

This naturalistic explanation of the prevalence of magic and religion in modern society of course raises the questions of the spread of such beliefs and practices, and to their relation, or even confrontation with science. This is an important question that deserves a lengthy treatment beyond the scope of this chapter (see McCauley 2011, this volume). Still, the naturalization thesis would predict that the phenomena, covered by the concepts religion and magic, are unlikely to disappear, as they are natural products of human cognitive architecture. Thus, breaking the spell of particular religious propositions (Dennett 2006) is unlikely to change people's minds, as explicit propositions, contrary to the understanding of many philosophers and theologians alike, are but a minor part of what constitutes religion.[8] This, however, does not mean that magical practices spread with equal ease in all societies. The transmission of ideas and practices not only depends on their cognitive optimality, but also on a number of other factors, such as their fitness in prevalent cultural models, their relation to social authorities and available economic resources (Sørensen 2004). Magic and religion are both relatively compartmentalized types of behaviour in modern societies, and there is no reason to believe that this systemic specialization will be rolled back in the near future. The battle between science on the one hand and religion and magic on the other is thus better thought of as a fight about legitimate discourses, authority and resources that naturally follow the differentiation of social systems.

This raises the question of the relation between magic and religion in modern societies. Magic, understood as ritual efficacy pertaining to concrete pragmatic aspects of the world, has to some extend been excluded from the dominant religious institutions of the Western world, most notably in Protestant denominations, though this has not made it disappear (see e.g. Inglis, this volume). Rather, it thrives outside organized religion, and sometimes it might even be the deciding impetus in the creation of new religions. The question is thus not so much whether magic survives in an age of modernity, as how the rationalization of belief systems that took place in the twentieth century and the accompanying rejection of explicit representations of ritual efficacy affects more traditional, organized religions. Organized Western religions might have aligned their theology to a modern, scientifically informed world-view, and thereby satisfied the need of their intellectual elite to diminish cognitive dissonance, but at the same time it has made its rituals less relevant for participants seeking pragmatic answers to real-world problems. In combination with the continuous loss of secular power, the lack of efficacious ritual actions – that is, the lack of magic – might explain the resurgence of interest in not only client-based magical practices but also in charismatic and evangelical forms of Christianity – all movements emphasizing the ability of ritual practices to influence relevant pragmatic concerns.

Acknowledgements

This work was made possible by the Danish Ministry of Science, Technology and Innovation's UNIK grant MINDLab at Aarhus University.

Notes

1. In later work, Stark gave up on the concept of compensators and rephrased it in terms of supernatural rewards. Even though this formed part of a more general relaxation of the strong version of RCT, it has no impact on the following discussion as Stark in fact emphasized the difference between religion and magic (Stark 1999; Stark and Finke 2000).

2. Stark and Bainbridge's theory has been widely criticized from several theoretical perspectives, with criticisms ranging from total dismissal to cautious approval. Thus, whereas Wallis and Bruce described the theory as 'entirely misconceived' (Wallis and Bruce 1984: 11), Simpson lauded the theory as 'the only extensive formal deductive theory of religion' (Simpson 1990: 367). The critique in the following sections only addresses features of the theory concerning the basis of human decision making and how this relates to the distinction between magic and religion.

3. In a later rendition of the theory, Stark radicalizes the division between beliefs underlying religion and magic (Stark 1999). Magic is understood as the manipulation of impersonal supernatural forces, in contrast to the personal forces underlying religion. This return to a Frazerian distinction, however, does not solve the problem, as it is unclear if people participating in religious rituals have representations of personal or impersonal forces in mind (or any at all). Stark's distinction thus ends up reproducing local theological interpretations instead of analysing individual motivational forces.

4. See Boyer (2001) and Atran (2002) for important general discussions, and Sørensen (2005b) for a review.

5. For a thorough discussion relating Malinowski's theory of culture to cognitive approaches, see Sørensen (2007c). For a non-cognitivist reinterpretation of Malinowski in terms of debates of performativity and rationality, see Tambiah (1990).

6. The literature on adaptive fitness within evolutionary theory and evolutionary psychology is extensive. See Buss (2005) for a helpful overview.

7. For a thorough discussion of earlier positions pertaining to this question, see Sørensen (2007a).

8. See Pina-Cabral (this volume) for a similar argument.

References

Ahlin, L. 2010. 'Back to the Classics: The Relation between Social Experience and Religiosity', *Nordic Journal of Religion and Society* 23(1): 27–51.

Andersen, P.B., and P. Lüchau. 2011. 'Individualisering og Aftraditionalisering af Danskernes Religiøse Værdier', in P. Gundelach (ed.), *Store og Små Forandringer: Danskernes Værdier Siden 1981*. Copenhagen: Hans Reitzels Forlag, pp.76–94.

Atran, S. 2002. *In Gods We Trust: The Evolutionary Landscape of Religion*. Oxford: Oxford University Press.

Bar, M. 2009. 'The Proactive Brain: Memory for Predictions', *Philosophical Transactions of the Royal Society B* 364: 1235–43.

Barrett, H.C. 2005. 'Adaptations to Predators and Prey', in D.M. Buss (ed.), *The Handbook of Evolutionary Psychology*. Hoboken, NJ: Wiley, pp.200–23.

Barrett, J. 1999. 'Theological Correctness: Cognitive Constraints and the Study of Religion', *Method and Theory in the Study of Religion* 11(4): 325–39.

Bauman, Z. 1998. 'Postmodern Religion?' in P. Heelas (ed.), *Religion, Modernity and Postmodernity*. Oxford: Blackwell, pp.55–78.

Beck, U. 1986. *Risikogesellschaft: Auf dem Weg in eine andere Moderne*. Frankfurt: Suhrkamp.

Beckford, J.A. 2003. *Social Theory and Religion*. Cambridge: Cambridge University Press.

Bersabe, R., and R.M. Arias. 2000. 'Superstition in Gambling', *Psychology in Spain* 4(1): 28–34.

Boyer, P. 1994. *The Naturalness of Religious Ideas: A Cognitive Theory of Religion*. Berkeley: University of California Press.

——. 1996. 'Religion as an Impure Object: A Note on the Cognitive Order in Religious Representations in Response to Brian Malley', *Method and Theory in the Study of Religion* 8(2): 201–14.

——. 2001. *Religion Explained: The Human Instincts the Fashion Gods, Spirits and Ancestors*. London: Vintage.

Boyer, P., and P. Liénard. 2006. 'Why Ritualized Behavior? Precaution Systems and Action Parsing in Developmental, Pathological and Cultural Rituals', *Behavioral and Brain Sciences* 29: 1–56.

Brubaker, R., M. Loveman and P. Stamatov. 2004. 'Ethnicity as Cognition', *Theory and Society* 33(1): 31–64.

Buss, D.M. (ed.). 2005. *The Handbook of Evolutionary Psychology*. Hoboken, NJ: Wiley.

Dennett, D.C. 2006. *Breaking the Spell: Religion as a Natural Phenomenon*. London: Penguin.

Dobbelaere, K. 2002. *Secularization: An Analysis in Three Levels*. Brussels: Peter Lang.

Duntley, J.D. 2005. 'Adaptations to Dangers from Humans', in D.M. Buss (ed.), *The Handbook of Evolutionary Psychology*. Hoboken, NJ: Wiley, pp.224–49.

Durkheim, E. 1965 [1915]. *The Elementary Forms of the Religious Life*, trans. J.W. Swain. New York: Free Press.

Eisenberg D.M., et al. 1998. 'Trends in Alternative Medicine Use in the United States, 1990–1997: Results of a Follow-up National Survey', *Journal of the American Medical Association* 280(18): 1569–75.

Evans-Pritchard, E.E. 1937. *Witchcraft, Oracles and Magic among the Azande*. Oxford: Clarendon Press.

Frazer, J.G. 1911. *The Golden Bough: A Study in Magic and Religion. Part I: The Magic Art and the Evolution of Kings*, vol. 1, 3rd edn. London: MacMillan.

Frith, C. 2007. *Making Up the Mind: How the Brain Creates Our Mental World*. Oxford: Blackwell.

Green, L., and J. Myerson. 2004. 'A Discounting Framework for Choices with Delayed and Probabilistic Rewards', *Psychological Bulletin* 130(5): 769–92

Huber, J., M. Kirchler and T. Stöckl. 2010. 'The Hot Hand Belief and the Gambler's Fallacy in Investment Decisions under Risk', *Theory and Decision* 68: 445–62.

Humphrey, C., and J. Laidlaw. 1994. *The Archetypal Actions of Ritual: A Theory of Ritual Illustrated by the Jain Rite of Worship*. Oxford: Clarendon Press.

Jones, O.D. 2005. 'Evolutionary Psychology and the Law', in D.M Buss (ed.), *The Handbook of Evolutionary Psychology*. Hoboken, NJ: Wiley, pp.953–74.

Kahneman D. 2011. *Thinking, Fast and Slow*. London: Macmillan

Kühle, L. 1999. 'Sekulariseringstesen i Religionssociologien: Reformulering eller Paradigmeskrift?' *Religionsvidenskabeligt Tidsskrift* 35: 43–60.

Kummer, H. 1995. 'Causal Knowledge in Animals', in D. Sperber, D. Premack and A.J. Premack (eds), *Causal Cognition: A Multidisciplinary Debate*. Oxford: Clarendon Press, pp.26–36.

Lawson, E.T., and R.N. McCauley. 1990. *Rethinking Religion: Connecting Cognition and Culture*. Cambridge: Cambridge University Press.

Lévy-Bruhl, L. 1985 [1910]. *How Natives Think*, trans. L.A. Clare. Princeton: Princeton University Press.

Loewenstein, G., and J.S. Lerner. 2003. 'The Role of Affect in Decision Making', in R.J. Davidson, K.R. Scherer and H.H. Goldsmith (eds), *Handbook of Affective Sciences*. Oxford: Oxford University Press, pp.619–42.

McCauley, R.N. 2011. *Why Religion Is Natural and Science Is Not*. Oxford: Oxford University Press

Malinowski, B. 1935. *Coral Gardens and Their Magic*. London: Allen and Unwin.

——. 1992 [1948]. *Magic, Science and Religion, and Other Essays*. Prospect Heights, IL: Waveland Press.

Nielbo, K.L., U. Schjoedt and J. Sørensen. 2013. 'Hierarchical Organization of Segmentation during Non-functional Action Sequences', *Journal for the Cognitive Science of Religion* 1(1): 71–97.

Nielbo, K.L., and J. Sørensen. 2011. 'Spontaneous Processing of Functional and Non-functional Action Sequences', *Religion, Brain and Behavior* 1(1): 18–30.

——. 2013. 'Prediction Error During Functional and Non-functional Action Sequences: A Computational Exploration of Ritual and Ritualized Event Processing', *Journal of Cognition and Culture* 13: 347–65.

Rappaport, R. 1979. *Ecology, Meaning, and Religion*. Richmond, CA: North Atlantic Books.

——. 1999. *Ritual and Religion in the Making of Humanity*. Cambridge: Cambridge University Press.

Schacter, D.L., D.R. Addis and R.L. Buckner. 2008. 'Episodic Simulation of Future Events: Concepts, Data and Applications', *Annals of the New York Academy of Science* 1123: 39–60.

Schjoedt, U., J. Sørensen, K.L. Nielbo, D. Xygalatas, P. Mitkidis and J. Bulbulia. 2013. 'The Resource Model and the Principle of Predictive Coding: A Framework for Analysing Proximate Effects of Ritual', *Religion, Brain and Behavior* 3(1): 39–86

Sherkat D.E. and C.G. Ellison. 1999. 'Recent Developments and Current Controversies in the Sociology of Religion', *Annual Review of Sociology* 25: 363–94

Shiner, L. 1967. 'The Concept of Secularization in Empirical Research', *Journal for the Scientific Study of Religion* 6(2): 207–20.

Simpson, J.H. 1990. 'The Stark–Bainbridge Theory of Religion', *Journal for the Scientific Study of Religion* 29(3): 367–71.

Sosis, R., and W.P. Handwerker. 2011. 'Psalms and Coping with Uncertainty: Religious Israeli Women's Response to the 2006 Lebanon War', *American Anthropologist* 113(1): 40–55

Sperber, D. 1996. *Explaining Culture: A Naturalistic Approach*. Oxford: Blackwell.

Staal, F. 1979. 'The Meaninglessness of Ritual Action', *Numen: International Review for the History of Religions* 26: 2–22.

Stark, R. 1999. 'Micro Foundations of Religion: A Revised Theory', *Sociological Theory* 17(3): 264–89

Stark, R., and W.S. Bainbridge. 1980. 'Towards a Theory of Religion: Religious Commitment', *Journal for the Scientific Study of Religion* 19(2): 114–28.

——. 1985. *The Future of Religion: Secularization, Revival and Cult Formation*. Berkeley: University of California Press.

——. 1987. *A Theory of Religion*. New York: Peter Lang.

Stark, R., and R. Finke. 2000. *Acts of Faith: Explaining the Human Side of Religion*. Berkeley: University of California Press.

Subbotsky, E. 2010. *Magic and the Mind: Mechanisms, Functions, and the Development of Magical Thinking and Behavior*. Oxford: Oxford University Press.

Sørensen, J. 2004. 'Religion, Evolution, and an Immunology of Cultural Systems', *Evolution and Cognition* 10(1): 61–73.

——. 2005a. 'Charisma, Tradition, and Ritual: A Cognitive Approach to Magical Agency', in H. Whitehouse and R.N. McCauley (eds), *Mind and Religion: Psychological and Cognitive Foundations of Religiosity*. Walnut Creek, CA: AltaMira Press, pp.167–85.

——. 2005b. 'Religion in Mind: A Review Article of the Cognitive Science of Religion', *Numen: International Review for the History of Religions* 52(4): 465–94

——. 2007a. *A Cognitive Theory of Magic*. Lanham, MD: AltaMira Press.

——. 2007b. 'Acts that Work: A Cognitive Approach to Ritual Agency', *Method and Theory in the Study of Religion* 19(3/4): 281–300.

——. 2007c. 'Malinowski and Magical Ritual', in H. Whitehouse and J. Laidlaw (eds.), *Religion, Anthropology and Cognitive Science*. Durham, NC: Carolina Academic Press, pp.81–104.

Tambiah, S.J. 1990. *Magic, Science, Religion, and the Scope of Rationality*. Cambridge: Cambridge University Press.

Tversky, A., and D. Kahneman. 1982. 'Judgment under Uncertainty: Heuristics and Biases', in D. Kahneman, P. Slovic and A. Tversky (eds.), *Judgment under Uncertainty: Heuristics and Biases*. Cambridge: Cambridge University Press, pp.3–20.

Vyse, S.A. 1997. *Believing in Magic: The Psychology of Superstition*. Oxford: Oxford University Press.

Wallis, R., and S. Bruce. 1984. 'The Stark–Brainbridge Theory of Religion. A Critical Analysis and Counter Proposal', *Sociological Analysis* 45: 11–27.

Zacks, J.M., and B. Tversky. 2001. 'Event Structure in Perception and Conception', *Psychological Bulletin* 127(1): 3–21.

Part II

§§

Beyond Science

Chapter Four

Moral Employments of Scientific Thought

Timothy Jenkins

Modern sciences share a number of characteristics concerning the kind of knowledge they produce, the communities of scientists who produce such knowledge, and the relation of the motivation behind the research to the discoveries made. From the social-scientific point of view, the interesting question is how the discoveries of science are recaptured by the categories of common sense and put to work in moral descriptions of the world, mappings that are very selective regarding which characteristics of scientific practices they choose to notice. These 'moral' employments of science fall under two broad headings. First, there are hybrids of various moral authorities – scientific and religious – that allow us to offer a description of the historical development of 'non-standard' religious forms in the last century. I also draw attention to the fluid relationship of mind and matter in these accounts. And second, there is a spectrum of literature, from Fantasy and Science Fiction to popular science, which plays on the same materials and issues, again in a strictly time- and context-bound fashion. This latter material (which includes, among others, the New Atheists' discussions of faith and science) may be said to represent an urban folklore, and is both diffuse and influential, serving to disseminate the ideas and forms of thought created by the movements of the first kind. In addition to identifying these areas, I offer some basic concepts to help think through the issues and a sociological description of these phenomena.

With regards to the present volume, the aim is to consider the relations between science and religion in contemporary modern societies, and to identify various ways that science is put to work in the lives of ordinary people in the domain of what would have been known previously as 'religious beliefs'. As well as defining a series of examples, I am also concerned to identify theory-laden terms that assist in the repair of the concepts of religion, rationality and secularization. I will offer a series of observations and try to sketch some terms I find useful in thinking about what I call 'improvisatory religion', taking the term from Orsi (1992). It is important to emphasize that this is a report on work in progress.[1]

Some Characteristics of the Modern Sciences

First, let me begin by making some observations about the practice of the modern sciences. Modern sciences share a number of characteristics concerning the kind of knowledge they produce, the communities of scientists who produce such knowledge, and the relationship between the motivation to research and the discoveries made.

Scientific discoveries emerge from a tissue of common-sense concerns and motives, but a discovery can only be made when scientists break decisively with that common-sense background. This approach derives from the work of Bachelard (1938), who influenced some of the central concepts employed by Bourdieu et al. (1991): this is a sociological account of the epistemological break.

The mark of such a scientific advance is that it is not, at the time, intuitively obvious but, on the contrary, reverses or turns upside down conventional expectation. Scientific thought develops against the categories of common sense, even though the initial motivation for research emerges from the concerns of the everyday world. This emphasis upon a break with common sense puts a question mark against theories which derive a scientific description from common-sense categories through increasing refinement whilst remaining in continuity with what seems self-evident – as is the case, I would suggest, with a good many psychological accounts in particular (although see McCauley, this volume).

Following on from the notion of a break with common-sense categories, we can suggest that the 'harder' sciences at least work through a dialectic of materialized theories (theories realized in equipment) and theorized materials (for example, the purified salts a chemist might work with), giving rise to a series of successive controlled approximations. The fascination and power of scientific thinking lies in the specificity of the understanding it produces in each case, including an awareness of the limits of its application. Therein too lie its disappointments, for it cannot readily generate universals.

The power of scientific discovery lies less than one might think in the universality or permanence of the truths the scientific community uncovers. Although the results of scientific discovery give rise to many effective applications, they are constantly open to revision and radical interpretation. The truths of science are not cumulative. Rather, the effectiveness of scientific discovery lies more in the fact that scientists form moral communities, with shared ideals, knowledge and practices. It is from their belonging to such groups, which have almost disappeared from many other parts of the modern world, that scientists are so productive, and that the authority they enjoy derives. They form in some respects the last pre-modern moral communities, and they are threatened by the same forces that threaten other forms of community: Weberian forces, secularization, the profit motive and so forth. Because of these characteristics, they are able continually to disturb or disrupt, in a smaller or larger-scale fashion, the categories of common sense.

Popular Apprehensions of Scientific Discoveries

Second, I offer some observations about thinking with science. From the social-scientific point of view, the interesting question is how the discoveries of science are recaptured by the categories of common sense and put to work in moral descriptions of the world, mappings that are very selective in what characteristics of scientific practices they choose to notice.[2] The characteristics of the advancement of science which we have identified, and in particular, that of the break with common-sense concerns, then have another face, for notable discoveries will first disturb and then, in time, be taken up by the wider population, who are not specialists, and put to work within the popular imagination of common sense. People use science to think with; that is, people employ representations of specific scientific discoveries as a part of their making sense of the world in which they find themselves. They may do so for a number of reasons: for interest, prestige, play or, most commonly, to contribute to popular theodicies: explanations of how the world works, and man's place in it, how things come to a good end, and how things go bad. I might offer a generalization of a formal kind: this kind of employment – of putting scientific discoveries to work – arises in a particular epistemological context, when previously secure forms of measurement collapse and predictions fail. The failure of measurement may well be the result of a scientific or technological advance. For example, the invention of space flight upsets a whole series of notions about distance and place – or, in another case, the invention of atomic weapons overthrows certain notions of boundedness and integrity – and both lead, or are implicated in, a series of improvised responses, including such forms as flying saucer cults or other kinds of millenarian movements (see Jenkins 2013). I draw attention to the formal nature of these disturbances, best described as the collapse of problems of measurement into problems of definition (following Ardener 2007), because otherwise they tend to be dealt with under psychological theories of compensation and the like, and this fails to do justice to the creativity of the responses.

Scientific advances in this sense are recaptured, and become part of the categories of everyday thought, and the consequences of this employment are rarely anticipated and may be, to a considerable extent, unpredictable; unpredictable because they are the products of collective human intelligence (although they show certain recurring patterns).

The Example of Newton's Discovery of Gravity

As an example of what I mean, consider the reception of Newton's discovery of the force of gravity, which excited extraordinary interest for an extended period. Experts still debate the precise nature of his theories, but the popular perception was clear: Newton was concerned with the influence bodies – in particular, planetary bodies – exert upon one another at a distance, and he offered a description of the regular movements of planetary bodies in terms of the gravitational forces exerted between them. And whatever Newton supposed gravity to be, many readers supposed 'gravity to be an innate property of bodies, and to act immediately at a distance' (Barrow 1986: 70).

Such views fed into contemporary debates which we might label anachronistically as being to do with 'physics': concerning the nature of matter and the forces to which it could be subjected. But they also underwrote more speculative or unorthodox popular contemporary accounts, including a renewal of astrology: for if it is the case that planets exert specific – though invisible – forces upon other bodies at a distance, it is reasonable to suppose that the relative position of the various planets at the time of a person's conception or birth may influence that person's life chances and possibilities, and that the influence of the planets may continue to act day by day.

We may reply that while it may seem reasonable superficially to suppose these connections, nevertheless it is a wrong supposition. It would be possible to introduce here an account of the conflicting 'language ideologies' employed by the positivist, scientific account on the one hand and the occult or metaphysical world-view on the other (again, see Jenkins 2013). But the point is that you can see how astrology in its modern form is essentially a meditation upon a popular understanding of Newtonian physics, a meditation indeed that exploits real ambiguities in the notions of force and influence in the theory.

In such an understanding, the prestige of science, of Newton's name in this case, lends itself to thinking about a series of human questions concerning problems of personal meaning and destiny, and how to account for good and bad happening in life. The term 'prestige' is meant seriously; science is taken to be an authoritative source for human understanding and wellbeing, and its discoveries are taken up and used to think with in a fashion that commands widespread assent (even if we ourselves do not subscribe to the particular use that is made of them in this instance). Part of any specific study then needs to consider the particular circumstances in which these accounts are first constructed, including the specific crisis in measurement to which they respond, through which their lasting plausibility is felt.

In fact, the influence of 'Newtonianism' in this sense spread widely; popular recensions of Newtonian physics concerning the nature of matter, the porosity of bodies and the influence of ill-defined, invisible forces in them link a range of nineteenth-century practices concerned with what we may term 'healing', activities that included, as well as early forms of medicine and what is now called psychiatry, such unofficial practices as mesmerism, spiritualism, spiritual healing, phrenology, herbalism and vegetarianism. These disciplines have been traced out by a number of authors, in particular Barrow (1986), whose work I have drawn upon in offering this sketch of the issues. A notable scientific discovery is put to work in a series of attempts to discern and assure human well-being.

Moral Employments of Scientific Discoveries by Religious Movements

In considering the popular uses made of scientific discoveries, then, we have to consider the milieu of reception, in which a range of unorthodox or alternative practices develop. For people are not content simply to read about the advances of science; they want to put them to work for their own advantage. These 'moral' employments of science fall under two broad heads: in the first place, the work of quite small movements that create new forms of thought; in the second, the various forms in which these ideas are disseminated more widely.

First, then, there are hybrids of various moral authorities – scientific and religious – that allow us to offer a description of the historical development of 'non-standard' religious forms (Fundamentalisms, New Religious Movements, New Age and so forth) in the last century. I have suggested the term 'improvisatory religion' to cover these movements; I would mention Harding's work on Fundamentalism (Harding 2000) and Bender's recent book on the New Age (Bender 2010), and I am myself engaged in a re-reading of Festinger's work (Festinger et al. 2008) on a flying-saucer cult in this perspective (Jenkins 2013). An important proviso: it is not clear that so-called 'mainstream' religions work any differently – but I have yet to investigate how to offer a re-description in this light, so we will stick with 'non-standard' or 'fringe' forms (saving a remark at the conclusion).

These improvisatory forms include both what appear to be intensifications of traditional religious concerns, such as the inerrancy of Scripture, the need for repentance and reform of life, and the imminence of judgement, and the outworkings of liberal Protestant thought that give the impression, if not of secularization, of the dilution and expansion of Christian categories to their limits, as in the perfection of the self, a this-worldly focus, and the loss of any concepts of sin, atonement or redemption. I have found the detailed social histories of Creationism by Numbers (1992) on the one hand and of New Thought by Braden (1987) on the other to be exemplary explorations respectively of these two tendencies.

A number of broad characteristics mark these kinds of enterprises, three in particular. They claim to have a scientific status, adopting a series of 'scientific' attitudes and methods and drawing upon the vocabulary of the sciences of the time. They look to education as the means of enlightenment and spreading the truth, and so to self-formation and self-perfection: they are 'auto-didactic' in form. And they are 'democratic' in the strict sense that they hold knowledge to be open and available to all (although they may well lack certain features of political liberal democracy). At the same time, they typically exhibit certain stylistic features; in particular, they appeal to immediate experience, they make premature generalizations and they identify imponderable universals or secrets; together, these features hinder this kind of approach precisely from developing scientific or critical thinking. They share, then, in the rhetoric of science without adopting the characteristics of scientific thinking noted at the outset, notably the initial break with common sense and the careful construction of controlled knowledge.

It is worth elaborating on this debt to scientific method, exemplified by the Spiritualist movement (see Barrow 1986; Moore 1989; Braude 2001), to make the point clear. Spiritualism built on a fascination with Mesmerism, the early 'science' of mental influence (see Darnton 1968), and also shared the presuppositions of that whole range of contemporary 'proto-sciences' listed earlier, as well as links to early forms of medicine and psychiatry, for we are dealing in a milieu in which contemporary divisions – of hard science, medicine and psychiatry on the one hand, and occult, pseudo-sciences on the other – were not clearly drawn. Then, Spiritualism responded particularly to the challenge and opportunities presented by popular New-tonianism. It could not have existed in the forms it took on, of invisible spirit penetrating porous materiality, without the theory of gravity and of influence at a distance. It was a transposition of a meditation on the nature of mind and matter, a transposition which claims that human matters – of thought, care, intention and affective relations – cannot be closed out by materialist accounts and which, in fact, we now know (thanks to Newton) do not need to be. In this perspective on the world, it is claimed that moral and personal matters have their place in scientific accounts. We will return to this distinction between a reductive and a non-reductive materialism in the next section. Lastly, Spiritualists reckoned themselves to be experimentalists, and not to take anything on faith. The séance focused on empirical demonstration: the practice of communication with known spirits. Instead then of the authority of religious dogma and institutions, Spiritualists adopted the authority of scientific practices, so that claims of contact with the dead were investigated under the 'test conditions' of the séance room, and contact with the dead offered 'scientific' evidence of Christian truths. Hence the repeated talk of 'independent confirmation' and 'testing', taken from scientific – indeed, laboratory – practices. Spiritualists were modern, progressive people, who drew their models from the latest scientific advances, in turn looking to gravity, mesmerism, electricity and the telegraph as key metaphors both to describe and to account for their experiences. They applied scientific discoveries and techniques to resolve the moral, spiritual and religious dilemmas of the period.

In sharing these broad characteristics, all the movements listed above form part of what one author calls a 'plebeian' culture, originating in a work-ing-class elite, linked therefore in their time to Nonconformity, Methodism and socialism, and showing a shared concern with the problems of self-def-inition, self-education and the control of man's destiny, and even with ex-planations of suffering and views of man's salvation. This is the triumph of a certain kind of Protestant thinking, principally of a Unitarian, Methodist kind, but whose utopian horizons may on occasion introduce an apocalyptic tone. In this milieu, confrontation with 'orthodox' structures (be they of science, medicine, education, the Church or the state) is a central part of the process of self-definition, and has served to protect from criticism the non-cumulative nature of these 'alternative sciences' and the non-falsifiable nature of their utopias and universals. These 'moral' employments of sci-entific discoveries are potentially profoundly polemical. In short, 'scientific knowledge' in these accounts plays the role of esoteric knowledge, a secret which the seeker after truth may be offered, initiated into and drawn deeper

into. In this way, it imitates the practices of scientific learning, in particular
benefiting from the break such learning makes with received wisdom, for
the unanticipated nature of scientific discoveries is used to justify the claims
of the occult sciences: just as we had no suspicion of the nature of gravity or
electricity or evolution, nor should we doubt the possibility of astrological
correspondences, thought transfer or reincarnation. So an important issue
is the development of a theory of the secret, drawing on the work of Simmel
(1950) and of Deleuze and Guattari (1980, chapter 10).[3]

Such approaches largely go unremarked as a class of activity and, when
remarked on, often partially or ill-understood, and yet they are enduring
and adaptable, for they take on new forms with each notable scientific advance, and are far more extensive than one might at first imagine. There is
indeed an increasing body of work (some of it listed above) that construes
the varieties of religious life from the late nineteenth century onward not as
independent growths nor as forms of throw-back to earlier practices, but as
informal or alternative contemporary attempts to think about – and, moreover, actively to respond to – questions of self and salvation, in response to
local turbulence (and, I would say, category collapse), employing the various
authorities available – most notably science and the Bible – in a variety of
combinations. This is then an important point: popular thinking does not
oppose science and religion, but employs various hybrid forms to try and
make sense of the world.

The Varying Relationship between Mind and Matter

Before looking at the dissemination of these ideas to a wider constituency, I
want to draw attention to a central feature of these movements we have been
considering: the relationship between mind and matter, which appears to
be particularly important in these acts of imagination. Some writers, stimulated by the power of the sciences to overthrow hitherto accepted categories, propose what one might call the scientistic claim that mind can be
explained fully in materialist terms. To make a claim, however, is essentially
a mental act. So others make a countervailing claim, not to deny the power
or authority of science but rather the reverse, to suggest that the sciences
should encompass a range of activities which hitherto have been excluded
from their consideration, taking into their consideration parapsychological
and supernatural or occult phenomena. These rival claims for the priority of
either mind or matter are not then simply opposed forms, for the definition
of each term changes according to the claim being made.

My concern here is to draw attention to the fact that the relation between mind and matter (or mind and body) alters over time. From the materialist perspective, the struggle is to see how much of 'mind' can be explained by 'matter' and, from the other side, an idealist defence is concerned to show how little a deterministic materialism can explain and how, in practice, acts of mind can have material effects. These dualistic claims and counter-claims – of what we might call a reductive and a non-reductive materialism – run through all our materials. I want to sketch briefly some of the shifts in the relation of mind to matter that occur in the long period we are considering, for the different movements that emerge correspond to some degree to these altered relations.

I have found a guide to this relationship in Papineau (2002). Papineau as a philosopher is concerned to show that material states (of the brain) can account for consciousness without remainder, and that it is now reasonable, with the current state of knowledge, to accept this claim. I do not necessarily follow him in this, but in an appendix he provides an account of the varying states over time of what he calls the 'completeness of physics' (ibid.: 233) to show why materialist claims were not accepted in the past but can now be.

Papineau begins at the Newtonian revolution. Previous 'mechanical philosophy' took it for granted that all physical action is by impact, and although Descartes had a theory of how the mind might have impact – 'the mind nudges moving particles of matter in the pineal gland, causing them to swerve without losing speed' (ibid.: 235) – this account was not given much credibility. Newtonian physics, however, allowed for forces other than impact. Newton thought of forces as disembodied entities, acting on the affected body from outside. An impressed force, as he called this, 'consists in the action only, and remains no longer in the body when the action is over' (ibid.: 238). Moreover, there could be impressed forces of different origins; the paradigm was gravity, pervading space from massive bodies and acting on anything that might be found there. But once you allow for forces distinct from the action of impact, there could in principle be similar disembodied special forces – such as magnetic, or cohesive, or even vital and mental forces. Papineau concludes: 'The Newtonian world of disembodied forces ... gives no immediate reason to view physics as complete' (ibid.).

Speculation about imponderable forces and their effects therefore flourished as the implications of Newton's discoveries became disseminated widely. As Barrow (1986) has investigated, a range of moral practices – theodicies – developed that allowed actions in the world that were primarily mental rather than physical in their causes, although any links between the investigations of scientists and philosophers on the one hand and plebeian groups and their various leaders on the other are bound to be loose, and to take time to become accepted, even as grounds for speculation. We are not talking about exact correlations but rather affinities or adhesions (though crossovers between the educated classes and the circles around group leaders are readily traceable).

The second moment of significance in Papineau's sequence concerns the emergence of the principle of the conservation of energy, which arose within the tradition of Newtonian mechanics and can be dated to the mid nineteenth century. This principle can be related to the acceptance and synthesis of two traditions: first, the idea that the sum of kinetic energy and potential energy remains constant, and second, the principle that heat and mechanical energy are equivalent (represented in Joule's law). These two were put together in 1847 as the principle of the conservation of energy by Helmholtz, who also dealt with apparent exceptions, bringing living systems within the sway of this mechanics. In this fashion, he opposed a tradition that appealed to vitalism – or the special powers and drives of living matter – and therefore initiated a tendency that would exclude any role for the physical causalities of non-material things such as spirit or mind.

With the rise of scientific thinking in the 1860s and 1870s, there was a push towards an increasingly reductive materialism, based on the principle of the conservation of energy. It did not exclude all animate forces, but it did demand that these special forces are conservative in their own right, or determined by the rule of the conservation of energy. Philosophers such as John Stuart Mill and Alexander Bain went so far as to argue that the conservation of energy, and in particular the notion of potential energy, supported the possibility of non-physical forces. The brain was thought of as a repository of 'nervous energy' that could be channelled in various ways and then released in action (Papineau 2002: 252).

We might see the challenges that Spiritualism faced in the 1870s and the development of Theosophy and Christian Science (see Meade 1980; Braden 1987; Braude 2001) as ways of playing around with these ideas. Their thrust is that minds – or mind-like activities – determine the realities of matter: they exploit the component elements and rules of the conservation of energy.

Papineau's third stage concerns the gradual tightening of the thesis of the completeness of physics during the twentieth century, increasingly excluding any notion of special mental or vital forces. He sees the crucial element in this process as evidence accumulating from physiology, as distinct from either physics or psychology. Increasingly detailed modern research has not indicated any anomalous physical processes within bodies, so that by the 1960s it had become difficult to continue to argue for special vital or mental forces (Papineau 2002: 253). Papineau mentions research on proteins: the identification of the role of enzymes and of basic biological cycles, together with the analysis of the structure of proteins and the discovery of DNA. In parallel, investigations in neurophysiology made it difficult to maintain that special forces operate inside living bodies; living processes seem to consist of nothing but 'familiar physical forces' (ibid.: 254). The emergence of physiology is therefore in Papineau's view the key that clinches the completeness of physics, against the background provided by the argument from fundamental forces.

However, in this period there was also a reintroduction of uncertainty into the nature of physics – at least as far as popular apprehension was concerned – in the discovery of Quantum Theory and the emergence of the Theory of Relativity, and then in Atomic Theory. Papineau tries to scotch the influence of the first on the claims he is setting forward for the completeness of physics, but it is clear that these two earlier theories allowed a new imaginative space for accounts of the effectiveness of mind, the power of thought, and the influence of spirits. We might look at the effervescence of the 1920s, or the new religious forms that emerged in the 1950s and 1960s, or indeed the role of particle physics in the present, to explore the claims made concerning the sciences of mind and matter and their uses by improvisatory religious groups in different periods. These claims and uses undoubtedly change and develop over time, playing with the latest advances, but there is little evidence that reductive accounts that see mind as a function or product of physical processes have triumphed. It is true that we could look at the Cognitive Science of religion as one kind of account of the completeness of physics, and we could also see the New Atheism of Dawkins and others as a proclamation of the same thesis, but neither have established their terms and the adequacy of their account to wide agreement; rather than representing a conclusion to the issues raised, they are rather actors in a long-running show, sharing many of the characteristics of the kind of movement in which we are interested.

In short, the relation between mind and matter, which seems so central to any consideration of the relations of 'religion' and 'science', is not a constant over the period we are considering, but on the contrary is a variable, one that has to be taken into account in giving a description of any particular moment.

Moral Employments of Scientific Discoveries in Literary Expression

It is important to understand that matters do not stop there, at the limits of the small-scale institutions of civil society which are studied by sociologists of religion. For there is also a vast spectrum of contemporary publishing that runs from overtly religious or cosmological speculation, through Science Fiction and Fantasy literature, to popularizing science texts, all of which play variations upon the motif of using contemporary science to think with whilst meditating upon the human condition. These employments may serve as a principle means by which the categories and ways of thinking that concern us become generalized. This is the second heading concerning moral employments of science.

This broad literary genre shares the characteristics of these unorthodox or alternative appraisals of the world discussed in previous sections, without necessarily seeking any practical outcome other than entertainment or enlightenment: they deal in representations of scientific discoveries, they are didactic, and they are frequently distrustful of institutional powers, to the extent sometimes of discerning conspiracies. In every case, they carry conviction through conveying esoteric knowledge to the reader. It is of interest to note that this spectrum is ill-defined, ill-studied (with certain honourable exceptions), and very popular: it sells well. There is much work to be done to characterize the genre: a pioneering work was by Q.D. Leavis (1968), and more recent work by Shippey (1982, 2000) compares the genre's underlying categories with those of folklore. Geraci's recent work on Artificial Intelligence and Science Fiction (Geraci 2010) expands the terms of the debate. In short, there is a series of overlapping genres that runs from Fundamentalism to *The Da Vinci Code* (Brown 2004) and beyond, which deserves, I suggest, greater attention and, indeed, respect, than it usually gets from academics.

The Da Vinci Code indeed presents all the features with which we are concerned. The crux of the story is a secret (a trivial secret, it turns out, but that is of no importance): it is an imponderable universal which permits a set of generalizations and appeals to experience, which are laid out by the narrator in a series of dialogues and a plot leading finally to the revelation of the secret. The knowledge at issue is 'scientific' ('symbological' in this instance), which can be handed on through a didactic education, and is potentially open to all. The knowledge is of course made-up in this case, but it is defended from examination by the invocation of a conspiracy by interested parties to prevent the secret becoming public knowledge. In brief, the structure of the plot is the revelation of esoteric knowledge deliberately concealed.

These kinds of concerns – particularly regarding publishing and the new media – are important in understanding the range and impact of contemporary forms of unorthodox thinking. The preceding account allowed me, for example, to suggest a way of reading Richard Dawkins's relatively recent book *The God Delusion* (2006), in a fashion that both may do justice to the text and also account for the success his writing enjoys and the authority he exerts over many readers (see Jenkins 2009). Dawkins can be located within the loosely constructed but long-established genre of 'thinking with science', as can the broader contemporary movement of 'aggressive atheism', with its characteristic liberal Protestant tropes that defined earlier movements, both religious and secular. And I think a good deal of controversial science, particularly of the evolutionist kind, can usefully be described in this fashion too.

Modern Theodicies

These sorts of account lack insight into the motivations and values of scientific research, and instead develop a rhetoric that draws upon the prestige and interest of the sciences without paying attention to their practices. In doing so, they share in the techniques and aims of a whole range of scientists who write for a popular audience and of writers who attempt to explain recent scientific advances to the same audience, who tend to create explanations of the nature of the world and evaluations of its possible futures that not only draw upon the prestige of the sciences but also utilize a concept of 'Science' (with a capital 's') as a cornerstone of these accounts.

A great part of the appeal of these books to their readers lies in the account they offer of the world and of the place of men and women in such a world: they offer a theodicy, an account of good and evil, of wisdom and folly, and of humanity's consequent well-being and woe. These accounts bear the characteristic marks of the genre outlined above: claiming a scientific status, looking to education to enlighten and spread the truth, and being 'democratic', holding knowledge to be open to all. In these respects, these theories – including Dawkins' – resemble accounts of the world that they would strongly reject, in particular, mesmerism, spiritualism, spiritual healing and phrenology. For these, as remarked earlier, were also widely held theodicies that built upon an appreciation of contemporary science, in this instance, popular apprehensions of Newtonianism. The reason that this comparison offers something more than a superficial resemblance is that these new works, of Dawkins and others, and of various evolutionists, rely upon an apprehension of Darwinism.

These books are not then what they appear to be; they are not 'scientific' in the strict sense, but popular science, with characteristic limitations and features, including the polemic against religion and their mix of appeals to immediate experience, premature generalizations and imponderable universals. Beneath the appeal to Science, embodied now in the genius of Darwin, we have a deliberate, skilful and rhetorical presentation of a theodicy, to be sold in the marketplace of such ideas, with the aim of persuading and even converting hearers to a secular salvation.

The success of these books may then be explained by their belonging to a tradition, going back two hundred years, of deploying simultaneously popular accounts of the Christian religion together with popular accounts of the latest scientific discoveries in order to offer some kind of moral picture of the present. The two major forms of authoritative truth available to us are brought into some kind of a relationship to explain who we are and where we are going and what our potential might be. The relationship will include aspects of cooperation as well as of opposition between the two forms of authority.

They therefore fit somewhere in a spectrum that includes not only spiritualism and astrology, but also, as hinted earlier, Fundamentalism and the New Age, Fantasy literature, Science Fiction and popular science, as well as a great deal more. As remarked, a good proportion of what is currently published and which sells well belongs to this kind of writing. To have begun to build a popular Darwinism, comparable to the popular Newtonianism of the nineteenth century, is a remarkable achievement, although the tribute may not be acceptable to the authors. And although they claim to be true accounts, that motif is part of the genre, as are the various stylistic and argumentative features we noted at the outset, not least the polemic, explicit and implicit, against established forms.

Dawkins, to take him as a typical case, is in these respects closer to Dan Brown (author of *The Da Vinci Code*) than he is to Gregor Mendel (the originator of genetics), and the reception (and success) of his writing needs to be thought about in these terms. He is offering us a secret, one that previously has been concealed from us by interested parties. This realization means it is quite difficult to appraise his account of religion, because it is a meditation upon some rather arbitrarily chosen aspects of the world, an assemblage using elements drawn eclectically to tell a certain kind of modern myth. It is perhaps worth adding that this kind of account aims quite as much at the elimination of sociological descriptions as legitimate explanations as it does religious ones, because of an underlying commitment to methodological individualism. Dawkins presents only a simulacrum of a scientific practice, and he would not sell well if he did otherwise. We might make a more general point, that methodological atheism is often an expression of the kind of phenomenon it is trying to study, or, to put it another way round (as a tentative proposal, to provoke counter-instances), natural scientific discoveries become interesting with respect to thinking about human societies and moral practices precisely at the point at which they are misapplied.

In Conclusion

Let me try and sum up. First, I drew attention to some sociological features of the practices of modern scientists: the break with common sense, the revisable construction of concepts, and the importance and coherence of the moral community to which they belong.

When we considered how common sense puts the discoveries of the sciences to work, I highlighted the importance of the break with common sense and suggested that the significant feature is that scientific (and technological) advances cause a collapse in previously secure forms of measurement. The improvisations or innovations that interest us are not initially in response to ethical concerns but rather to an epistemological dilemma: the collapse of problems of measurement into problems of definition. This leads to what Ardener (2007) calls a 'prophetic condition', where individuals articulate responses in existing language forms to the new conditions they have perceived, responses which make sense to the groups and movements they gather around them (but which are often mistaken from the outside as offering predictions under the old system of measurement).

Whilst this prophetic condition is stimulated by an epistemological dilemma, the response offered inevitably has moral dimensions, and takes the form of a theodicy, an explanation of how the world operates and what is humanity's place in it, offering an account both of evils and suffering and a prospect of well-being. Scientific discoveries are taken up and elements put to work to serve these narratives, with certain features – such as the break with common sense – being used in new ways to serve as confirmation of the scheme offered.

This kind of thinking centres on the possession of what may be called a 'secret', the function of which is principally to order people into two classes, those who are 'in' the secret, and those who are not, but may potentially be recruited (or betray it). Perhaps the vital feature of the approach I am seeking to identify is that it brings to prominence ways of thinking and acting that displace educated, academic approaches from any kind of hegemonic claim over the exercise of intelligence. Such ways of thinking imitate academic thought, but also exploit and parody it to pursue political, moral and religious ends. As a consequence, educated academic thinking of the kind with which we are especially familiar becomes part of a wider social field, one kind within a wider genus, and we may be surprised by the resemblances and overlaps both in process and in motivations with other kinds of thought that emerge once this displacement has been recognized. I have drawn attention in particular to both the centrality and the mutability of the opposition between mind and matter in these complex improvisations.

In brief and in sum, the crucial features of the kind of phenomena I am seeking to isolate are the 'epistemological break', 'parameter collapse', 'theodicy' and 'secrecy'. These broad features allow us to draw together a disparate series of social movements over the last two centuries that exhibit certain family resemblances; these will contain elements that allow them to be classified as political, cultural, economic – or lunatic – phenomena according to circumstance; they may equally as well be 'secular' or 'religious' in form, or a mixture. It also allows us to bring into consideration a wide range of publishing, both in fiction and non-fiction, which show many of the same characteristics and which also serve as a laboratory for further experiment and innovation, at the same time acting to disseminate the concepts and categories in question.

Two remarks, finally, about the distinction between 'fringe' and 'mainstream'. First, significant thinking, it appears, is largely done in the margins of society, and heterodox thought becomes mainstream over time. In the West, we are all now more or less liberal Protestants in many of our basic categories, wherever we situate ourselves; much of our common sense, about progress and self-perfection, is defined by Unitarian or Methodist invention – a sobering thought. Second, a defining characteristic of the present period – in the sense of a striking feature, though not necessarily an important one in the long term – may be the disappearance of any assured discrimination between what counts as 'mainstream' and what counts as 'fringe'. Postmodernity may simply be a certain and temporary loss of a social hegemony; the interesting features of Modernity may lie elsewhere, in the sort of features to which I have drawn attention, and which are the concern of this volume.

Notes

1. This chapter both repeats material from and expands on Jenkins (2009).
2. Amongst the various examples in this volume, I draw attention in particular to Melhuus's discussion of the embryo, and Sansi-Roca's description of 'scientific spiritualism', both of which share a strongly historical perspective.
3. See also Jenkins (1999, 2013).

References

Ardener, E. 2007 [1989]. 'The Voice of Prophecy', in *The Voice of Prophecy and Other Essays*. London: Berghahn, pp.134–54.
Bachelard, G. 1938. *La formation de l'esprit scientifique*. Paris: Vrin.

Barrow, L. 1986. *Independent Spirits: Spiritualism and English Plebeians, 1850–1910*. London: Routledge and Kegan Paul.

Bender, C. 2010. *The New Metaphysicals*. Chicago: University of Chicago Press.

Bourdieu, P., J.-C. Chamboredon and J.C. Passeron. 1991. *The Craft of Sociology: Epistemological Preliminaries*. New York: de Gruyter.

Braden, C.S. 1987 [1963]. *Spirits in Rebellion: The Rise and Development of New Thought*. Dallas: Southern Methodist University Press.

Braude, A. 2001. *Radical Spirits: Spiritualism and Women's Rights in Nineteenth Century America*. Bloomington: Indiana University Press.

Brown, D. 2004. *The Da Vinci Code*. London: Random House.

Darnton, R. 1968. *Mesmerism and the End of the Enlightenment in France*. Cambridge, MA: Harvard University Press.

Dawkins, R. 2006. *The God Delusion*. London: Bantam.

Deleuze, G., and F. Guattari. 1980. *Mille Plateaux*. Paris: Minuit.

Festinger, L., H.W. Riecken and S. Schachter. 2008 [1956]. *When Prophecy Fails*. London: Pinter and Martin.

Geraci, R.M. 2010. *Apocalyptic A.I.: Visions of Heaven in Robotics, Artificial Intelligence and Virtual Reality*. New York: Oxford University Press.

Harding, S.F. 2000. *The Book of Jerry Falwell: Fundamentalist Language and Politics*. Princeton: Princeton University Press.

Jenkins, T. 1999. 'Secrets of the Spirit World', in *Religion in English Everyday Life: An Ethnographic Approach*. Oxford: Berghahn, pp.221–37.

——. 2009. 'Closer to Dan Brown than to Gregor Mendel: On Dawkins' *The God Delusion*', *Scottish Journal of Theology* 62(3): 269–81.

——. 2013. *Of Flying Saucers and Social Scientists*. New York: Palgrave Macmillan.

Leavis, Q.D. 1968 [1932]. *Fiction and the Reading Public*. London: Chatto and Windus.

Meade, M. 1980. *Madame Blavatsky, the Woman behind the Myth*. New York: Putnam.

Moore, R.L. 1989. *In Search of White Crows*. Oxford: Oxford University Press.

Numbers, R. 1992. *The Creationists: The Evolution of Scientific Creationism*. Berkeley: University of California Press.

Orsi, R. 1992. 'Beyond the Mainstream in the Study of American Religious History', *Journal of Ecclesiastical History* 43(2): 287–92.

Papineau, D. 2002. *Thinking about Consciousness*. Oxford: Oxford University Press.

Shippey, T. 1982. *The Road to Middle Earth*. London: Allen and Unwin.

——. 2000. *J.R.R. Tolkien: Author of the Century*. London: Harper Collins.

Simmel, G. 1950. 'The Secret and the Secret Society', in K. Wolff (ed.), *The Sociology of Georg Simmel*. New York: Free Press, pp.330–78.

Chapter Five

The Social Life of Concepts

Public and Private 'Knowledge' of Scientific Creationism

Simon Coleman

I begin with a secular parable about knowledge, evidence and belief. Many years ago I was standing on top of a cold, windy hillside in South Wales after two weeks of working on what my fellow workers and I had all believed was a Palaeolithic cave site. I say 'believed' because after a fortnight's digging we had found precisely nothing. Addressing his crestfallen team on that windy day, the director of the dig – bravely summoning up a combination of hope and irony – announced that we had indeed made an important discovery: that there was something called 'negative evidence', and that it was there in abundance in the empty cave site in Wales. We knew, in effect, that there was nothing to know.

I mention this long-distant experience in a book on knowledge and belief because of more recent questions raised in my mind by a small field project of my own that uncovered evidence with the initial appearance of being decidedly negative – indeed, evidence that appeared to be pointing to the decided absence of something looked for. What I had been looking for was a certain kind of knowledge among my informants, and it simply did not seem to be there.

Let me explain. It is true that some of this chapter is going to be about the lack of a certain kind of knowledge among Christian creationists. But I am writing not to engage in the usual secular scientific ritual of accusing such believers of being incapable of understanding evolutionary theory. Instead, I want to point to what I think is a different and for me more interesting kind of absence. Much of this chapter, then, is about the relative lack of interest or engagement in creationism as a practical issue or a salient ideology in the independent evangelical churches that I encountered in the north and south of England, the apparent lack of much systematic production of knowledge that could unambiguously be regarded as creationist in content or intent. Having said that, my argument is going to be that what appears from one perspective to be a lack is actually something more significant, a more implicit location of 'creationist' discourse and practice in areas it did not initially occur to me would be promising areas to excavate. So one of the lessons of the following ethnographic parable is going to be that an apparent absence can imply a different kind of plenitude, can point to a different kind of significance and construction of a different kind of 'knowledge'. In that sense my approach will be similar not only to the unfortunate director of the Welsh excavation, but also to a famous example provided by a different searcher for the truth, Sherlock Holmes, in the story 'Silver Blaze'.[1] At one point in the investigation of the case of a missing horse, the police detective, Inspector Gregory, says to Sherlock Holmes:

> 'Is there any other point to which you would wish to draw my attention?'
> 'To the curious incident of the dog in the night-time' [Holmes replied].
> 'The dog did nothing in the night-time' [Gregory responded].
> 'That was the curious incident', remarked Sherlock Holmes.

Yet, while many of the believers I shall be referring to seem to have been largely unengaged in public, defined discourse on creationism in the UK, they contrast with others who have been busy shaping knowledge of and about creationists, often in the name of secular science, and these latter are also going to be referred to in the following. In some respects, indeed, my own original interest in and understanding of scientific creationism was moulded by the occasionally intense public debates generated by the topic, by popular and social scientific models of conflict between 'science' and 'religion' emerging out of the antagonism between religious and secular interest groups, particularly in the US, but also to some degree in the UK. We shall see that things look very different if one turns away from overtly public arenas towards seeing creationism in 'everyday' terms, integrated into congregational life and wider forms of worship, religious narrative and belief, so that it actually becomes both more and less than a concept. This relatively jagged juxtaposition of public and private prompts us to do more, I think, than just focus on realms of the domestic and the everyday that we often see as the prime anthropological province of investigation. In other words, what are we to make as anthropologists about creationism as public discourse? What happens when religion does not just appear in public, but is somehow constituted through the process of *going* public?

Of course we can talk about these questions by assessing common tropes of opposition between secularization and post-secularization, reason and religion, religion and modernity and so on. But I want to think about it in slightly different ways as well, even though at this point I shall be engaging more in a thought experiment than in reasoning from ethnography. For it seems to me that debates over creationism are especially interesting for anthropologists because they embody subject matter in which we have a particular kind of stake: human evolution is after all one of the things that we study. At the same time, we are interested in the construction and representation of knowledge itself, and therefore in a meta-analysis of evolutionism and creationism as discourses about humanity. What I shall be suggesting is that by looking at who is making the running in public constructions of evolutionary and creationist discourse in the UK we can start to ask some questions not only of Christian believers, but also of 'secular' scholars, including anthropologists. We are also prompted to reflect on distinctions between public and private forms of knowledge, and indeed on marginality and centrality in the construction of 'societies of knowledge', as well as what we might call 'societies of situated ignorance'.

Everyday Creationism

My research has consisted of two sets of activity. An initial project in the 1990s involved an exploratory set of in-depth interviews conducted by me and the American anthropologist Leslie Carlin with thirty-four evangelical but largely non-charismatic Christians recruited largely by snowball sampling from three congregations, two in the south of England and one in the north. Leslie had initially been attracted to the topic by discovering another kind of absence, when teaching evolutionary theory to anthropology students in the US and the UK: while her American students often saw the acceptance or rejection of evolutionary theory as a key point in articulating both personal identity and political orientation, her British students both took evolutionary theory for granted and were largely comfortable with the idea of entertaining alternative points of view. So we then began to explore what we called the 'cultures of creationism' (Coleman and Carlin 2004), the various ways in which both evolutionary and various forms of anti-evolutionary theory have been expressed in different parts of the English-speaking world, and the cultural and structural reasons for those differences (see also

Numbers 1992). But after attending a lecture given by a creation scientist at a public event staged at our own university, we also became interested in the articulation of creationism and creation science amongst British evangelicals. In the congregations that we looked at, all interviewees identified themselves as supporting a creationist position of some sort, and many had read the classic text of many creation scientists worldwide: John Whitcomb and Henry Morris's *The Genesis Flood: The Biblical Record and its Scientific Implications* (1961). However, while a few were members of UK-based creationist organizations, the vast majority were not.[2]

The main point to make here is about our methodology: we were trying to locate creationist discourse and practice in the context of congregational or personal devotional life,[3] rather than in activist organizations as such; and, although we could not do extensive participant observation, we worked on placing what people said about creationism in relation to their readings not just of Genesis but of the whole Bible as a guide for life; and indeed to how they thought not just about science, but also about belief.

Before I say more about what we found I want to juxtapose this work with my second encounter with creationism, some ten years later, when I was asked to act as an advisor to a report called 'Doubting Darwin', produced by the British think-tank Theos as part of a wider survey of evolutionary and non-evolutionary beliefs in the UK (Pharaoh et al. 2009). That study, based largely on fifty interviews with people the researchers call 'opinion-formers' –church ministers, activists, teachers and students – found evidence for a wide variety of ideological stances that are explained in the text but that I need not go into here: 'young Earth' creationism, 'old Earth' Creationism, intelligent design and so on, as well as Islamic creationism. For my purposes, the important dimensions of the study relate to its conclusions about the UK. The investigators found that, while some informants were afraid of being 'outed' as creationists in public, many were unconcerned about the issue, and church ministers in fact noted that their 'beliefs about evolution were a relatively minor concern in daily life, a comparatively unimportant aspect of their work or of their identity' (ibid.: 107). Indeed, many creationist leaders interviewed were running small churches, so that such views had to blend in and not prompt conflicts in relation to cross-cutting pastoral, social and theological ties. As one minister put it: 'Do we have the luxury of sitting around and making daisy chains? ... I tend not to preach about creationism. [Though] I have been working on it personally to get it more settled in my mind. But I am more concerned that we are united and I don't want to bring anything in that would be divisive' (ibid.: 108). This kind of positioning led the writers of the report to conclude that supporters of creationism, including of the more recent intelligent design strain, did not constitute a 'movement' in the UK since they displayed little ideological unity and were dispersed both geographically and politically (ibid.: 13).

Such relative fragmentation and lack of fervour, especially when compared with the US, needs to be understood in relation to the smaller numbers of evangelicals in the UK, the greater fusion even now of Church and state, and the relatively centralized character of the media, electoral and educational systems, even if all of these are shifting (and perhaps crumbling). So in the UK there seem to be long periods of inattention paid to the issues by opinion-formers on either side of the argument punctuated by moral panics in which a secular or religiously neutral order is restored. For instance, when a number of pro-creationist schools were proposed in the north of England in the spring of 2003, Richard Dawkins, then Oxford professor of the public understanding of science, led the opposition by dismissing the juxtaposition of evolution with a faith position as a form of 'educational debauchery'.[4] More recently, Michael Reiss, the Royal Society's director of education – both a Church of England clergyman and a biologist – was forced to resign after addressing the British Association for the Advancement of Science and arguing that school teachers should accept that they were unlikely simply to change the minds of pupils who held creationist beliefs. As he put it: 'My experience after having tried to teach biology for 20 years is if one simply gives the impression that such children are wrong, then they are not likely to learn much about the science ... There is much to be said for allowing students to raise any doubts they have ... and doing one's best to have a genuine discussion'.[5] His remarks were publicly represented as having caused uproar among some of his fellow scientists.

The Theos report notes that if there ever could be a uniting, galvanizing effect on sceptics towards evolution, it would, ironically, come precisely from the dismissive comments of figures such as Richard Dawkins (Pharaoh et al. 2009: 14). We shall consider this issue later. For the time being, the point is that we see here a religio-political context that often encourages public quiescence, or at least a diversion of energy in other directions, among most British evangelicals. And we also see distinct parallels between the findings of the Theos report – focused, remember, on so-called creationist activists – and those of the interviews conducted by Leslie Carlin and myself as we talked to members of congregations who were more diffusely supportive of creationist and creation science positions. In fact, Leslie and I found little consensus, even among members of the same congregation, over what creationist position to take – young Earth, old Earth, and so on. Many informants reported that they had not really decided what their position was, that it was an ongoing process and that creationism was not in fact central to core principles of Christian identity; that even if they were in favour of some version of a creationist position, it would still be perfectly possible to be Christian without being a creationist. Others went further. One man put the ethnographers in their place when he noted: 'I actually avoid debating with creationists ... It bores me largely, that sort of debate'. Or again there was the following response from a young student taking a PhD in science, 'Well, at one level ... the issue doesn't interest me that much, [though] it may sound a bit odd'. Here, the reference to 'it' sounding odd referred – fascinatingly, I think – to the fact that he was in fact a paid-up member of the Biblical Creation Society in the UK. Or once more, there was some significant hair splitting from another informant, this time an older man, responding to our question of whether he would describe himself as a creationist, 'Well, I probably wouldn't call myself one, but I probably am one'. These kinds of attitudes went along with another standpoint that initially surprised us: that almost all informants were actually extremely wary about the teaching of creationism in schools. In other words, they disliked the idea of giving the responsibility of imparting such knowledge to a potentially secular teacher, and moreover in a public context away from the context of living faith as practised at home or in the church.

At this point, the temptation is perhaps to go back to the image with which I began this chapter, of standing on the Welsh hillside and admitting that the evidence is negative: it is time to move on and try to dig up evidence for creationist discourse somewhere else. But I think that there is something else going on here, that these apparent absences or apathies are actually directing us to reframe our search for a more productive layer of creationist ideas and practices – even of a different form of knowledge. Let me start by looking briefly at the idea of an 'everyday' type of creationism, a concept with a particular kind of social life. The notion of 'everyday' is actually borrowed here from the work of Joel Robbins (2001) on millenarianism among the Urapmin of Papua New Guinea, a group of a few hundred people who converted to Pentecostalism in the 1970s. Robbins draws a distinction between the kind of heightened millenarianism that causes people to abandon work and await the end of the world (and which does occasionally happen among the Urapmin), and the more everyday sort – that which forms part of the background expectation and self-construction of believers. It is this latter sense of a creationism that is more implicit, more formative of the subject in a chronic, diffused way that I am interested in. The point is reinforced by my appropriation of Appadurai's (1986) 'social life of things' when talking of a concept such as creationism, since I am interested in the way that Appadurai calls attention to how meanings derive from human transactions and circulations, and the ways in which value can derive from social relations. In other words, adapting such ideas for my purposes: How is creationism constructed and circulated as a concept or as a wider form of discourse in a social setting such as a congregation?

To these points I want to add just one further piece of theoretical background, focusing on work that has highlighted the limitations of intellectualizing or indeed proposition-based conceptions of belief. As Galina Lindquist (2008) has pointed out, such analytical strategies can prompt us into over-emphasizing the centrality of referential meaning when even a faith such as Western forms of Christian fundamentalism must be seen as embodied as well as thought, located in buildings and practices as well as principles. Or we might again point to the ambiguities of the word 'believe' as laid out by anthropologists such as Robbins and, before him, Malcolm Ruel (1982), for whom 'believing that' – a propositional orientation – can be distinguished from 'believing in' – where belief is rooted more explicitly in issues of social relationship and trust. So I want to argue for an analysis that searches for creationism as embodied practice, as embedded in wider conceptions and social relations of the believing subject – a subject whose commitment to the faith is an ongoing process.

The English informants whom Leslie and I interviewed seem, in retrospect, to be pushing us in this very direction. Admittedly, in our interviews we encountered the familiar tropes of creationism as a useful means to engage non-Christians in debate. As one man put it, 'It is an excellent way of witnessing ... talking about things that interest them, you know, because they're all interested in dinosaurs and fossils and this sort of thing'. ('They' in this quote refers to non-believers.) We also found the common evangelical trope of Genesis itself as the key point in an intellectual pack of cards, so that its discrediting would precipitate a collapse in the rest of the Bible. However, more striking and more common were attempts to move creationism towards a discussion of creation – to 'de-ism' it, so to speak, to deny the validity of separating out creationist debates from wider considerations of the construction of the self as a believer. Thus a former biology teacher, no less, stated: 'I'm not sure I'm terribly happy with creationism as a term anyway ... It's important to say that in talking about creationism I'm really saying I believe in the biblical account of creation', and a more recent convert told us, 'I think what I've realized is that the only reason I believe in creation at all is because of what the Lord's doing in my life'. This latter response was just one of many examples of a shifting of our questions on people's views of creationism into a discussion of ongoing belief in, and relationship with, divinity. And for a young trainee barrister, the debate also led her to considerations of the self as moral agent, as she noted that, 'the creation story fits in very well with the New Testament as it gives us a sense of responsibility ... We were created by God and have a responsibility to obey God'. Leslie and I vividly remember another interview that we carried out with a leading activist in British creation science circles, which took place in his office in the university where he worked as a leading research scientist, and which ended not with his summarizing his thoughts on creationism but with a much more generalized testimony as to the importance of having faith. Incidentally, we see another intriguing conflation or paralleling of creation, creationism and the construction of the religious subject in an American example Leslie Carlin and I have used before (Coleman and Carlin 2004: 7) where we quote a *New Scientist* interview with Bob Willis, head of the Creation Science Association of Mid-America, who is both an activist in the fertile US context but also replies in an intriguing way when he talks about how he was converted to creationism. Willis notes that reading Darwin was one catalyst, but in addition:

> I was not a Christian – I didn't know Christianity from the sole of my foot. But I became a creationist – an anti-evolutionist creationist – by a series of, some would say, unusual events. One was a traumatic personal event that caused me to rethink the meaning of life and to seek other solutions from the lifestyle I was living.[6]

This is creation science discourse framed by and constituted within the language of personal testimony, and a trajectory of the subject from ignorance, through personal trauma, into a new way of seeing and acting within the world.

It is important to emphasize here that none of our British informants professed themselves to be anti-science, and indeed we encountered a disproportionate number of natural science PhDs in our interviews because of the nature of the networks we were following. What informants were generally against was a turning of creationism into a form of distorting public discourse. As one man put it, 'I am concerned that it's possible to take creationists' viewpoints to such a degree that it's the only thing the Bible is on about'. The point being made is that, although informants might attend study days on creationism or read literature on the subject, they often have deep misgivings over it becoming a self-contained object of circulation and self-presentation to others, taken away from wider considerations of congregational and family life. At times, indeed, such views were expressed explicitly in relation to the American contexts in which creationism and creation science have been seen to thrive. One young man called jokingly for a form of British, as opposed to American, fundamentalism, but more seriously talked of how he preferred to deal with the topic by making it an object of prayer with a friend – like him, a natural science PhD student – whom he regarded as his prayer partner. So these attitudes lead us to a perhaps coun-ter-intuitive orientation, at least from a social-scientific point of view, that such believers are broadly supportive of creationism but also mistrustful of it, indeed sometimes see it as inimical to sincere belief in its most extreme forms of articulation and circulation in the public sphere. Publicness and piety contend in specific ways here. An attempt to demonstrate the truth of the Bible in rational terms is seen as moving the believer towards a problem-atic doctrine of works, rather than faith. As one middle-aged woman put it, 'I accept creation because I accept what the Lord wrote in the Bible, but I don't need to prove it'. Similarly, an older man invoked a much-used biblical image that takes us back to questions of the nature of evidence, in referring us to Hebrews 11: 1: 'Now faith is the substance of things hoped for, the evidence of things not seen'.

We are very far here from creationism as a system of knowledge. If anything, we are encountering people who are resisting such an approach, even though they are perfectly capable of dealing with such systems. Fur-thermore, as scholars such as Chris Toumey (1994) have shown in his work in North Carolina, the distance between creationism articulated in public debate and the ambiguities of more private discourse can be considerable in any context, even that of the US. So the real point here so far has been to find new ground in which to explore creationism as practice and even, in Foucauldian terms, less an object of debate and more a technology of the self, part of a wider set of ideological resources through which to constitute the self as believer. And if we accept this argument we might or might not agree with the statement often made by believers that only those who 'be-lieve' can truly understand God's words in the correct way, but we are surely given food for thought in considering whether Michael Reiss – sacked from his public role – or Richard Dawkins might be the more effective interlocu-tor with self-professed creationists in a school classroom.

Creating 'Science'

And so we come to the second half of this chapter, the second context of knowledge construction about creation and creationists, and one based much more speculatively on general observation rather than fieldwork or interviews. My question now becomes: How are we to understand the de-bates through which creationism is presented and, I would argue, recreated in public? Of course simple public/private distinctions are flawed, as some of my previous argument has indicated, but on the other hand we have seen how some British informants have felt constrained from talking in secular contexts about their beliefs, and about moving from congregational contexts into those where terms of discourse cannot be controlled, such as schools.

My strategy in thinking about public debate is admittedly an incomplete one, not least as I do not focus here on the public activities of creationists themselves, but I hope it will allow us to consider some key contrasts in the articulation of knowledge. It will also, I hope, move us from overt to more implicit, but I think equally important, aspects of the debate.[7]

To start with the (perhaps overly) obvious. Undoubtedly one of the major catalysts of moral entrepreneurship on Britain and beyond in relation to debates around creationism and creation science has been Richard Dawkins. As already mentioned, Dawkins is the describer of the juxtaposition of evolution with a faith position in schools as 'educational debauchery', but he was also for much of his career a professor for the public understanding of science. 'Public understanding' in such terms presumably implies less the task of mediating between public and private forms of knowledge and more one of interpreting science for the lay public, but the title still implies the need to articulate forms of knowledge in public space within what is called in this volume a 'society of knowledge'. As is well known, Dawkins has been a tireless activist in various aspects of the public realm, ranging from his numerous books, articles and lectures to his sponsoring of a famous advertising campaign on British buses in 2009, organized by the British Humanist Association, with posters bearing the curiously uncharismatic exhortation: 'There's Probably No God. Now Stop Worrying and Enjoy your Life'.[8] Dawkins's Foundation for Reason and Science lists as its mission the aim 'to support scientific education, critical thinking and evidence-based understanding of the natural world in the quest to overcome religious fundamentalism, superstition, intolerance and human suffering'.[9] In the past, Dawkins has debated with creationists, including a 1986 Oxford Union Debate involving himself, John Maynard Smith (professor of biology at the University of Sussex) and the creationists A.E. Wilder-Smith (a professor of pharmacology) and Edgar Andrews (a materials scientist and president of the Biblical Creation Society). While it was said of T.H. Huxley that he was Darwin's bulldog, Dawkins can clearly look after himself. In the imagery favoured by Sherlock Holmes in 'Silver Blaze', he is a dog who both barks *and* bites.

The significant point for our purposes is what kind of knowledge, and what kind of public understanding of science and religion, are being promoted by a figure such as Dawkins? One way to approach such knowledge is, so to speak, to view it from within. It is surely worth noting the recent comments of fellow evolutionary biologist David Sloan Wilson (2008) that situate Dawkins intellectually, arguing that while some scholars in the latter's field have suggested that religion has proved adaptive by aiding survival through promoting the formation of bonds, Dawkins rejects such a social explanation because it relies on group selection – the differential survival of harmonious societies – rather than one-to-one competition (see also Midgley 2008: xix). While the political resonances of such a view are argued by some to be deeply individualistic in themselves, Wilson refers to a different kind of constituting metaphor, what he calls Dawkins's 'demonic meme hypothesis' (Wilson 2008: 134), through which selfish memes inhabit our minds in a pattern comparable to a kind of spiritual possession.

Whatever we think of these ways of characterizing Dawkins's work, I think we can see his attacks on religion as also and inevitably forming religion as an object of discourse, as a phenomenon to be discussed but also known, in two further significant ways. First, there is simply the sense of religion as 'Religion' with a capital 'r', so to speak, a phenomenon that can be isolated and potentially expurgated while the rest of society carries on. For Wilson, the problem, however, lies precisely in the approach of issuing monolithic statements about religion, as opposed to using the tools of evolutionist analysis to explain religious diversity as one might biological diversity (ibid.: 129). Mary Midgley (2008: xviii) puts the point in another way in her comments on Dawkins, arguing that we cannot grasp the range of religion by reducing it to a single local model that is then simply universalized.

Second, we need to ask what this 'local model' consists of. Dawkins himself puts it in the following way in *The God Delusion*: 'I do have one thing in common with the Creationists. Like me, but unlike the [Neville] Chamberlain school, they will have no truck with NOMA [non-overlapping magisteria]' (Dawkins 2006: 67–68). Here is a dig at Stephen Jay Gould's (and of course others') suggestion that religion and science might be doing essentially different things, and at the same time it seems to me that this is a form of intellectualism being presented under the guise of evolutionary biology (see Brooke 2008: 157). Such intellectualism performs an important function: it justifies the joining of religion and science and their representatives in a common, potentially public sphere of debate, where concepts can be debated. This work of conjoining is vital, indeed, to a process of delegitimization, to a mutual construction and then distancing of religion and science. There is of course a history to this, including the emergence of Christian fundamentalism itself as a religion of opposition, willing at times – and especially in the US – to combine tribal exclusiveness with engagement in the public sphere. But as Midgley also points out (2008: xix), when Dawkins declares 'I shall suggest that the existence of God is a scientific hypothesis like any other' (Dawkins 2006: 51), he surely displays a startling lack of interest in the workings of language, as do those who support his position. It seems to me that we not only see here the translation of religion into a framework of public disconfirmation, but also in effect a performative act, a creation and not merely a definition of religion as interlocutor.

To all of which we might well say, so what? Dawkins is likely to illustrate the extreme end of a particular spectrum of approaches. Somebody has to. In response I would say the following. Firstly, that in the public sphere, what Midgley has termed the 'cold war' approach has been, as she puts it, 'accepted without comment by many as rational and proper' (Midgley 2008: xviii). Elsewhere, I have also quoted the example of evolutionary biologist Steve Jones, certainly no Richard Dawkins in his approach to argumentation, nonetheless announcing to a well-known book festival that he was simply giving up debating with creationists, and doing this in a talk entitled 'Why Creationism is Wrong and Evolution is Right' (Coleman 2011: 183).[10] What is being created here is a particular way in which to represent but also create knowledge, not least by publicizing and then marginalizing what is claimed to be an alternative system of equivalent knowledge. Secondly, as part of such knowledge construction, we are also being presented with a particular methodology for understanding a phenomenon such as religion. Here Wilson, with his own adoption of a Sherlock Holmesian analogy, argues that in a subject such as religion, as indeed with cultural evolution, Dawkins – the champion of reliable evidence – has not conducted empirical research, preferring to play the role of Mycroft Holmes, who sat in his armchair and let brother Sherlock do the legwork. I hope we might be able to think back briefly to my comments on everyday creationism and the complex, embodied construction of the religious subject, but rather than dwelling in any detail on those points I want instead to suggest that the Dawkins approach, the authoritative albeit controversial promotion of a certain version of the knowledge society, also runs the danger of propelling us towards a certain kind of ignorance. Let me explain what I mean.

On Knowing about Not-knowing

In previous work I have argued that we need what one might call an anthropology of 'Dawkinsism' as well as creationism, involving an understanding that both represent sometimes conjoined cultural phenomena, but that we need also to see them as involving particular, wider modes of practice and sets of assumptions (Coleman 2008). The idea of Dawkinsism may seem to have a facetious dimension, but it is meant to have a serious intent in the very movement of Dawkins into an 'ism'; in other words, in the movement away from a person to the wider cultural phenomenon that he has come to represent. This movement might also be seen as a translation of Dawkins as moral entrepreneur into an anthropological object of investigation, and as such should also carry out ethnography on those who subscribe to a Dawkins-like world-view, their modes of expression, moral frameworks and so on. There are many ways in which we might study this phenomenon. The deployment of language is likely to be one fascinating area; another is its dealing with such religious themes as, say, aesthetics or 'secular' theodicy; yet another is the trope, evident in religious and other texts, of retranslating Dawkins's discourse into religious categories – saying that he is *really* a secular fundamentalist, preacher manqué, and so on – and this last approach can among other things be seen as a counterpart of Dawkins's framing of religion as a set of hypotheses. For the purposes of this chapter, however, I prefer to argue that Dawkinsism can be seen not merely as a form of knowledge, but also as a form of ignorance.

In making this claim I draw on a recent paper by Roy Dilley (2010). Dilley's thesis is that that knowledge and ignorance must be regarded as mutually constitutive in terms of how a dialectic between knowledge and ignorance is played out in specific sets of social and political relations. Ignorance – not knowing – can be seen as an absence in and of itself or as a willed and intentional stance towards the world, different stances that I personally think of as ignorance and ignorance.

Dilley notes that his initial thoughts were prompted by a nineteenth-century St Andrews philosopher, James Frederick Ferrier, who was father of the term 'epistemology', but also gave birth to the idea of 'agnoiology', the theory of ignorance, so that the science of knowing could be contrasted with the doctrine of those things of which we are necessarily ignorant. We might think of this, says Dilley, as science versus 'nescience', the latter defined as the lack or want of knowledge.

As Dilley points out, knowledge and ignorance, science and nescience, are not to be seen as timeless universals in a discourse of philosophical speculation; nor are they devoid of moral value. In fact, they must be seen as located in ethical discourses about knowing and not-knowing. Ignorance as innocence is possible to posit, as in the case of Adam and Eve prior to the Fall. In contrast, the state of ignorance as nescience can also carry the ethical imperative for expunging ignorance by revealing knowledge – an argument with moral valency for both medieval theologians and post-Enlightenment scientists, but also, in all probability, for the unfortunate director of the dig on that Welsh hillside who refused to countenance the possibility that two weeks of archaeology had produced no knowledge at all. For my purposes, the most significant part of Dilley's argument relates to his stating the need to uncover not only social practices of knowledge, but also how varieties of ways of knowing are contingent upon how ignorance and not-knowing are framed. Creationism, as we have seen, emerges from several different sites of production, but there is a disjunction between it as a type of knowledge emergent through the formation of the subject on the one hand, and as a means of interlocution in a public sphere that is both agnostic and agonistic on the other. Many of the believers whom I mentioned shied away from the latter precisely because it could not comprehend the sense of knowing of the former, rooted in the life of congregation and family. Dawkinsism requires 'science' and 'religion' to be interlocked as well as interlocutors, but in the process creates nescience as well as science, agonistic constructions for public debate where knowledge of a concept such as creationism that might be provided not only by religious experience, but also by ethnography, is made marginal. In one extraordinary video made by Dawkins himself that I have previously observed on his website, he sits by a fire in a comfortable living room and reads out emails sent to him by religious opponents accusing him of various forms of blasphemy. Dawkins is careful to retain the grammatical errors and profanities of the writers, and is speaking both to the video audience and to an audience in the room, off camera, who laugh along with him at the vituperation being showered on him. In voicing these texts, Dawkins is also performatively constructing the ignorance of his religious opponents and of the religion that they espouse. But in my terms, he is also constructing a form of ign*o*rance – of the kind of work discussed in the first part of this chapter. Mary Midgley refers to the cold war created by simplistic opponents of science and religion, but I am also pointing to a much more implicit yet no less important undermining of a key component of a knowledge society: an indifference to a social-scientific view of the world, and thus not to a simple absence of knowledge (such as the lack of archaeological material in a Welsh hillside) but to the creation of an absence, a muting of other disciplinary apparatuses.

We can see the ironies here if what is presented as the public understanding of science entails a lack of understanding of both 'the public' and of alternative modes of 'secular' understanding – in other words, if science also creates significant forms of nescience. But we might argue that what is at stake is also a matter of simple effectiveness: an approach that also helps precisely to create or at least provoke its own opposition is not one that is likely to see the end of religion in the world. Brooke notes that, 'If the goal is to proselytise on behalf of Darwinian science, to transform it into an atheistic ideology can be to shoot oneself in the foot' (Brooke 2008: 157), not least as such an approach does not come close to comprehending or having any relevance to the kinds of religious knowing we see in the congregations I have described. To deploy a further canine image, it is barking up the wrong tree. At the same time, as social scientists we hardly have cause to be satisfied at our own relative failure to bark at all. As others have noted (e.g. Engelke 2008: 3), socio-cultural anthropology lacks an effective evidential language with which to engage colleagues in other human sciences, the humanities and the natural sciences, or actors and interest groups in the wider world. Our discipline is still largely unable at present to create a truly public version of itself, even over a topic that is supposedly within our own remit. We have been unable to produce a professor of the public understanding of social science with the charisma and influence of Dawkins. That – in the context of discussing the workings of a knowledge society – is perhaps the greatest shame of all.

Notes

1. Originally published in the collection *The Memoirs of Sherlock Holmes* (1894).
2. The majority of our interviewees were aged 18 to their mid 70s; they had at least undergraduate degrees, and a few had PhDs in the natural sciences. Congregations represented were both broadly evangelical and in one case Pentecostal.
3. Compare Jenkins (this volume) on how science is captured through common-sensical and moral descriptions of the world.
4. Retrieved 10 June 2014, from: http://news.bbc.co.uk/2/hi/uk_news/education/2982933.stm.
5. *Guardian*, 11 September 2008. Retrieved 10 June 2014, from: www.guardian.co.uk/science/2008/sep/11/creationism.education.
6. 'Take Me To Your Leader', *New Scientist*, 22 April 2000. Retrieved 10 June 2014, from: www.jodkowski.pl/ek/TWillis002.html.
7. In considering how creationism is transferred and translated into the public sphere, there are parallels to be drawn with Melhuus's discussion (this volume) of how the embryo is both an object of scientific knowledge and the subject of intense moral engagement, constructed through different regimes of knowledge.
8. For the campaign logo, see: www.humanism.org.uk/bus-campaign.
9. Quoted from the website of the Richard Dawkins Foundation for Reason and Science. Retrieved 23 June 2011, from: http://old.richarddawkins.net/pages/mission.
10. See *Guardian*, 30 May 2006.

References

Appadurai, A. 1986. 'Introduction', in A. Appadurai (ed.), The Social Life of Things: Commodities in Cultural Perspective. Cambridge: Cambridge University Press, pp.3–63.
Brooke, J.H. 2008. 'Can Scientific Discovery Be a Religious Experience?' in A. Bentley (ed.), *The Edge of Reason? Science and Religion in Modern Society*. London: Continuum, pp.155–64.

Coleman, S. 2008 'Science Versus Anthropology, Not Religion', in A. Bentley (ed.), *The Edge of Reason? Science and Religion in Modern Society*. London: Continuum, pp.39–45.

——. 2011. 'Actors of History? Religion, Politics and "Reality" within the Protestant Right in America', in G. Lindquist and D. Handelman (eds), *Religion, Politics and Globalization: Anthropological Approaches*. Oxford: Berghahn, pp.171–88.

Coleman, S., and L. Carlin. 2004. 'The Cultures of Creationism: Shifting Boundaries of Belief, Knowledge and Nationhood', in S. Coleman and L. Carlin (eds), *The Cultures of Creationism: Anti-evolutionism in English-speaking Countries*, Aldershot: Ashgate, pp.1–28.

Dawkins, R. 2006. *The God Delusion*. London: Bantam.

Dilley, R. 2010. 'Reflections on Knowledge Practices and the Problem of Ignorance', *Journal of the Royal Anthropological Institute* 16(2): 176–92.

Engelke, M. (ed.). 2008. 'The Objects of Evidence', *Journal of the Royal Anthropological Institute*, special issue, 14(supplement).

Lindquist, G. 2008. 'Loyalty and Command: Shamans, Lamas, and Spirits in a Siberian Ritual', *Social Analysis* 52(1): 111–26.

Midgley, M. 2008. 'Foreword', in A. Bentley (ed.), *The Edge of Reason? Science and Religion in Modern Society*. London: Continuum, pp.xvii–xxiv.

Numbers, R. 1992. *The Creationists: The Evolution of Scientific Creationism*. Berkeley: University of California Press.

Pharaoh, R., T. Hale and G. Rowe. 2009. *Doubting Darwin: Creationism and Evolution Scepticism in Britain Today*. London: Theos. Available online at: http://campaign-director.moodia.com/Client/Theos/Files/TheosDoubtingDarwin.pdf.

Robbins, J. 2001. 'Secrecy and the Sense of an Ending: Narrative, Time and Everyday Millenarianism in Papua New Guinea and in Christian Fundamentalism', *Comparative Studies in Society and History* 43(3): 525–51.

Ruel, M. 1982. 'Christians as Believers', in J. Davis (ed.), *Religious Organization and Religious Experience*. London: Academic Press, pp.9–31.

Toumey, C. 1992. *God's Own Scientists: Creationists in a Secular World*. New Brunswick, NJ: Rutgers University Press.

Whitcomb, J.C., and H.M. Morris. 1961. *The Genesis Flood: The Biblical Record and Its Scientific Implications*. Philadelphia: Presbyterian and Reformed Publishing Co.

Wilson, D.S. 2008. 'Why Richard Dawkins is Wrong about Religion', in A. Bentley (ed.), *The Edge of Reason? Science and Religion in Modern Society*. London: Continuum, pp.119–37.

Chapter Six

The Embryo, Sacred and Profane

Marit Melhuus

While scientists are claiming the human embryo for research into what is presented as one of the most promising fields in modern biomedicine – stem-cell research – the embryo is being subjected to philosophical, theological, ethical and political examination worldwide. The 'modern' embryo is imbued with qualities that make it an exceptionally vibrant entity, and the various perceptions of the embryo are neither localized nor limited to one belief system or cosmology. Quite the contrary. The contemporary embryo articulates particular shifts in technoscience, circuits of licit and illicit exchange, systems of governance and regimes of ethics and values (Collier and Ong 2005: 4). At issue is what kind of entity the embryo is – what 'work' it does – and hence, what purposes it can be made to serve. What is it about the human embryo that gives it such a vital presence in contemporary bio-politics? In what follows I hope to shed some light on this question.

I focus on a few aspects of the debates that have been generated around the moral status of the embryo, with a specific emphasis on the distinctions that are brought to bear on delineating the embryo, as well as the characteristics with which it is endowed. In this effort, I draw on both philosophical and theological arguments as well as policy issues to illustrate the kinds of domains within which the embryo moves. This includes a brief comparative exercise regarding legislation of embryo research as well as a consideration of one specific argument in that regard: the so-called 'twinning argument'. I also give some consideration to the issue of the 'spare' embryo.

In an article on embryo tales, Lynn Morgan demonstrates how the early embryologists at the beginning of the nineteenth century, 'breathed life into their specimens, animating them to tell embryonic tales' (Morgan 2003:

290). She argues that embryos were invoked as political actors and agents as early as the 1910s and 1920s to underscore her main point: that the embryo does not take its meanings from its immanent qualities, but rather that the meanings ascribed to the embryo – and its image – depend on the context in which they are visualized (ibid.: 262). At the time, the issues to which the embryo spoke were evolution, race problems and the relationship of humans to animals. Today, we know, embryos tell a very different story. As Franklin states: 'From a speculative entity in the seventeenth century, the modern embryo has emerged as a scientific fact of embryology. Successfully extracted from the "dark continent" of the maternal body, or created in the petri dish, it has emerged as an "individual" in the late twentieth century' (Franklin 1999: 163).

Over the last few decades, with the advent of reproductive technologies and the promise of stem-cell research, the human embryo has moved with a particular forcefulness into the public sphere. It is inscribed in discourses on kinship, in medical science, in religious, bioethical and moral discourses, as well as political ones. The embryo is both an object of knowledge, a scientific artefact as well as the subject of intense emotional and moral engagement. It is subject to different regimes of knowledge, inscribed in a form of epistemological pluralism (Blume, this volume). The embryo commands new attention while it works on peoples' imaginations. I say 'new' because the embryo has been embedded in the abortion issue for a long time, even though the main focus in those debates has been on the foetus.

By this very statement, I have confronted one of the many questions that surround the embryo – namely its definition, or delimitation. What exactly is the human embryo? For some, the foetus and the embryo are the same entity – in fact, that is the whole point: to ensure/convince that there are no qualitative markers that distinguish an embryo from a foetus. For others, it is precisely the distinction between an embryo and a foetus that is essential. It is this distinction that enables a redirecting of the circuits/relations that an embryo may enter. Others yet have created an altogether different entity – the pre-embryo – in an attempt at 'certain' classification (Mulkay 1997; Sirnes 1997).[1] At stake is the ontological status of the embryo – its very nature.[2]

Opinions about the 'nature' of the embryo flourish transnationally and cross culturally. In some senses the embryo is a global entity – but like all things global, it gains its particular meanings through local contexts. However, a local context may in one instance be a national legislation or a *fatwa* – and in the next instance an international, interdisciplinary conference on stem-cell research. Nevertheless, there is one conspicuous fact about the embryo: there is no consensus on what it is and what it may be used for – be it within or between nation-states, bioethicists, scientists, religious denominations or the public at large. It is this very diversity that makes the human embryo such a conspicuous entity.

Within contemporary biomedicine and biopolitics, the embryo represents an especially controversial and potent site. It draws together opposing views, even beliefs, working at the interface between politics, science and religion. Thus there are many different voices that converge on the embryo, and one problem is to find adequate ways to do justice to these different perspectives while paying attention to the positions from which they are spoken. Not only has the embryo become the subject of parliamentary debates, it is, as mentioned, also intensely discussed amongst theologians, bioethicists and scientists. This is particularly salient regarding research on embryos,[3] but also within reproductive medicine, the embryo brings problematic issues in its wake (Melhuus 2012a). These are tied to the use of pre-implantation diagnosis (PGD) and the possible selection of embryos with desirable traits; to the storage (cryopreservation) of embryos and the fate of supernumerary embryos (left over after IVF cycles); as well as to questions pertaining to the ownership of embryos.

First Distinction: Reproductive/Regenerative

There is one term and two distinct qualities that constitute the contemporary embryo. The term is 'potential', and the qualities reproductive and regenerative. The potential with which the embryo is endowed draws its force from these inherent capabilities, which have to do with future human life and the future of human beings. What makes the embryo such a vital matter in contemporary biomedicine is that it possesses at one and the same time both reproductive and regenerative potentials. These potentials imply qualitatively different ascriptions, which are mutually exclusive while mobilising very different sets of relations. In its reproductive capacity, the embryo represents a potential human being, a unique individual (totally independent of where it is gestated). In its regenerative capacity, the embryo represents a potential cure for serious illness, as it is the source of embryonic stem cells. These are termed 'totipotent' – having unlimited capability.[4] It is these as yet undifferentiated cells that can potentially constitute the basis for regenerative medicine and stem-cell-based therapy.

The embryo embodies at one and the same time two very different potentials. These potentials feed off each other while at the same time displacing each other. Both as a reproductive and as a regenerative entity, the embryo represents new life, but in different ways. However, the embryo cannot serve both purposes at the same time. These two potentials are mutually exclusive. These are two different trajectories to which an embryo can be made to work, where pursuing one implies negating the other.

The embryo, then, is at once singular and universal (in the sense of being interchangeable). In its unique capacity it can only move in particular reproductive relations (although irrespective of its genetic origins); that is, kinship relations. In its universal capacity it can circulate more freely; it can be put to work elsewhere. Stem-cell lines originating from embryos are exchanged among scientists, research groups and pharmaceutical companies. The distinction between the reproductive and regenerative capabilities of the embryo renders the embryo ambiguous, and activates a moral dilemma between the respect due human life in an early phase and the obligation due humanity to alleviate serious illness. This dilemma is often phrased in terms of 'the moral status of the embryo'.

The Moral Status of the Embryo

The moral status of the embryo has been one way of framing the debate – or setting the agenda – about the embryo and the uses (or not) to which the embryo can be subjected. This debate is not new (re abortion issue), but it is increasingly actualized, especially in conjunction with stem-cell research. One example is a Norwegian Research Council (NFR) research project entitled 'The Moral Status of Human Embryos with Special Regard to Stem-cell Research and Therapy', led by the Norwegian theologian and bioethicist, Lars Østnor. The project, he states, was motivated by 'the burning ethical questions raised by stem cell research and eventual therapy' (Østnor 2008: vii). According to Østnor, to grant something (human, animal, plant) some form of moral status implies that we as moral agents have ethical obligations towards it, and ascribing a moral status to the human embryo implies that they have rights to protection of life, body and health (Østnor 2007). Thus, the status attributed to the human embryo will necessarily impinge on the uses to which it may be put. Is the human embryo 'a ball of cells and nothing more', or does the embryo 'from conception onwards [have] the status of humanity'? (Bruce 2005).

Thus, we can formulate a second distinction that characterizes the embryo: that is the distinction between human life and human being. There are those who claim that the moment of conception confers complete human dignity on the embryo.[5] It follows from this that no research (on the embryo) whatsoever would be morally acceptable, as that would violate the right to life and protection from harm. This argument is not necessarily tied to a religious belief – but there are certain religious congregations or religious persons that argue this position more forcefully than others. For example, it appears that the preoccupation with the moral status of the embryo is a more acute Christian concern than it is either a Jewish or Muslim one (see Zoloth 2002; Al-Aqeel 2005). However, within the different Christian churches, there is no consensus on this issue. There is no disagreement that the embryo is human life, but there is dispute about whether the embryo is at its very conception a human being. If the embryo is coextensive with humanity, it is sacred. Within Christianity, this latter argument is forwarded with reference to the Bible, and the claim that humans are created 'in the image of God' (see Baune et al. 2008: 9).[6] This position is congruent with a potentiality argument that states that that which has the potentiality of becoming a developed human being with a moral status has a right to life.

However, those who argue for research on embryos perceive the nature of the embryo differently. Most importantly, they do not accept that there is a continuous, undifferentiated development of the embryo. Rather, they argue that there are distinct stages in this developmental process, and that these can be identified. One such stage – or marker – is the so-called primitive streak, which occurs about fourteen days after fertilization, when the first visual signs of organ formation appear. It is this entity (before the primitive streak) that was coined the 'pre-embryo' in the British parliamentary debate (see Mulkay 1997, and below). For others, it is the attachment of the embryo to the womb that is significant, and some claim that the significant marker is the appearance of brain activity (about fifty days after fertilization). Others yet might use markers such as 'ensoulment' – stressing that the early embryo is not a fully 'ensouled' person, and may then be used for research or 'in the service of human healing' (e.g. Zoloth 2002: 73). Hence, these 'markers' draw their legitimacy from very disparate and maybe even incongruent realms, underscoring the ambivalence and uncertainty surrounding the delimitation of the embryo.

Examples: The UK and Norway

Let us now look at debates concerning the embryo in two countries: the UK and Norway.[7] The embryo was the subject of intense public and political debate in Britain throughout the 1980s. In his detailed study of the embryo research debate in the UK, Mulkay demonstrates how opinion changed over time, from close to being banned until, 'In 1990, embryo research emerged ... with recognition in law as a legitimate area of scientific enquiry' (Mulkay 1997: 2). People had changed their minds (e.g. ibid.: 59–62). Mulkay explores the complexities involved in gaining a majority for research, not least the impact of the pro-research lobby. He argues that it was the invention of the pre-embryo that facilitated the acceptance of embryo research.[8] As he says, 'acceptance of scientists' definition of the experimental subject of embryo research made such research permissible' (ibid.: 61). This acceptance, he notes, has to do with the increased contact between parliament and the scientific community, as well as a general concern for control over genetic disorder. According to Sirnes (1997), through the notion of the pre-embryo, those arguing for research were able to present an alternative understanding of the nature of the object. The pre-embryo was constructed as an object of science. This transformation enabled them in turn to redirect and shift the terms of the argument (ibid.: 226). Moreover, and importantly, the position of the various churches, indeed even within the Church of England itself, was, as Mulkay indicates, 'by no means uniform and by no means consistently negative' (Mulkay 1997: 96, 108). Hence, there was not one authoritative religious voice. For example, the Archbishop of York, primate of England, argued on behalf of embryo research (ibid.: 96; see also Sirnes 1997: 237).

Although the debates were framed in terms of religious thinking as against scientific, rational thinking, Mulkay argues that the main difference between these opposing views is not the structure of the moral argument, but rather the difference in opinion regarding the nature and moral standing of the embryo (Mulkay 1997: 102). In the British case, the pro-research lobby imposed on the debate the cultural authority of science. The successful establishing of a qualitative distinction which allowed for a re-creation of the embryo – as coming into being after fourteen days – was central. Research could be carried out until the primitive streak – but not after.

In the Norwegian parliamentary debates, no such term as the pre-embryo was introduced, and according to Sirnes (1997) part of the problem for those arguing for permitting research was that they were not able to establish any significant distance from the object of research.[9] They were unable to create a concept/entity similar to that of the pre-embryo, which could be used to ground a rational scientific argument. In fact, Sirnes claims that 'science' was not present as a partner in the debates (ibid.: 239), in sharp contrast to the British case.[10] He argues that the concept of the pre-embryo acknowledges the link to humanity (as 'not-embryo' for example would not), while at the same time implying a qualitative difference in development stage (ibid.: 214). Moreover, he suggests that the notion of the pre-embryo should not be understood as a scientific concept, but rather as one that bridges (mentally) the relation between science and politics (ibid.: 215).

The terms used in Norwegian to characterize the embryo are most commonly fertilized egg (*fertilisert egg*) or incipient life (*spirende liv, gryende menneskeliv*). The fertilized egg is in fact for most (whether religious or not) coterminous with incipient life. In the Norwegian case, then, no room was given for establishing any definitive moment that would separate the fertilized egg from its further successive stages. As Sirnes states: 'the decisive human criteria was neither to be separate nor distinct. Therefore they [the politicians] were unable to create a theology-free space for the first two weeks of the life of the fertilised egg' (ibid.: 240).

Moreover, Sirnes makes an interesting point regarding notions of personhood and the individual. In the British debates there was an intense focus on the distinction between the human being and the human person, or person and non-person.[11] It is not enough to be human, you also have to be a person in order to have value (ibid.: 231). Those against embryo research claimed that the embryo was a person. However, those arguing for research did so on the basis of a notion of individuality (or the individual). In their understanding, the pre-embryo could not be an individual – partly because it would at one point split into the future embryo and the placenta (and thus it is composed of different matters, not all of which will form the individual); partly because it was not until the formation of the primitive streak that the embryo could potentially split into identical twins (see below for the 'twinning argument'). However, in the Norwegian case, Sirnes suggests that individual, person and human were used synonymously, expressing the same thing (ibid.: 234). The person is nothing different nor more than a human. Therefore the Norwegian debate was not framed in the same conceptual distinctions as the British one. This implied that individuality was not a central criterion. Rather than focus on individuals, the Norwegian ontology (according to Sirnes) tended to be about some mutual human value – common to all – that had to be protected. 'Incipient life' could be understood as such a common value. The Norwegian notion of 'incipient life' is not about unique individuality (expressed through genes), but embraces that which is common to all humans. It is this common quality (underpinning all humanity) that is significant – and not the specific quality which separates one individual from another. The British however were concerned with what distinguishes one individual from another. Only when a human being is constituted as distinct is it inviolable (ibid.: 234).

Such debates about the embryo reflect socio-cultural distinctions between the notions of human, individual and person. By pointing to different articulations of such fundamental socio-cultural factors (that is, what constitutes personhood), Sirnes demonstrates how notions of the inviolable differ in the UK and Norway (ibid.: 235). Significantly, these differences in the understandings of what the embryo is perceived to be also leads to different policies when it comes to research on embryos. Until 2007, Norway had in fact banned all research on human embryos.[12] When the Norwegian Parliament passed an amendment permitting research on supernumerary embryos, the majority gained the vote because certain parties had shifted their position. Moreover, the legislation was not based on a radical change in perceptions of the embryo; rather, it had to do with more pragmatic arguments related to the destruction of supernumerary embryos.

The Twinning Argument

The twinning argument is a reasoning which tries to bridge the gap between two different strands of thinking in order to accommodate a position which will allow for research on embryos without undermining Christian ethics. It can, perhaps, be seen as a 'moral employment' of science (see Jenkins, this volume). The argument is congruent with a notion of 'pre-embryo', in that it establishes a crucial differentiating point between the moment of conception and the beginning of an individual life. It does so through a particular example: the case of the creation of identical twins.[13] Thus, a new element is introduced that is not bound by the fundamentalist view, nor is it trapped by the gradualist position. Central to Kenny's argument is the 'beginning of individual human life' (Kenny 2008: 167).[14] Kenny turns to the Warnock (and Harries) Committee and its contribution to the debate on the moral status of the embryo by offering a new *terminus ante quem* (that is, a finishing point of a process), namely that of fourteen days, the time of the primitive streak.

The argument is that the line of development from conception to foetal life is not the uninterrupted history of an individual. Foetus, child and adult have a continuous individual development (and are coextensive), which the gamete and zygote do not have.[15] In the case of identical twins, there will be two different human individuals, each of whom will be able to trace their life trajectory back to the same embryo, but neither of whom will be the same individual as (identical to) the embryo. In other words, to count embryos is not the same as to count human beings, as one single embryo may produce two individuals. To make his argument, Kenny makes a point of differentiating the foetus from the embryo. The foetus is seen as identical with the adult human, that is, it is the 'same individual as the human child and adult into which ... it will grow' (ibid.: 171). The embryo, however, is not. An embryo can potentially produce two individuals, and it is this fact that is deployed to create a moment of significant differentiation. The moment where one entity splits into two is seen as the defining moment of individuality. This is sustained by another fact: that neither of the two individuals is identical to the embryo.

This is a retrospective gaze with regard to the moment of individuation of the human being. It is the point to which you can trace your actual origin (that is, the moment of splitting) which becomes decisive (and not the more universal claim that all humans develop from embryos). In this view, the embryo in its earliest days is not an individual human being. 'In its early days a single embryo may turn into something that is not a human being at all, or something that is one human being, or something that is two people or more' (ibid.: 172). The argument is sustained by appealing to a notion of identity which differentiates between specific identity and individual identity: 'Two things may be identical in the sense that they answer to the same specification [e.g. DNA], and yet not be identical in the sense that they are two different things, not a single thing' (ibid.: 172).

These are the arguments put forth by a philosopher to reject the protection of the embryo. In Kenny's words: 'The preservation of the life of the mother, the fertilization of otherwise barren couples and the furthering of medical research may all ... provide reasons to override the embryo's protected status' (ibid.: 173). Thus, Kenny formulates an argument that would allow for research on embryos based on a particular understanding of the individual and identity.[16] To what extent this argument is 'local' – in that it relies on a specific notion of the individual (Kenny is British) – and to what extent the argument may gain adherents more generally is a point I am unable to pursue. However, in the context of this chapter, where the focus is to indicate the kind of work the embryo does, this argument is interesting as it is an attempt to circumvent a notion of the embryo as coextensive with humanity, in order that embryo research be permitted. Moreover, the twinning argument is yet an illustration of what the embryo mobilizes in terms of intellectual power in order to resolve its status – which in turn (in so far as the argument wins ground) will have implications for its 'purpose'.

The Problem of the Spare Embryo

In 2005, the then US president, George Bush, declared: 'There is no such thing as a spare embryo. Every embryo is unique and genetically complete, like every other human being' (quoted in Solberg 2006). President Bush's statement reflects a position not commonly held in Europe. I let it stand as a backdrop to my further discussion of what is denoted as 'supernumerary embryos'. These come into being in conjunction with *in vitro* fertilization (IVF). Usually, in the course of a cycle of IVF treatment (and as a consequence of hormonal treatment), more eggs are intentionally produced than is normal. Of these, several are fertilized, but not all the fertilized eggs are necessarily employed in one cycle. In Norway, for example, the practice is to insert one embryo, whereas in other countries two or three may be inserted. The remaining embryos that have not been used in an IVF cycle, if deemed of good enough quality, are frozen for use at a later date. Those embryos that have not been used – or whose time in cryopreservation has for example exceeded a specified regulatory storage time – are (by some) considered as surplus or supernumerary. These may also be called 'spare'. These embryos may potentially be used for research.

There are two forms of research on embryos. One is to improve the techniques and procedures of *in vitro* fertilization – that is, research that will enhance the reproductive potential of embryos. The other is stem-cell research, which implies redirecting the potential of the embryo towards regenerative medicine. In both cases, spare embryos are needed. Women all over the world are being asked to decide on the fate of their unused embryos – whether they should be 'discarded, donated, sold, turned into spare parts, [or] experimented on' (Thompson 2005: 253). These women are also subject to different regulatory regimes.

The issue of 'spare' embryos raises many questions. First and foremost, this is tied to whether they can – or cannot – be destroyed. If destruction is allowed, under what conditions should it be permitted? If destruction is not allowed, then what should be done with stored embryos that will not be used for reproductive purposes or have for other reasons been abandoned? In the US (and in contrast to Europe) this is an acute issue. As Thompson states (with reference to the US): 'A trend over the last decade and a half has arrived at a point where no eggs or embryos can be left unaccounted for and their enumerated fates are fiercely debated' (Thompson 2005: 250). This in turn points to another question regarding spare embryos: Who actually owns them and has the right to decide their fate?[17] And finally, granted that embryos are a scarce resource, is it foreseeable that embryos can be created for the mere purpose of research or procurement of embryonic stem cells?[18]

In lieu of the discussion of the debate on the moral status of the embryo, it is not difficult to grasp that the destruction of embryos would be highly problematic for many people. Yet in Norway (and elsewhere in Europe) this is a routine practice. Thus, in a certain sense and at a specified time, embryos are de facto medical waste. Yet due to regenerative medicine, with a need for embryonic stem cells, this 'waste' can be transformed to 'non-waste', serving another purpose. This is the potential that supernumerary embryos have come to represent, and which may provoke anxiety.

In Norway, for example, an embryo may be stored for five years, at which point it is destroyed. Interestingly, in the debates on whether to permit research on embryos, destruction itself was not the main issue, although there were voices that also raised this question.[19] Rather, the debates turned on the difference between destruction and research: whether those embryos, which in any case would be destroyed, would not serve a better purpose if their use in research was permitted. And 'purpose' is a central concern. There were those that argued that research on embryos represents an instrumentalization of human life, as the fertilized egg becomes a means rather than an end in itself. Another argument forwarded was that the embryo becomes the object of an intervention that will not serve the embryo itself, but rather serve a purpose for which it was not created. Thus one position forwarded was to permit research that would better the method of IVF, but not research to create cell lines. The former would be in line with 'the purpose' of the embryo, whereas the latter would not.

Within the context of reproduction, the self-purposefulness of the embryo (as a potential human being) provides its moral status. Within the context of research and regenerative medicine, this purposefulness becomes alienated.[20] Thus, yet again, the challenge is to find moral arguments to justify the use of embryos for research. One such argument is pragmatic and utilitarian: better to use embryos that in any case would be destroyed for research that could serve to alleviate serious illness for humans more generally. In other words, the embryo would then serve a universal purpose: to better the condition of humanity.

The issue of 'spare' embryos points to yet another domain where embryos are active, moving biopolitics in different directions. What the embryo 'is' or is perceived to be is critical for the kinds of circuits the human embryo may enter. This in turn is influenced by the kinds of ethical and value regimes in which the embryo is inscribed.

By Way of Conclusion

Over the past few decades, the human embryo has gained iconic status. It has moved into the public domain, occupying a significant yet controversial space, where science, religion, technology and ethics meet. It is widely recognized that the human embryo has potential – but what kind of potential is being referred to is not necessarily clear. This is reflected in the very ambiguity surrounding the embryo – and its purpose. As we have seen, the embryo attracts different interests. It means different things to different people: experts such as scientists, theologians and bioethicists (as well as anthropologists), as well as politicians and 'ordinary' men and women all have an interest in and even a claim on the embryo.

Debates on the moral status of the embryo take us to the heart of anthropological concerns: about what constitutes a person, about the beginnings and ends of life, about matters that are vital to any and all social communities (although not necessarily, or even usually, framed in terms of the embryo). The debates also reflect systems of classification regarding biological matter and the attempts at reclassification of this matter. This reclassification entails transposing the embryo from its biological/scientific realm (of 'facts') to a moral, even religious one (of 'value'). Or vice versa. This is one of the ways contemporary biopolitics is articulated.

Embryos have (again) become matters of state – albeit it in a somewhat different way than the question of abortion (although some of the arguments and interests may overlap). One difference is the way the embryo is perceived and discussed as an entity in its own right. As Franklin observes: 'From a legal non-entity, it has become a civil subject, accorded the attention and respect of parliamentarians and the protection of the state. Clearly these changes in meaning of the embryo cannot be separated from the wider social relations which accord it particular conventions of recognition' (Franklin 1999: 163). The embryo is viewed as separate and apart from the body within which it might potentially be gestated. Although arguments in the abortion debates also claim individual and autonomous status for the embryo and/or foetus, a woman's right to self-determined abortion is grounded in the innate relational quality of a woman to the embryo she carries.

The embryo has been removed from its localized and particular origin. It is now pictured as something out there – and not something internal to the body. This process has come as a consequence of developments in reproductive medicine and in the public eye, and, perhaps more significantly, through the actual visualization of the embryo (by way of ultrasound). However, that image of the embryo is one which works in a different direction than an image of the embryo as a bunch of pluripotent cells. What is surprising is how rapidly this objective view of the embryo has become naturalized, while at the same time the embryo is being animated in other ways. The embryo has gained another purpose.

One way to understand this shift is the distinction between the reproductive and the regenerative potentials of the embryo. I return to my initial remarks. As a regenerative entity, the embryo is disassociated from its reproductive capacity. It does not need a womb to do its work. It can, as it were, be put to work elsewhere – without regard for its 'original purpose'. Nevertheless, it is the reproductive capacity of the embryo that represents the moral impediment to its regenerative use. It is the fact that the embryo has the potential of becoming a human being that creates moral and ethical problems. This potentiality is – by many – granted a special status. Bringing regeneration and reproduction into the same sphere implies a reconfiguration of the embryo. This reconfiguration, in turn, presupposes that the embryo is disembedded and decontextualized. Scientific developments (within biomedicine – both reproductive and regenerative) have been conducive to the recontextualization of the embryo. However, this process of re-embedding is complex and multifaceted. I have illustrated just a few ways that this occurs. Moreover, the many contexts within which the embryo is now articulated do not necessarily overlap, nor are they congruent. On the contrary. Yet, they are mutually implicated. It may well be that the very debates about the moral status of the embryo implicates science and scientists in ways that have perhaps been difficult to foresee. However, the reverse is also true: the promise of science in reproductive and regenerative medicine involves people – and states. The embryo animates these different domains, bringing them together. At the same time, the embryo is animated, in that disparate views converge on the embryo. All the while, the fact remains that there is no consensus about what this vital entity – at once both the sacred and profane – embodies, and that is perhaps the very source of its spirit.

Acknowledgements

This chapter draws inspiration from several seminars and public meetings held in Norway over the past few years, where I participated partly as 'fieldworker' (the seminars being ethnographic field sites in their own right), partly as interlocutor. These are 'Religion and Bioethics', a research course organized by Jan Helge Solbakk, Rikshospitalet, Oslo, in December 2005; 'Religion and Biotechnology', an open meeting organized by the Norwegian Biotechnology Advisory Board, December 2005; 'The Stem Cell Challenge', organized by the Norwegian Biotechnology Advisory Board in May 2007; two gatherings organized by Lars Østnor (and his project group) at MF Norwegian School of Theology (Det teologiske menighets fakultet) on 'The Moral Status of Human Embryos with Special Regard to Stem-cell Research and Therapy' in May and December 2006; and 'Preimplantasjonsdiagnostikk og forskning på befruktede egg: etiske og samfunnsmessige dimensjoner', a meeting organized by the Norwegian Research Council in April 2006. I use this opportunity to thank Heidi Fjeld for constructive comments on an earlier version of this chapter. All translations from the Norwegian are my own.

Notes

1. The pre-embryo is used to refer to the human organism during a period of approximately two weeks between fertilization and the emergence of the first structural features (Mulkay 1997: 31), the appearance of the 'primitive streak'.

2. Thompson employs what she calls, 'the ontological choreography of embryos in ARTs – [that is] what their ontological status is and how they coordinate very different kinds of time scales, matter, ideas, and organization' to describe what she terms the biomedical epoch (Thompson 2005: 250).

3. See Walters (2008) for an overview of the state of research on embryos in the world.

4. When a sperm and egg cell unite, they form a one-celled fertilized egg. This cell is totipotent – it can give rise to any and all human cells, such as brain, liver, blood or heart cells. In the first hours after fertilization, this cell divides into identical totipotent cells. About four days after fertilization, these cells begin to specialize into pluripotent cells that can give rise to most, but not all, of the tissues necessary for foetal development (see the web pages at: http://biomed.brown.edu/Courses/BI108/BI108-2002-Groups, retrieved 29 June 2010; and: www.medterms.com/script/main/art.asp?articlekey=18, retrieved 20 June 2010). However, see Bobbert (2008: 244), who says that this difference does not reflect a scientific consensus, and asks whether moral status can be attributed to embryonic stem cells.

5. That would be the position of the Catholic Church. For a short presentation of the views of different churches, including the Lutheran, see Niekerk (1994), Østnor and Thunberg (1995) and Østnor (2005). Unfortunately the publication of the edited volume of Marcia Inhorn and Soraya Tremayne (*Islam and Assisted Reproductive Technologies*, Berghahn Books, 2012) came to my attention after finishing the final draft of this chapter. This volume brings vital knowledge about Islamic perceptions of the embryo which I have not been able to integrate into this chapter.

6. This argument, often termed 'the creation argument', has to do with 'an expression of human uniqueness and of humanity's special role within creation, in contrast to all else that exists' (Baune et al. 2008: 9). The dispute about the moral status of the embryo might also fruitfully be read against Coleman's chapter on scientific creationism (Coleman, this volume).

7. The following comparison between the UK and Norway draws mainly on Mulkay (1997) and Sirnes (1997). Whereas the former concentrates on the debate in the UK, the latter is a comparative analysis of the debates in the British and Norwegian parliaments.

8. See also Spallone (1989: 53–54), who states: 'the coining of the term pre-embryo was a political act' (ibid.: 53). It was preferred to other terms such as conceptus, zygote or pro-embryo.

9. Sirnes bases his arguments on the early debates, that is, those in the late 1980s and early 1990s, which in Norway culminated with the passing of the first Bio-

technology Act in 1994. See also Franklin (1999) for an analysis of the British debates from an anthropological perspective, with a specific view to kinship.

10. Moreover, Sirnes argues that in Norway the relationship between science and religion is/was different (from that of the UK), and that the outcome of the debate in Norway can be explained through this difference.

11. Franklin also makes the point that there was an 'explicit concern for the personhood of the embryo' in the British parliamentary debates, linking the shared definitions of embryonic personhood to its biogenetic basis and its unique individuality (Franklin 1999: 133).

12. Suggestions to permit research on the human embryo were put forward with the first act to legislate assisted conception in 1987, but did not gain a majority. Neither the first Biotechnology Act, passed in 1994, nor its subsequent revision in 2003, opened the way for research on embryos. For an ethnographic account of Norwegian biopolitics with a focus on law, biotechnology and kinship, see Melhuus (2012a: 89–108), which specifically explores the moral status of the embryo. See also Melhuus (2009, 2012b).

13. The argument is taken from Anthony Kenny, partly from a conference presentation (which I attended in 2006) and from the later publication (Kenny 2008). For a different argument related to twinning, and the question of divisibility, see Munthe (2011).

14. Kenny points to the fact that, since 1869, the dominant position of the Catholic Church has been to take conception as the beginning of individual life, although for most of its history this has been a minority view (Kenny 2008: 169).

15. A gamete is a mature germ cell able to unite with another cell in sexual reproduction; a zygote is the cell formed by the union of two gametes.

16. Both Øyvind Baune and Dagfinn Føllesdal have critical comments and counterpositions to that of Anthony Kenny. For those interested, see Baune (2008) and Føllesdal (2008). See also Steinbeck (2011).

17. I am not familiar with the different legislations regarding ownership of embryos, but in the case of Norway, a couple does not 'own' its embryos, in the sense that they have exclusive rights over them. They cannot, for example, demand to have an embryo delivered from a Norwegian clinic in order for it to be used in a clinic abroad. However, informed consent is required for the use of embryos for purposes of research.

18. However, there are now techniques that can create entities that will provide embryonic stem cells, so called therapeutic cloning, through techniques such as somatic cell nuclear transfer (SCNT) or altered nuclear transfer (ANT). The advantage of ANT is 'that nothing that could become a human being is destroyed' (Baune et al. 2008: 16).

19. For a presentation of some of the main arguments regarding the revision of the Biotechnology Act (especially with regard to embryo research), see the Norweagian parliamentary bill, 'Om lov om endringer i bioteknologiloven (preimplantasjonsdiagnostikk og forskning på overtallige befruktede egg' ('Parliamentary proposition concerning changes to the biotechnology law,

including research on supernumerary embryos'), Odelstings Proposisjoner 26 (2006/2007).

20. See Bobbert (2008: 240) for objections to embryo research. She, among other things, points to the problem of transferring embryos form one context to another (from reproductive to regenerative).

References

Al-Aqeel, A.I. 2005. 'Ethical Guidelines in Genetics and Genomics: An Islamic Perspective', *Saudi Medical Journal* 26(12): 1862–70.

Baune, Ø. 2008. 'Can the Distinction between the Moral and the Descriptive Support a Full Moral Standing of the Embryo?' in L. Østnor (ed.), Stem Cells, *Human Embryos and Ethics: Interdisciplinary Perspectives*. Springer, pp.149–66.

Baune, Ø., O.J. Borge, S. Funderud, D. Føllesdal, G. Heiene and L. Østnor. 2008. 'The Moral Status of Human Embryos with Special Regard to Stem Cell Research and Therapy', in L. Østnor (ed.), *Stem Cells, Human Embryos and Ethics: Interdisciplinary Perspectives*. Springer, pp.1–20.

Bobbert, M. 2008. 'Human Embryos and Embryonic Stem Cells: Ethical Aspects', in L. Østnor (ed.), *Stem Cells, Human Embryos and Ethics: Interdisciplinary Perspectives*. Springer, pp.237–50.

Bruce, D. 2005. 'Therapeutic Use of Cloning and Embryonic Stem Cells', unpublished paper presented at 'Open Meeting on Religion and Biotechnology', Oslo, 12–15 December, Rikshospitalet.

Collier, S., and A. Ong. 2005. 'Global Assemblages, Anthropological Problems', in A. Ong and S. Collier (eds), *Global Assemblages: Technology, Politics and Ethics as Anthropological Problems*. Malden, MA: Blackwell, pp.3–21.

Franklin, S. 1999 [1993]. 'Making Representations: The Parliamentary Debate on the Human Fertilisation and Embryology Act', in J. Edwards, S. Franklin, E. Hirsch, F. Price and M. Strathern, *Technologies of Procreation: Kinship in the Age of Assisted Conception*. London: Routledge, pp.127–70.

Føllesdal, D. 2008. 'The Potentiality Argument and Stem Cell Research', in L. Østnor (ed.), *Stem Cells, Human Embryos and Ethics: Interdisciplinary Perspectives*, Springer, pp.137–48.

Inhorn, M., and S. Tremayne. 2012. *Islam and Assisted Reproductive Technologies. Sunni and Shia Perspectives*. New York: Berghahn Books.

Kenny, A. 2008. 'The Beginning of Individual Human Life', in L. Østnor (ed.), *Stem Cells, Human Embryos and Ethics*. Springer, pp.167–76.

Melhuus, M. 2009. 'Qui a peur de la "société de tri"? Les biotechnologies, l'individu et l'État', *Ethnologie francaise* 39(2): 253–64.

———. 2012a. *Problems of Conception: Issues of Law, Biotechnology, Individuals and Kinship*. New York: Berghahn.

——. 2012b. 'Hva slags mening gir sorteringssamfunnet? En hendelse og noen refleksjoner omkring kunnskap, likhet, valg, individ og samfunn i Norge', *Norsk Antropologisk Tidsskrift* 23(1): 33–47.

Morgan, L. 2003. 'Embryo Tales', in S. Franklin and M. Lock (eds), *Remaking Life and Death: Toward an Anthropology of the Biosciences*. Santa Fe, NM: School of American Research, pp.261–92.

Mulkay, M. 1997. *The Embryo Research Debate. Science and the Politics of Reproduction*. Cambridge: Cambridge University Press.

Munthe, C. 2011. 'Divisibility and the Moral Status of the Embryo', *Bioethics* 15(5/6): 382–97.

Niekerk, K. 1994. *Teologi og bioetik*. Aaarhus: Aarhus Universitetsforlag.

Østnor,L. 2005. 'Embryoets moralske status i lys av kristent menneskesyn', *Religion og livssyn: Tidsskrift for religionslærer foreningen* 17(12): 5–14.

——. 2007. 'Stem Cell Ethics', unpublished paper presented at the conference 'The Stem Cell Challenge', organized by the Norwegian Centre for Stem Cell Research and the Norwegian Biotechnology Advisory Board, Oslo, 14 May 2007.

——. 2008. 'Introduction', in L. Østnor (ed.), *Stem Cells, Human Embryos and Ethics*. Springer, pp.vii–ix.

Østnor, L., and A.M. Thunberg. 1995. 'Fertilized Eggs and Pre-implantation Diagnosis: A Letter to a Medical Researcher', in V. Mortensen (ed.), *Life and Death: Moral Implications of Biotechnology*. Geneva: Lutheran World Federation, WCC Publications, pp.50–63.

Sirnes, T. 1997. 'Risiko og meining: Mentale brot og meiningsdimensjonar i industri og politikk. Bidrag til den sosiale stadieteorien', PhD diss. Bergen: University of Bergen.

Solberg, B. 2006. 'Person or Not Person? That is Not the Question', unpublished paper presented at the conference 'The Moral Status of the Human Embryo with Special Regard to Stem Cell Research and Therapy', Norwegian School of Theology, Oslo, December.

Spallone, P. 1989. *Beyond Conception: The New Politics of Reproduction*. Gramby, MA: Bergin and Garvey.

Steinbeck, B. 2011 [1992]. *Life Before Birth: The Moral and Legal Status of Embryos and Fetuses*. Oxford: Oxford University Press.

Thompson, C. 2005. *Making Parents: The Ontological Choreography of Reproductive Technologies*. Cambridge, MA: MIT Press.

Walters, L. 2008. 'An Intercultural Perspective on Human Embryonic Stem Cell Research', in L. Østnor (ed.), *Stem Cells, Human Embryos and Ethics*. Springer, pp.91–110.

Warnock, M. 1985. *A Question of Life: The Warnock Report on Human Fertilisation and Embryology*. Oxford: Basil Blackwell.

Zoloth, L. 2002. 'Reasonable Magic and the Nature of Alchemy: Jewish Reflections on Human Embryonic Stem Cell Research', *Kennedy Institute of Ethics Journal* 12(1): 65–93.

Chapter Seven

The Religions of Science and the Sciences of Religion in Brazil

Roger Sansi

In Brazil, the supposed contradiction between religion and science is full of ambiguity. In fact it could be argued that in their different incarnations, 'religion' and 'science' have been mutually constitutive, in similar ways that Cuba has been 'enchanted by Science', according to Palmié (2002, 2011). First, many of the religions of the Brazilian elites have historically made a claim to be religions *of* science: from the Freemasonry, of which even the emperor-scientist of Brazil during the nineteenth century was a member (Moritz-Schwartz 1998), through the Positivist Church, which was the religion of choice of the military elites who overthrew the Empire; and finally and most of all, throughout the twentieth century, spiritualism, which has been one of the main religions of the Brazilian middle classes (Giumbelli 1997). Secondly, the study of the 'religions of the other inside', as it were – Afro-Brazilian religions, Amazonian shamanism, so-called 'popular Catholicism' – have been at the core of the development of the social sciences in Brazil since its very origins. These 'other' religions were discovered as such by early social-science researchers; before that, these popular and subaltern practices were not defined as religion but as sorcery, and therefore as an object of persecution, not knowledge (Pares and Sansi 2011).

In fact, the drive of the elites towards 'scientific' religions and the scientific study of religions can be described as two opposite movements, which have been dialectically related. The second of these was key in the attempt to separate science and religion itself. This science of religion, mainly anthropology throughout the twentieth century, has researched the 'authentic' religions of the 'other within' – so-called Afro-Brazilian religions – but it would rarely study the scientific religions of the elite: Freemasonry, the Positivist Church and spiritualism. Partially, I would argue, this is because they were perceived precisely as hybrids between religion and science. One of the main objectives of the social sciences in Brazil, and of anthropology most of all, would have been to disentangle these hybrids, to purify the authentic religions and cultures of Brazil, as an 'other' to modern universal science and modernity in general. By the same token, the legitimacy of 'scientific' religions was questioned, since the new 'pure' scientists – psychologists and anthropologists – would separate the study of religion from the practice of religion; they would define themselves precisely as agnostic and philistine students of religion, and not religious practitioners – in opposition, for example, to spiritualists, for whom their religious practice is at the same time a process of scientific learning. And yet, very early on, this radical distinction was questioned: since the 1930s, most anthropologists working on Afro-Brazilian religions have ended up becoming active practitioners, even priests, of that religion. Their books have become objects of theological study by Afro-Brazilian religious practitioners themselves. Thus today, 'science' and 'religion' seem to be ambiguously reversible.

The Religions of Science

To explain this convoluted story, I shall start by going back more than a hundred years, when the 'science of religion' was still not established in Brazil. In 1904, sixteen years after the abolition of slavery and the declaration of the Republic of Brazil, a journalist known as João do Rio wrote a series of articles, latter published as a book, *The Religions of Rio*, describing the myriads of different religious practices one could find in the then capital of the republic, Rio de Janeiro (Rio 2006). These included evangelical churches, the Maronites, spiritualism, the Positivist Church, a religion called the Priestesses of the Future, satanism and African sects such as candomblé. All these religions coexisted, he said, in a country that was apparently Catholic. In the late nineteenth century, however, Catholicism was not having its best day. The Catholic Church had been very openly criticized by the free-thinking intellectual elites of Brazil as one of the main reasons for the backwardness of the country. The Emperor of Brazil, Pedro II, was himself a Freemason, and a devout believer in scientific progress. He had often complained of his destiny of being Emperor, when he, by his personal inclinations, would have rather been a natural scientist. In 1874, the bishops of Olinda and Pará caused a scandalous public conflict when they expelled from the church priests who were also Freemasons. The reaction of the prime minister, the viscount of Rio-Branco, also a Freemason, was incredibly radical: he ordered bishops' imprisonment. This did not last long, but it made obvious the confrontation between the Empire and the Catholic Church, and questioned the hegemony of Catholicism.

In 1889, a year after the abolition of slavery, the first republic of Brazil was proclaimed, and some of the key characters of this declaration, like Benjamin Constant, were active members of the Positivist Church, inspired by the sociologist Auguste Comte. Positivism was extremely influential at the turn of the century in Brazil.

As one could assume, one of the central tenets of the new Constitution of the republic was freedom of religion, but there were some contradictions. Article 157 of the penal code of 1890 explicitly persecutes 'spiritualism'. The law condemns those who 'practice spiritualism, magic and its sortileges, use talismans and cartomancy to awake feelings of love and hate, cure ... healable or non-healable ills, [and] fascinate and subjugate public credulity' (Maggie 1992: 22–23). In other words, spiritualism was not recognized as religion, but as charlatanry. As Yvonne Maggie (ibid.) has explained, policemen and judges in the late nineteenth century did not persecute all spiritualist practices as such, but only those which were seen as being used for evil purposes; what was condemned was the exploitation of people through their belief in spirits, but not the belief in spirits itself. Analysing court cases of the early republican period, Maggie concludes that all the discussion is built around a common belief: the existence of spirits that can be incorporated and the possibility that some of these spirits produce evil charms (*feitiços*); the law was used against sorcery. This belief in sorcery, Maggie argues, was shared also by the police, the judges and the whole apparatus of the state. This shared belief is in fact one of the main topics of João do Rio's book. Sorcery, for him, was mainly identified with African ritual practices, including but not only candomblé. Sorcery was not practised by Africans or black people alone; indeed, the opposite was the case: African ritual practitioners provided the means, but these means were used by people from all social, cultural and racial backgrounds. It was in fact the elites of Rio, do Rio argued, who maintained and perpetuated the existence of sorcery: 'We live under the spell... [I]t is us who ensure its existence, with the affection of a businessman for his actress-lover' (Rio 2006: 50).[1]

Sorcery was a kind of ironic inversion of social rules. In a country still strongly divided by the hierarchies of recently abolished slavery, the entire city seemed to be enchanted by the sorcery of the former slaves, which promised their clients all that they desired and could not obtain through the formal codes of the civilized world. Blacks and their sorcery, but specially their hypocrite clients, who succumbed to their superstitions and lower passions, were the cause of the backwardness of the country. Sorcery is like the lover one cannot do without, but which cannot be recognized in public, in relation to the Catholic Church, who would be, following the logic of do Rio's point, the wife. For João do Rio, 'civilization' of the elites of Rio de Janeiro was only a public show of hypocrisy, hiding an intimate barbarism. African ritual practices were only the more open, evident manifestation of the barbarism of the country, but this barbarism could also be found among the elite. The problem of sorcery, from the point of view of the authorities and the elites, was then not a specifically African problem, but a problem concerning the whole of Brazilian society.

It is interesting to note that at the end of the nineteenth century, the discourse on the causes of this sorcery was different from the traditional scholastic discourse of the Catholic Church. The cause was not the Devil, as the Inquisition and canon law proposed, but racial degeneration and miscegenation. This was not an offence to God, but to nature. The rule of sorcery over Brazilian society is not just a result of the Devil, or a manifestation of the (sinful) human condition, as it had been for Catholic theologians. It is the result of the specific social and racial situation in Brazil at the end of the nineteenth century. What was this situation? Brazil had abolished slavery as late as 1888. After abolition, the majority of the inhabitants of Brazil were descendants of slaves of African origin. The racial and evolutionary theories imported from Europe at that time describe Africans as sub-humans. But what is worse was that, according to these European theories, the elites of Brazil were not that great either: they were descendants of the Portuguese, who, after all, were not really a particularly evolved race according to imperialist northern European standards. And the religion of this elite was Catholicism, which was described as a backward, medieval religion, not very different from the superstitious practices of Africans.

This point is explicitly made in the novel *O Feiticeiro* (1897), or 'The sorcerer', written by the Bahian Xavier Marques. One of the characters, the mother-in-law of the main character, goes to church, where she buys a breve, a sort of amulet, 'against *feitiços* and invasions of the devil and against all the devilish dangers that can happen in life' (Marques 1975:112).[2] After this, the author writes: 'Her own religion, the religion of her parents, also feared and tabooed magic charms and enchantments. If they were not real, would the holy books talk about how to fight against them? Therefore, everybody had to believe them and fear them' (ibid.: 122).[3] Sorcery was, for Marques, the result of ignorance, and fear. It was not just the case that people made use of sorcery because they were sinners. They used sorcery because their religion, Catholicism, would have educated them to fear the Devil, and in the necessity of having magical protection against him. The problem was thus not just African cults. The problem was Catholicism too, and how uncannily similar one and the other were.

In the long run, even the hierarchy of the Catholic Church thought there was a problem! After the First Vatican Council, the Church of Brazil intended to extirpate the vices and superstitions of traditional popular Catholic practice, in a process of 'Romanization'. Azzi (1976) summarizes four points about this project. First, to impose the primacy of the clergy on the traditions of colonial Catholicism, which had hitherto had few priests and been mainly articulated through lay practices like lay brotherhoods and the devotion to saints and sanctuaries. Second, to fight popular legends, myths and thaumaturgic practices; in other words, to fight sorcery. Third, substituting the primacy of familial and local relations, where the father or the owner was in charge of religion, by the authority of the priest. Fourth, this priestly authority would limit the social character of popular religiosity, based on festivals, to foster a more individualized, private and ascetic faith. Summing up then, the role of the priest was to install orthodoxy, separate religion from folklore and superstition, and replace traditional, medieval Luso-Brazilian Christianity with a modern, orthodox practice.

Romanization was unquestionably a modernization project, and also very clearly anti-popular and anti-traditional. Public festivals of devotion were now considered to be non-religious and profane, maybe even anti-religious, obscene and barbaric remains of pagan cults. Likewise, the direct, almost idolatrous relationship between people and images of saints had to be limited and mediated by the priests. It is important to understand that this vision of popular religious practice as subversive, later appropriated by social scientists, is first an interpretation of the Catholic Church itself. At the time, the Catholic Church saw the popular classes more as enemies than partners. Its only option was to forge an alliance with the free-thinking elites, joining forces against the feared populace that was emerging from slavery.

An example of this new strategy in Bahia concerns the suppression of the Lavagem de Bonfim. The church of Bonfim is a sanctuary with an image that is famous for its miracles. The Lavagem de Bonfim, the 'cleansing' of Bonfim, was a popular festival in which the devotees of the saint came to the church to clean it. This is a traditional practice that can still be found in Portugal today. But in Bahia, the Lavagem became a massive event, and the authorities feared that it could become a focus of riots and subversion.

The Lavagem de Bonfim was forbidden by Bishop Luiz Antônio dos Santos in December 1889, a year after the abolition of slavery, in agreement with the governor of Bahia, Dr. Manoel Victorino Pereira. For the authorities, Bonfim was a an African 'pagan' ritual in the open air (*candomblé a céu aberto*). The strategy of the Church from then on was to identify practices of popular Catholicism that were beyond their control and infected with 'paganism'. And paganism, in Bahia, had a clear origin: Africa (see Sansi 2005).

The repression of the Lavagem de Bonfim was not an isolated act. The 1890s was a time of increasing repression of religious practices that were deemed potentially dangerous for the newly formed Republic of Brazil, a repression that had the open approval of the hierarchy of the Catholic Church. The more large-scale and famous example is the war of Canudos, in the backcountry of Bahia, described by Euclides da Cunha (1944). Canudos was a sort of new Jerusalem, funded by a self-assigned prophet, Antonio Conselheiro. A mass of poor peasants followed him to the middle of nowhere, to the desert of Canudos. After a series of skirmishes with federal troops, the federal government started seeing Canudos as a reactionary menace to the recently established republic, and kept sending bigger military expeditions to exterminate the 'new Jerusalem', which were invariably defeated, more by the hostility of the land than by the followers of Conselheiro. The final expedition was one of the biggest military campaigns in the history of Brazil, and ended in mass slaughter. The fight against Canudos was a colonial war and a civil war at the same time, a war against the barbarism that Brazilians were afraid to find within themselves.

The Science of Religion

Euclides da Cunha was not the only one to write about Canudos. Raymundo Nina Rodrigues, a forensic doctor, wrote an article in which he described Canudos as an episode of collective hysteria. Rodrigues kept the head of Antonio Conselheiro in his museum of 'anthropology' to study it. Mysteriously, the museum burnt down a few years after.

Rodrigues's analysis of Canudos unquestionably lacks the subtlety of Euclides da Cunha, but maybe we should not judge him for this. In a classic study, Rodrigues wrote the first anthropological ethnography of Bahian candomblé (Rodrigues 1935). For Rodrigues, candomblé was not *feitiçaria*, or sorcery, but a fetishist cult, a religion. Rodrigues was the first to propose that it was necessary to make a clear distinction between sorcery and fetishism, which means also a clear distinction between African and Catholic religion, at least in practice (Rodrigues 1935: 15).

Rodrigues was also a racist, a man of his time. But he did not take a moral position: he did not try to fight sorcery, the *feitiço*, but quite the contrary, he tried to defend the practitioners of candomblé from the police. For Rodrigues, black people should not be judged under the same civil codes as white people, since they were physically and mentally different, that is inferior: they were like children (Moritz-Schwartz 1993), and their cults stemmed naturally from their childish mentality. Like children, they should be taken care of by scientists and doctors, not punished by the police.

Rodrigues had a scientific interest in the cults: he was interested in describing the phenomenology of possession in terms of psycho-pathology. From his scientific standpoint, he was detaching himself from the world ruled by the hidden hand of sorcery: he was an exterior, impartial, objective, agnostic and paternalist observer, neither a practitioner, nor a client, nor a repressor. He was the first 'scientist of religion' to assist openly in candomblé cults, not hiding himself; but at the same time, he remains outside its magic. He was an 'anti-fetishist' in Latour's (2010) terms: a modern intellectual, who does not try to fight the fetishes, but instead points to the head of the fetishist, as the root of the fiction of the fetish. He acknowledged that many times possession was just a simulation, but most of the time it was sincere. He tried to find its 'natural causes' in a mental condition, somnambular hysteria (Rodrigues 1935: 109–40), a sickness stimulated by the rituals of the cult. He conducted experiments using hypnosis to artificially induce trance states, with quite quirky results, and he quickly understood that ethnographic observation was the only way to properly understand trance. He observed ethnographically the candomblé houses of Bahia, particularly the house of Gantois, helped by the babalawo, or candomblé priest Martinano de Bonfim. For Rodrigues, as I mentioned, candomblé was not sorcery but a 'primitive religion', the outcome of the 'primitive mind' of the black, which was in an inferior stage of evolution. Following Tylor and Thierry Lefèvre, he classified candomblé as 'animist fetishism', a cult that had originated in West Africa among the Yoruba, and which was evolving towards polytheism (ibid.: 28). For Rodrigues, the Yoruba in Brazil preserved their religion, almost in a pure African form. This was not the case with the syncretic cults, which mixed divinities from different origins: African, Catholic and indigenous.

The paternalist medicalization of candomblé that Rodrigues introduced implies a paradox. If writers like João do Rio and Xavier Marques placed blacks and whites at the same level, both being slaves of sorcery, Rodrigues takes his racist assumptions to their final consequences, making a sharp distinction between the researcher and the object of research. Candomblé is a question of Africans and their inferior mentality, and its sorcery, the *feitiço*, is just a childish fiction.[4] For Rodrigues, the real problem, worse than racial difference was racial mixture. Racial mixture inevitably brings degeneration, since physical and mental differences among races make them naturally different, and incompatible. Thus, it is understandable that Rodrigues sees 'syncretistic' cults as degenerate.

Although highly respected in his time, Rodrigues's advice of substituting police repression with the medicalization of candomblé proved unsuccessful. It took almost thirty years until a disciple of Rodrigues, Arthur Ramos, came back again to the study of candomblé. Combining psychoanalysis with Lévy-Bruhl's theory of pre-logical mentality, Ramos explained the psychological 'primitivism' of the blacks in Brazil more in terms of lack of education than biological determinism, thus abandoning the racial assumptions of his predecessor. But he was only substituting cultural determinism for racial determinism. For Ramos, possession was a 'regression', a lack of control over the expression of the unconscious (Ramos 1957: 245); it expressed 'a complete eroticization of the body, a hysterical attack, a symbol of coitus' (ibid.: 344). For Ramos, this lack of control could be overcome with education (ibid.: 27), which would involve learning to control the body and the unconscious. Brazilian blacks were to learn to embody civilization as a 'second nature'.

Ramos also emphasized the distinction that Rodrigues had introduced between fetishism as religion and *feitiçaria*, and he defined it in sociological terms: sorcery is something private, individual and socially persecuted, following Mauss and Durkheim, while religion remains public and a central social institution; magic is directed to private interest, to practical ends, while religion is directed towards public interest. In this sense, what happened in Brazil was that under the imposition of Catholicism, the more so-called 'primitive' religions of the Africans were reduced to marginal practices, to the *feitiço*. The *feitiço* is the result of a de-Africanization: when Africans were unable to keep together their religious community and religious traditions, they became sorcerers, without 'culture', only guided by personal interest (ibid.: 164). Only those people able to keep together their traditions and a sense of community, such as that of the Yoruba/Nagô, where able to keep their religion, their fetishism. For Ramos, the Nagô are 'a black aristocracy' in Bahia, superior to Africans of other origins. Thus, racist theories of miscegenation as degeneration were substituted by sociological theories of syncretism as decadence.

In Ramos and Rodrigues we find delineated the three main problems around which the Afro-Brazilianist literature will focus from then on: possession, sorcery and syncretism. After them, it is definitively established that the candomblé of the traditional houses of Bahia has to be understood as a 'religion', and that these preserve 'pure' Yoruba African traits, as opposed to other more syncretic cults, which were 'sorcery'. Thus the science of religion was established by building its absolute African 'other'.

This transition from scientific religions to the science of religion can be exemplified more thoroughly by the example of the Mental Hygiene Service (MHS), established in Recife in the 1930s (Stone 2011). Only at that time did Rodrigues's project to medicalize Afro-Brazilian religions start to take shape, albeit not for long. This service, organized by medical doctors with training in psychology, public health and anthropology, had a special unit dedicated to the control and study of spirit possession. Before the constitution of the MHS, practices of spirit possession were often persecuted by the police as forms of sorcery and charlatanry. The MHS managed to secure protection from the police for houses where possession ceremonies were performed, under the argument that they were a public health problem more than a public order problem. But in fact they went much further than that. The MHS made a clear distinction between spirit possession rituals performed by Afro-Brazilian sects and the practice of spiritualism. At that time, many spirit possession cults in Recife were moving in an unstable territory between one and the other in a continuum that was organized by degrees, from 'low spiritualism' (sorcery) to 'high spiritualism' (medicine). Low spiritualism was an object of police persecution, while high spiritualism was respected, basically because its practitioners belonged to the elites. The MHS's work was partially a subversion of these categories. By imposing a clear distinction between spiritualism and Afro-Brazilian ritual practices, the MHS in fact privileged the second, as authentic, 'pure' cultural practice, as opposed to the first, spiritualism, which was defined as an unstable mix of religion and science. In fact, the issue at stake was also the legitimacy of different forms of medicine, or science: the psychologists and anthropologists in charge of the MHS were keen to distinguish themselves very clearly from spiritualists, and to delegitimize the practice of the latter. By the same token, they became protectors of 'lower spiritualism', which from now on was defined as African religion. In this sense, at the same time that psychology and anthropology were constituted as distinctive sciences, so was African religion constituted as a distinctive entity. As a result of these processes of distinction, the intermediate hybrid practices between science and religion, like spiritualism, have since been mostly ignored as objects of study by the sciences of religion in Brazil.

From Religion to Culture

However, in one sense Rodrigues and the doctors of the MHS did not succeed. They managed to construct Afro-Brazilian religion as a separate object of study, a religion of the 'other', separated from the ambiguous stickiness of sorcery. And yet this religion of the 'other' could not be constrained by the domain of medicine. From the 1930s onwards, Afro-Brazilian religions started to appear in public as something more than a public health issue; they started to appear as 'culture', that is to say as cultural manifestations, as art, a culture that was central to the constitution of Brazilian identity. And it was not medical scientists but modernist artists and writers, like Mario de Andrade and Jorge Amado, who started to facilitate this change in public perception. These authors did not see the practices of candomblé, such as spirit possession, as manifestations of illness, inferiority, deviation or irrationality, but rather as works of art, manifestations of liberation. They were followed by many anthropologists, national and international, such as Melville Herskovits, Roger Bastide and Pierre Verger, for whom spirit possession was not a 'problem', but instead a manifestation of culture, of different notions of the person, of particular techniques of the body. Becoming an object of culture and art, Afro-Brazilian religions were thus not only to be studied, but also admired. From the 1940s, it became a must for intellectuals and artists in places with a strong Afro-Brazilian religion, like Bahia, to visit the candomblé houses and take inspiration from them (Sansi 2007). Some candomblé houses became 'court' societies, inhabited by the cultural elites of the city.

The intimacy between candomblé and the cultural elites was so strong that many artists and anthropologists became initiated in candomblé. Pierre Verger is probably the most famous of them, but there are many other cases, most of them scholars of candomblé, people like Vivaldo Costa Lima, Julio Braga, Juana Elbein and Gisele Binnon Crossard. These belong to candomblé houses, and some have even become priests of the religion. The transit in fact is two-way: many people raised in the cults have ended up studying anthropology and become active 'practitioners' of social science (see Silva 2001).

In fact, over the last few decades, the 'pure' forms of African religion in Brazil have been increasingly popular amongst the upper-middle classes in Brazil, at the same time that spiritualism has lost ground. It could be argued that this is partially due to the higher prestige that 'African' religions have, precisely because they are seen as culturally respectable and interesting objects of study for social scientists. On the other hand, spiritualism has become increasingly ambiguous, divided between science and religion.

And yet, spiritualism is very present in so-called 'African' religions, even if the countless elements and traces of spiritualism, which we can find in everyday so-called Afro-Brazilian or 'popular Catholic' practice, go unremarked on or taken for granted by the scientists of religion. It is quite clear to any student of Afro-Brazilian religions that the idioms used by their practitioners to explain their practices – terms like *incorporar* (to incorporate), *espiritu* (spirit), *materia* (the body who incorporates), and even notions of the 'evolution' of spirits and so on – come from spiritualism. Candomblé practice is also full of arcane Freemasonic symbols. In fact it is known that many of the founders of candomblé in the nineteenth century were also Freemasons (Parés 2006). Furthermore, there is reference to psychological and psychoanalytic terms, such as *inconsciente* (the unconscious). There is nothing exceptional in this use of scientific terms if we look at those who are candomblé practitioners today. These are not the absolute 'other within' of two hundred years ago – that is, African slaves – but may be middle-class people of any racial and cultural background, many with a university education, many anthropologists, medical doctors, psychologists and scientists. So it is not strange that they use the language of their realm of expertise to explain their faith. To an extent this is partially a paradox; but in another sense, by proposing to 'purify' religion from science, the social scientists have created a realm of pure authentic religions of the 'other' – the African, indigenous or lower-class 'other'. The purity of these authentic religions has, paradoxically, been so seductive that many middle-class intellectuals have ended up becoming members of them. Just as people a hundred years ago would be members of the local Freemasonic lodge, the Positivist Church or the spiritualist centre, now they practise candomblé.

Multiplicity

One of the main effects of the hegemony of the sciences of religion in Brazil is the containment of spirit possession within the framework of African religions, when in fact so called spirit possession seems to be common to many other religions, indigenous or European, like spiritualism. But saying that spirit possession seems to be a wider phenomenon in Brazilian society, not simply confined to supposedly Afro-Brazilian cults, and even less to people of African descent, I do not want to suggest that spirit possession is a cross-cultural phenomenon as some recent cognitive theories of spirit possession imply (Cohen 2007; Cohen et al. 2011). More than seeing spirit possession as a cross-cultural phenomenon, what I find striking about spirit possession in Brazil is its historicity and multiplicity – it contains in one all the cultures that could be possibly 'crossed through'. The world of the spirits of candomblé and spiritualism embodies in its imaginary the totality of the multiple 'others' than inhabit the self of the past, all its possible histories. For example, Madalena, a black woman from Bahia, had amongst her spirits not only African queens and kings, but also Indians from the Amazon,

sophisticated European gypsy women and street urchins from the metropo-
lises of the south of Brazil (*meninos da rua*); as it were, her spirit pantheon
was a miniature reproduction of Brazilian society as a whole, lodged inside
her body. Just as she can be possessed by Amazonian Indians and European
gypsies, so I have seen professors of anthropology and psychology being
possessed by the spirits of African kings and indigenous American hunters.
Spirit possession appears to be an open door to multiple personhood, a radically embodied multiplicity (Anjos 2006; Matory 2009).

  This raises the question: Can one be a scientist and be possessed? I
am afraid that I can only say that, in my experience, the answer is: Yes. Of
course, not all scientists will be possessed by spirits, but that does not really
depend on the scientists as much as on the spirits: it is they who decide who
will be their 'horse', who will be the vehicle of possession. Academic degrees
are no obstacle for the spirits. How does that affect their brain? I do not
know. I can only say, from participant observation, that the people who become possessed are fully functional, rational thinkers and speakers in other
contexts – such as academic conferences. And they don't have mental illnesses as far as I know. They do not have a multiple personality disorder
either. Perhaps it is just their world, which expresses its flamboyant multiplicity through them. But at the same time that spirit possession is a form of
embodying a multiple history, it can also become a discourse through which
this history is objectified, segregated, 'purified', by assigning to some people
or 'culture' the exclusive rights to be possessed by spirits – for example, 'African religions' as opposed to spiritualism.

  In many ways it has been one of the tools through which these cultures
have met, assembled or embodied, or have been segregated, 'purified' or
objectified. Spirit possession has helped bringing peoples from different
origins together, but it has also been used to justify their segregation. Let
me explain this point a bit further: to see spirit possession as a cross-cultural
phenomenon seems to imply at least a couple of assumptions. First, the
very idea of 'cross-cultural' seems to presuppose that cultures are separate
entities out of history, but also that this separation can in a way be crossed
if we step outside these cultures, and that if we cross from one to the other
perhaps we can lurk somewhere behind – the sea of nature, perhaps. In other
words, it is a politically correct way of talking about universals. But in fact
the relationship between cultures is not a gap to be crossed by comparative
analysis but by the thread of history, which brings cultures together or
separates and objectifies them in different times and places; 'cultures' as
separate entities are only temporary objectifications of a historical, global
process that we ourselves are immersed in. The idea of being able to step
outside this flow of history and identify its elements as discrete units, out of

time, implies a lot of assumptions – for example, the assumption that the very concepts that we use can also be outside history. But the concept of spirit possession, for example, like many others, is the result of a particular historical process that has been at the same time the product of situations of cultural encounter and the tool through which cultures have been separated or segregated – objectified, as it were. As Paul Christopher Johnson has recently argued, modern concepts of spirit possession emerge precisely at the same point that, or as a counter-image to, modern notions of the rational, autonomous, self-possessed individual, the natural mind/body dyad that some seem to think is a part of our intuitive knowledge (Johnson 2011: 389). The mythical and practical site of this counter-image was Africa in the eighteenth century, the place of anti-modernity for contemporary Europeans. The modern concept of possession emerges as a projection on the African 'other', in complementarily to its twin concept, the fetish. In the same way that the fetish is an aberrant concept, since it implies the notion of an object that becomes a person, spirit possession implies the notion of a subject that becomes an object. Fetishism and possession would be the key concepts of a supposedly anti-modern, fetishist, religious African ontology. Defined in these terms, via the labour of the negative, they were used by European slave traders and philosophers from Bosman to Hegel to establish what constituted modern, European naturalist scientific epistemology, based on a strict separation of humans as persons from things as objects (Sansi 2011).

Of course, this naturalistic ontology has never been fully accomplished as a political project (Latour 1992), and we have lived ever since in the hybrid stage of a world that is supposedly divided between culture and nature, the human and the non-human, the made and the given, religion and science, even if our everyday life constantly tells us the opposite – sometimes through moderately counter-intuitive events, like spirit possession; sometimes through highly counter-intuitive ones, like an economic crisis.

The colonial Atlantic world has always been at the centre of these processes of the production of concepts, objects and things, the enslavement of Africans being one of its constitutive elements. To their enslavers, it seemed that it was the fetishism of Africans, their religious fatalism, their confusion of objects with people, what inevitably led them towards their enslavement. Places like Brazil – which were neither purified, naturalist Europe, nor fetishist, dark Africa – were caught a little in between, at a counterpoint. There, apparently, anything could (and can) happen, from European scientists becoming fetishists to priests of spirit possession cults becoming doctors of social anthropology. Interestingly, as Johnson (2011), Matory (2009) and many others have noted, embodied spirits seem to thrive amongst travelling communities. Not only African spirit possession cults but also European spiritualism seem to have grown exponentially at moments of mass migration or colonialism – and in fact their periods of expansion during the nineteenth century coincide, again in uncanny ways. But of course spiritualism was ultimately much more dangerous for the imperial project of the West that African fetishism, since spiritualism contained in it a radically different concept of the person from the self-appointed European, modern model of the self-possessed individual, being at the same time a fully modern, European project. Spiritualism is a manifestation of the multiple souls of the West, and as such it was a danger because it could question not just its difference and exceptionality from the Rest, but also its internal unity, its purity as a 'culture' even if this was a culture of science – a culture that defined itself as 'universal'.

I hope that this chapter has shown not just how difficult it is to disentangle science from religion when we don't simply compare them from a theoretical and formal standpoint, and instead we look at them as 'forms of life' (Salazar, this volume). But going further than that, I have not just looked at science and religion as 'forms of life' from an ethnographic perspective, but also as historical formations that in many ways have been mutually constitutive; they have been 'purified' or objectified in the past through their contra-position. By looking at the history of the relationship between one and the other in Brazil, in particular through the practice and/or the study of spirit possession, I have tried to show how this process of 'purification', or the separation of one from the other, hasn't been totally successful. And maybe we don't need to be upset about that fact.

Notes

1. *[V]ivemos na dependencia do feitiço ... somos nos que lhe asseguramos a existencia, como carinho de um negociante por uma amante atriz.*
2. *Antes do Carnaval, obrigaram-na a sair e ir a missa ... A viuva ... indicou o Breve Santissimo da Marca contra feitiços e infestos do dominio e contra todos os perigos diabólicos que podem acontecer na vida.*
3. *A sua religião, a religião dos seus pais também temia e prevenia os maleficios e Coisas feitas. Se estas não tivessem alguma realidade, os livros santos cogitariam de as conjurar? Logo, era todo o mundo a crêr e todo o mundo a temer.*
4. Rodrigues recognized that white people are also clients of candomblé (Rodrigues 1935: 97). This issue does not seem to be the centre of his concerns, however, and did not undermine his racist assumptions.

References

Anjos, J.C.G. 2006. *No território da linha cruzada: A cosmopolitica Afro-brasileira*. Belo Horizonte: UFRGS.

Azzi, R. 1976. *O catolicismo popular no Brasil*. Vozes: Petrópolis.

Cohen, E. 2007. *The Mind Possessed: The Cognition of Spirit Possession in an Afro-Brazilian Religious Tradition*. Oxford: Oxford University Press.

Cohen, E., D. Espirito Santo, A. Halloy and P. Liénard. 2010. 'Around Emma Cohen's *The Mind Possessed*', *Religion and Society: Advances in Research* 1: 164–76.

Cunha, E. da. 1944 [1902]. *Rebellion in the Backlands*. Chicago: University of Chicago Press.

Giumbelli, Emerson. 1997. O Cuidado dos mortos: Uma história da condenação e legitimação do Espiritismo. Rio de Janeiro: Arquivo Nacional.

Johnson, P.C. 2011. 'An Atlantic Genealogy of "Spirit Possession"', *Comparative Studies in Society and History* 53: 393–425.

Latour, B. 1993. *We Have Never Been Modern*. Cambridge, MA: Harvard University Press.

———. 2010. *On the Modern Cult of the Factish Gods*. Durham, NC: Duke University Press.

Maggie, Y. 1992. *Medo do feitiço: relações entre magia e poder no Brasil*. Rio de Janeiro: Arquivo Nacional.

Marques, X. 1975 [1897]. *O feiticeiro*. Rio de Janeiro: Civilização Brasileira.

Matory, J.L. 2009. 'The Many Who Dance In Me: Afro-Atlantic Ontology and the Problem with "Transnationalism"', in T. Csordas (ed.), *Transnational Transcendence: Essays on Religion and Globalization*. Berkeley: University of California Press.

Moritz-Schwartz, L. 1993. *O espetaculo das raças: Cientistas, instituições e questão racial no Brasil, 1870–1930*. São Paulo: Companhia das Letras.

———. 1998. *As Barbas do Imperador: Um monarca nos trópicos*. São Paulo: Companhia das Letras.

Palmié, S. 2002. *Wizards and Scientists: Explorations in Afro-Cuban Modernity and Tradition*. Durham, NC: Duke University Press.

———. 2011. 'From Enchantment by Science to Socialist Sorcery: The Cuban Republic and its Savage Slot', in L.N. Pares and R. Sansi (eds), *Sorcery in the Black Atlantic*. Chicago: University of Chicago Press, pp.121–44.

Parés, L.N. 2006. *A formação do Candomblé: história e ritual da nação jeje na Bahia*. Campinas: UNICAMP.

Parés, L.N., and R. Sansi (eds). 2011. *Sorcery in the Black Atlantic*. Chicago: University of Chicago Press.

Ramos, A. 1951. *O Negro na civilização brasileira*. São Paulo: C.E.B.

Rio, J. do. 2006 [1906]. *As religiões do Rio*. Rio de Janeiro: Editora José Olympio.

Rodrigues, N. 1935 [1896]. *O animismo fetichista dos negros baianos*. Rio de Janeiro: Civilização Brasileira.

———. 1977 [1936]. *Os Africanos no Brasil*. São Paulo: Companhia Editora Nacional.

Sansi, R. 2005. 'Catholic Saints, African Gods, Black Masks and White Heads: Tracing the History of Some Religious Festivals in Bahia', *Portuguese Studies* 21: 182–200.

———. 2007. *Fetishes and Monuments: Afro-Brazilian Art and Culture in Twentieth-century Bahia*. Oxford: Berghahn.

———. 2011. 'Sorcery and Fetishism in the Modern Atlantic', in L.N. Parés and R. Sansi (eds), *Sorcery in the Black Atlantic*. Chicago: University of Chicago Press, pp.19–41.

Silva, V.G. 2001. *O antropólogo e sua magia*. São Paulo: EDUSP.

Stone, D. 2011. 'Charlatans and Sorcerers: The Mental Hygiene Service in 1930s Recife, Brazil', in L.N. Parés and R. Sansi (eds), *Sorcery in the Black Atlantic*. Chicago: University of Chicago Press, pp.95–120.

Chapter Eight

Science in Action, Religion in Thought

Catholic Charismatics' Notions about Illness

Maria Coma

I begin this chapter with a testimony, narrated by a guest preacher at a Spanish Catholic Charismatic Renewal national conference in 2011.

> One day, after a healing mass I officiated in Maracaibo [Venezuela], a young couple came to me. They asked for a special blessing and laying on of hands for their five-year-old son. The little boy, Miguel, had a malignant brain tumour and was heading to the United States, where he would undergo a very risky operation. I acceded to their request and prayed over Miguel. As I was told later, the surgery went well and physicians were able to remove 80 per cent of the tumour, but 20 per cent remained. After coming back to Venezuela, Miguel and his parents attended healing masses weekly. One month later, medical examinations showed that the malignant tumour had entirely disappeared.

This testimony illustrates the theme I wish to explore: how the biomedical and the religious intersect in Catholic charismatic healing practices. Charismatic healing consists of a set of ideas concerning health and illness, as well as a number of ritual practices aimed at healing body, mind and soul. Those representations and practices are not isolated from other ways of understanding and addressing human suffering. Where physical illness is concerned, for example, healing rituals are combined with medical care, as in the case of Miguel, who received the priest's blessings and prayers, attended healing masses and also had surgery to remove his tumour.

This chapter analyses the way in which Catholic charismatics deal with illness in everyday life, and pays special attention to the different articulations between biomedicine and religious beliefs and practices. In accordance with the proposition put forward in this volume, of exploring the relationships and articulations between science and religion as two different modes of thought or ways of engaging with the world, the following aims to show how such articulation occurs in a particular ethnographic context.

In the first section I set out the theoretical framework that forms the basis of my reflections, and contextualizes my ethnographic data. I draw upon the recent work of Robert McCauley (2011, this volume), in which he explores scientific and religious thought from the perspective of cognitive science. In his reflections on science and religion, McCauley introduces an important distinction between science and technology, one that aids understanding of Catholic charismatics' views of biomedicine and its relationship with religion in healing processes.

The second section features a characterization of the Catholic Charismatic Renewal and the movement's notions and practices related to healing. It is followed by a presentation of ethnographic materials obtained through nine months of fieldwork with a charismatic prayer group based in Barcelona. During my fieldwork, I had the opportunity to participate in the ritual activities of the prayer group, which included weekly prayer meetings, as well as occasional healing masses and regional and national conferences. I completed the observations arising from my fieldwork by conducting a number of unstructured interviews with members of the prayer group.[1] Healing narratives and reflections on health and illness were a common topic of conversation with my informants, and became a central point of my interviews too. Three ethnographic accounts of charismatic healing are used to illustrate how biomedicine and religious beliefs work together in situations of physical illness.

The principal aim of the final section is to show how science and religion are related in charismatic healing. Combining theoretical reflections with ethnographic materials allow me to clarify what roles biomedicine and religious beliefs and practices play in Catholic charismatics' experiences of healing processes.

Science and Religion

Robert McCauley has recently examined scientific and religious thought (McCauley 2011, this volume). After recognizing that science and religion have a common concern for explanation, the author explores both the cultural manifestations and the cognitive foundations of each. Doing so leads him to show how science and religion are related, and how their efforts to provide explanations differ.

McCauley argues that, according to recent developments in the cognitive science of religion, natural cognition facilitates religious thinking while it hampers scientific inquiry. In other words, religion and its forms of explanation are 'natural' because they make intuitive sense to us. In contrast, the kinds of explanation provided by science do not come naturally to human minds, and thus could be seen as 'unnatural'. McCauley uses the term 'natural cognition' to refer to 'the subterranean parts of our mental lives that constitute our fast, (mostly) unconscious, automatic, effortless, intuitive thought', as opposed to 'unnatural cognition', a form of 'slower, conscious, controlled, effortful, reflective thought' (McCauley 2011: 4). A distinction should be made between the two types of natural cognition, namely 'practised naturalness' and 'maturational naturalness'. Practised naturalness concerns cultural activities – invented at some point in human history – that, once acquired through specific instruction and extensive practice, become automatic and unconscious. Writing and riding a bicycle are examples of such 'second-nature' activities. Like practised naturalness, maturational natural cognition is automatic and unreflective. However, it differs from the former in that it arises early in life, and it addresses the most fundamental problems with which humans have to deal, such as recognizing faces or avoiding contact with contaminants. Additionally, maturational cognition functions regardless of cultural input, that is, it does not rely on any kind of instruction, preparation or artefact. This is the type of natural cognition on which McCauley focuses to compare science and religion.

The author begins his argument about the comparative unnaturalness of science by recognizing that not all aspects of scientific thought are cognitively unnatural. Making sense of the world is a psychological inclination of human beings, one that is expressed by science's drive for explanatory theories. As stated before, that is a common feature of both science and religion. So, what is it that makes scientific efforts to provide explanations unnatural? McCauley points to the sophistication and systematicity which characterize the production and assessment of empirical evidence in science. The generation of empirical data and the criticism of theories which constitute scientific activity require skills 'foreign to the natural proclivities of human minds' (ibid.: 138). The contents of new scientific theories are out of kilter with common views of empirical matters, and constitute a challenge to our intuitions and common sense. Thus, in order to develop such theories, scientists have to get round multiple cognitive biases and errors to which human beings are prone. Overcoming such cognitive limitations is the aim of a number of scientific tools and cultural arrangements that play a pivotal role in science. Such cultural support (the institution of science, with its professional associations, journals and so on) is responsible for a crucial aspect of scientific progress, namely the critical assessment of scientific theories.

Science is, on the whole, an 'unfamiliar activity' that humans do not acquire naturally. It involves forms of thought and practice which are very difficult to master, and is actually restricted to a narrow community of scientific researchers. The emergence, development and persistence of science rely on strong cultural support that constitutes proof of its rarity and unnaturalness. This point can be illustrated by the scarcity of science in human history, the most prominent episodes being Ancient Greece and the period of modern science that began in Europe four centuries ago.

In contrast to the rarity of science, religion dates from our prehistoric past, has recurred throughout history and exists in every human culture. Besides, and unlike science, religion strongly relies on humans' standard cognitive equipment. In McCauley's words, 'Religion ... employs ideas and forms of thought that are naturally appealing to the human mind, because they are rooted in maturationally natural cognitive dispositions and the kinds of knowledge they support, which are available to most children by the time they reach school age' (ibid.: 154). In his consideration of religious cognitive products, the author discusses the counter-intuitive properties that have been commonly attributed to religious beliefs and could diminish religion's naturalness. According to McCauley, popular religion involves only modestly counter-intuitive representations of a sort of special agent. They are normal variations of cognitive activity, which result from limited violations of maturationally natural knowledge.[2] Modes of religious thought, meanwhile, are sustained by basic cognitive skills, the most important of which is the ability to detect agents and their actions. Religious representations of superhuman agents serve explanatory purposes by allowing for the generation, comprehension and transmission of religious stories, beliefs and rituals. Religion's explanatory theories are thus embedded in myth and ritual, the languages through which religious knowledge is conveyed. The acquisition of religion, then, does not depend on explicit instruction, nor does it require specialized intellectual skills, contrary to the case of science. Instead, it relies on basic cognitive dispositions that human beings come by easily.

The above considerations show that religious systems strongly depend on our most basic cognitive resources. Therefore, religious ideas and forms of explanation seem more familiar and intuitive than their scientific counterparts.

McCauley's reflections on religious and scientific thought are essential to an understanding of the roles that both religious and biomedical representations play in charismatic healing. The considerations outlined previously suggest that science, as a theory of reality, is more cognitively costly and demanding than religion. We could hold, then, that religious explanations are naturally appealing, in contrast to biomedical explanations, which require a lot of cultural support. That is an audacious statement though, and I wish to introduce some nuances and qualifications to the characterizations of biomedicine and religious thought alike.

Firstly, it is not my intention to equate science and biomedicine. Biomedicine undoubtedly has a scientific dimension, manifested in its efforts to produce knowledge of the human body. It creates a set of representations of health and illness, and seeks to explain them by conforming to scientific methods. There is far more to biomedicine than that, however. It involves applying the aforementioned knowledge to patients through a range of different technologies and procedures. Additionally, as medical anthropologists have pointed out, it is embedded in sets of social relationships. In other words, medical representations and practices are not isolated from other social spheres, such as the political, economic, social and religious domains (Lindenbaum and Lock 1993; Good 1994).

McCauley carefully examines the distinction between science and technology I have just briefly outlined. According to him, scientific theory and material technology have always been closely connected, but have become inextricable since the nineteenth century, biomedicine being a perfect illustration of that inextricability. Still, there is no confusing the two. In contrast to science, technology has existed throughout history and across cultures. Its ubiquity renders material technology independent from science, and that has actually been the case for a long time. The fundamental difference, however, lies in orientation. While technology is aimed at the practical, science is characterized by an 'abstract theoretical interest in understanding nature for its own sake' (McCauley 2011: 97). The distinction between science and technology allows us to consider the different aspects of biomedicine. In the following, we will examine how science and technology become culturally embedded in a religious context.

Concerning religious ideas, the simplified picture just sketched out merits further examination, for not all such ideas are naturally appealing in equal degree. Some of them, as we will see, are directly based on our intuitive knowledge, and pose us no problem in terms of acquisition. The optimally counter-intuitive character of some religious beliefs makes them attention grabbing and facilitates their circulation (Boyer 2001). Not all religious representations fit so well with our cognitive dispositions though.

Strong cultural support is required for highly counter-intuitive beliefs to be transmitted. Such transmission is effectuated, according to Harvey White-house (2004), either through a doctrinal or an imagistic mode of religios-ity. Whitehouse's well-known theory of modes of religiosity distinguishes between the doctrinal mode – consisting of high-frequency, routinized ritu-als in which verbal communication is a central element – and the imagistic form of religiosity – based on particularly intense experiences. Charismatic healing is a rich system of representations and practices which includes the different types of beliefs described above.

The Catholic Charismatic Renewal

The Catholic Charismatic Renewal (CCR) originated as a movement in the United States in 1967, and constitutes a synthesis of Catholic and Pentecostal elements. It is part of the second Pentecostal revival, which took place in the 1960s, when members of non-Pentecostal churches who received the gifts of the Holy Spirit started renewal movements within their own churches (Rob-bins 2004: 121). The movement expanded rapidly across Catholic countries, and has now spread worldwide (Csordas 1997, 2011). Despite having diverse local and national characteristics, it is generally agreed that Catholic char-ismatics seek to revitalize the Catholic Church through the influence of the Holy Spirit.[3] Also referred to as Pentecostal Catholics, Catholic charismatics claim to offer an experience-based religiosity in which the believer cultivates a personal relationship with Jesus and direct access to the Divine is granted through spiritual gifts or charisms. Those gifts include glossolalia and faith healing, and they constitute proof of the presence of the Holy Spirit in the lives of their receivers.

The CCR began as a network of informal prayer groups, but a second form of organization soon emerged in the shape of covenant communities marked by a higher degree of discipline and commitment. The movement today is made up of associations of the two kinds, in addition to national and international institutional structures, such as the International Catholic Charismatic Renewal Services. In Spain, the movement mainly comprises prayer groups of ten to forty people, who gather in parishes or, to a lesser extent, private homes for weekly charismatic prayer meetings. Besides such meetings, group participants attend occasional healing masses, weekend re-treats and regional or national conferences (Csordas 1997, 2011; Hébrard 1991).

Catholic Charismatic Healing

In 1974, divine healing was introduced to the CCR by the Dominican priest Francis MacNutt. At the CCR's international conference in Notre Dame, Indiana, MacNutt performed the movement's first healing rituals, and thus became its chief spokesperson regarding healing practices. Healing rituals rapidly increased in popularity over the following years, and today lie at the heart of charismatic ritual practice (McGuire 1982; Csordas 1994). The centrality of charismatic healing is reflected in the scholarly literature on the movement. Authors such as McGuire (1982), Charuty (1990) and Csordas (1994) have paid special attention to healing rituals, and ethnographies of the CCR's diverse local expressions highlight ritual healing practices.[4]

Healing is one of the gifts that the Holy Spirit bestows upon the faithful for their personal spiritual growth and that of the Church. Catholic charismatic healing rituals, however, have to be understood within a broader framework of religious beliefs. Firstly, God is described as a loving, caring superhuman agent. He is not regarded as a distant, authoritative entity, but rather as a friend who wants His people to be happy and healthy. Therefore, concerning illness and suffering, '[charismatics] have largely abandoned a notion of redemptive suffering in favour of the notion that God desires everyone to be healed' (Csordas 1994: 43). They also believe that Jesus is alive today. Through the intimate relationship that charismatics develop with Him, God is made present and active in everyday life. Divine presence can be perceived in a number of situations and acts, such as ritual, bible reading, the words of a fellow believer or holy coincidences. Illness is no exception. Being alive today, Jesus continues to heal the sick as He did in the gospels two thousand years ago. Because divine power has no limits, no disease can resist His healing touch, and God is believed to cure the most serious and devastating illnesses affecting humans. This point can be illustrated by the widespread circulation among Catholic charismatics of testimonies of the remission of cancer or AIDS and the disappearance of disabilities, such as the one with which I began this chapter.

What do Catholic charismatics mean by healing though? To what do their notions of health and illness refer? Close observation of those representations and their associated ritual practices show that charismatic healing is not equivalent to conventional biomedical healing. Catholic charismatics often associate healing with salvation, the latter being a process originated by conversion. Conversion is seen as a means of healing modern suffering, and healing, like salvation, as a process of becoming closer and closer to God. According to Csordas, healing is a vehicle for the creation of a sacred self, a self that is essentially healthy. 'Healing is not only the relief of illness and distress, and not only a "sign to unbelievers" of divine power, but an instrument for molding the sacred self' (Csordas 1994: 25). Along similar lines, McGuire links the charismatic notion of health to the idea of wholeness and oneness with the Lord. It is not defined as a state or condition, but as a process that needs healing in order to succeed. 'Humans have broken lives, broken relationships with others and with God, and broken, imperfect bodies. Healing makes whole these fractured lives, the relationship with God being the highest goal of wholeness' (McGuire 1982: 154).

God's love and goodness lie at the very heart of charismatic representations of healing. Whatever humans intuitively consider good is seen by charismatics as coming from or relating to God. The idea of Him as a superhuman agent full of goodness and love seems to profit from our hard-wired concepts of good health, happiness and joy. Thus, assimilating such a representation of the Divine, one in which God wants us to be happy and healthy, is not a difficult task.

It is not easy, however, to believe that chronic disease can be cured or that the paralysed can stand up and cast aside their wheelchairs. Catholic charismatics have come to the Renewal as adults and live in a world in which faith is only one option among others (Taylor 2007). Additionally, even within the realm of faith, conventional Catholicism does not place as much emphasis on God's healing powers as charismatics do. When presented with accounts of successful faith healing, charismatics affirm their validity but also express astonishment, acknowledging that it is difficult for them to believe in such miracles. Thus, the transmission of the idea that Jesus heals today as He did in the Gospels requires considerable cognitive investment. Such transmission is effectuated through a doctrinal form of ritual, described above in the outline of Whitehouse's theory of modes of religiosity. Charismatic rituals place great emphasis on the idea that Jesus heals. In a ritual context, that emphasis takes the form of verbal communication, with preachers reiterating over and over that Jesus has the power to heal any disease, and that believers should not hesitate to ask Him for a cure. Beyond the context of ritual, accounts of miraculous healing are constantly repeated in informal settings. The transmission of ideas about God's healing powers also has an imagistic aspect, specifically the performance of healing prayers, which involves the laying on of hands and the utterance of performative words, resulting in an intense experience for the believer. The idea that God has the power to heal is thus successfully transmitted through both verbal communication and ritual performance.

On a more practical level, charismatics have developed a healing system that identifies three different aetiologies of affliction, specifically bodily illness, emotional affliction and the influence of evil spirits. Each of those aetiologies corresponds to one of the three dimensions of the charismatic person, namely body, mind and soul, and is addressed by means of a specific healing prayer. The different types of illness can be combined if, for example, physical pain is a sign of a more profound emotional affliction. Bodily illness has environmental or accidental causes, and is addressed by means of a prayer of physical healing consisting of the laying on of hands and the utterance of a prayer. The second kind of affliction is emotional, and is addressed by means of a prayer for inner healing or the healing of memories. Charismatics regard emotional problems as the result of traumatic life events. Consequently, the healing prayer focuses on each stage of the supplicant's life, from conception to the present moment. When traumatic events or relationships arise, Jesus is introduced as an actor who heals the painful situation. Finally, the adverse effects of sin and evil spirits are treated by means of the prayer of deliverance, in which spirits are commanded to depart in the name of Jesus. Deliverance is not equivalent to the exorcism of demonic possession, in which a demon takes total control of a person. Demonic possession can only be addressed by a priest, for only they are allowed to perform the rite of exorcism.[5]

Such healing prayers take place in a variety of forms and contexts, from huge rallies and healing masses with multiple patients to private intercessory prayers or individual requests. Their performance commonly includes techniques such as, again, the laying on of hands and the utterance of specific prayers. While some healing is dramatic and miraculous, the majority of healing rites consist of partial relief from suffering or recovery from minor ailments. The type of healing that sustains the charismatic healing system is characterized, according to Csordas (1994), by an 'incremental efficacy' that allows for a modulation of disability, which is understood as a mode of engaging with the world.

These brief notes on charismatic healing clearly show that CCR participants' understanding of illness, healing and health does not correspond to the biomedical definition of those concepts. Catholic charismatics and biomedicine have developed different representations of health and the lack thereof, address different objects and use distinct healing methods. Thus, one might question the appropriateness of establishing a relationship between the two. However, after acknowledging the importance of such differences, I wish to focus on the articulations that exist between the two. I will restrict my analysis to physical illness, a type of affliction that both healing systems define in similar ways and to which the largest proportion of the ethnographic data I have collected refers. Catholic charismatics do not ignore the role of biomedicine in processes involving physical illness (nor in certain emotional afflictions). As we have seen in the example of Miguel's malignant tumour and its removal, biomedicine and religion can and do work together.

Intersections between Biomedicine and Religious Belief

Charismatics do not regard the relationship between religious and biomedical healing as contradictory or disjunctive.[6] Patients who participate in healing prayers are not asked to give up their medical treatment, and the work of physicians is not questioned or criticized. On the contrary, biomedicine is integrated into a broader framework of religious beliefs. For charismatics, God is the 'divine physician' and His healing powers are greater than those of conventional doctors. Doctors, their knowledge and their practice are part of the healing powers of God. They are created by Him for the benefit of humankind and are seen, just as healing prayers are, as a divine instrument of healing. For that reason, charismatics always pray for physicians before surgery or medical appointments. They ask God to bring light to doctors so that they will diagnose problems correctly, prescribe the right medicines or succeed in surgical procedures. As Isabel, a 59-year-old woman who went through several illnesses during my fieldwork, once told me, 'Physicians are an instrument of God and I pray before any operation. I pray for the doctor's hands to be His instrument, because all actions are a work of the Lord'.

As we will see below, charismatics consider biomedicine a tool of God. They attribute meaning to the religious sphere – that is, to the ultimate cause of healing – while biomedicine is stripped of its explanatory capacities and simply functions as a technology. Biomedicine addresses the issue of 'how', but not that of 'why', for explanation is taken from a religious stance. Biomedicine is assimilated and integrated into a broader framework of religious representations. This allows for the establishment of a non-conflictual relationship between biomedicine and religious ideas concerning suffering and illness.

Three ethnographic examples of the different ways in which biomedicine and religion work together in processes of healing illness and suffering follow. I will show how cooperation between the two healing systems takes different forms, and occurs at different stages of the healing process.

Divine Healing

Charismatics believe that God's healing powers go far beyond those of physicians, and accounts of complete cancer remission or wheelchair users regaining their ability to stand up are widespread among prayer-group participants. Despite the popularity of such miraculous healing, the prayer-group participants I interviewed had no personal stories of this kind. What they shared with me were testimonies of the healing of minor ailments or spontaneous recovery from illnesses that would have required difficult or risky medical treatment, as in the case of Guillermo, a prayer-group leader and intercessory team member. Severe leg discomfort led him to see a physician, who, after several tests, noted a deterioration in the head of his thigh bone, a cause of femoral necrosis. If the necrosis had progressed as expected, the only solution would have been to replace the damaged femoral head with a prosthesis. There was no need for surgery though. The intercessory team prayed over Guillermo and the members of his prayer group included requests for the recovery of his health in their daily prayers. The two forms of prayer succeeded, according to Guillermo, in curing his necrosis, for when he returned to the doctor's surgery, the doctor found that all signs of the femoral deterioration had completely disappeared. Divine healing takes different forms, and does not necessarily occur at the very moment the healing prayer is performed, nor is it always accompanied by a special physical or emotional sensation. In this case, Guillermo cannot identify a particular moment at which the healing took place, and it was the physician who confirmed it through medical tests.

In this example, God heals Guillermo's femoral head and restores it to a healthy state. The medical treatment suggested for thigh-bone necrosis is thus not needed. However, although the healing is attributed to God, the role of biomedicine should not be overlooked. Guillermo combines prayers with appointments with his doctor, and it is the physician who both diagnoses the problem and certifies the disappearance of the necrosis and the bone's recovery. Cooperation is thus established between biomedical and religious ways of addressing Guillermo's pain. However, biomedicine and religion do not have equal status. Biomedicine, despite being crucial to the healing process, in that it provides diagnosis and certifies recovery, is subordinated to religion, because the ultimate cause of Guillermo's healing is God's action. In other words, biomedicine is the means to God's end, the way in which divine intervention is made manifest.

Patient Improvement and the Success of Medical Treatment

Personal accounts of healing reported to me often consisted of attributing the patient's full recovery or improvement to God's intervention. Such cases differ from those of the previous category in that medical treatment does not constitute an alternative to divine intervention. On the contrary, the biomedical system takes full charge of the patient, and medical treatment leads to them being healed or to an improvement in their condition. That was the case with Isabel, who was diagnosed with type 2 diabetes and was having trouble coping with it. Receiving a great deal of medical attention reassured her, but she was very scared of fainting or falling over in the street. Day by day, she ceased doing the most basic household chores, and became very dependent on her husband and daughters. She experienced fear and anxiety related to her condition, which led her to measure her blood glucose levels several times a day, and she panicked whenever they were dangerously low. Every Friday evening, during prayer meetings, Isabel asked God for healing, and requested that prayer-group participants include her suffering in their daily prayers. Healing eventually occurred at the CCR's annual national conference in Madrid. The 2011 conference's guest preacher was well known for his healing charism. After a healing prayer, he asked for the ten people who had just been healed of diabetes to stand up, and Isabel was among those who did so.[7] Two months later, I interviewed her and asked about her diabetes. She told me: 'In Madrid, there was a big change. I said to myself, "Lord, I'm in your hands", and I lost all fear. Now I'm doing well, I feel calm and relaxed, and my diabetes is stable. I don't need to take pills any more. I'm on a diet and I only have minor problems when I don't follow the physician's advice'.

Isabel's healing does not involve the complete remission of her illness, but rather a substantial improvement in her condition and her way of coping with it. Her words illustrate how biomedical and religious understandings of 'healing' differ considerably. According to biomedical science, diabetes is a chronic disease for which no cure exists, except in very specific situations. It can, however, be controlled by managing blood sugar levels and keeping them close to normal. This stabilization of the condition is what Isabel considers 'healing'. Among Catholic charismatics, healing includes not only bodily changes that result in the disappearance of illness and the restoration of health, but also partial healing and improvements in the patient's condition. They are all manifestations of God's activity in a person's life, opportunities for becoming closer to the Divine and engaging in a process that ultimately leads to oneness with the Lord.

Despite their different representations of healing, the two healing systems again intersect in this example and are articulated in a particular way. Isabel receives medical treatment, but prayers result in God being present throughout the entire process of her illness. Divine presence, particularly manifested during the mass healing rituals at the national conference, ensures Isabel's improvement and loss of fear.

Diagnosis

God's healing powers are not limited to curing or improving a patient's condition. They also extend to the initial phase of medical treatment, during
which the study of symptoms leads to a diagnosis, in accordance with which
medical treatment is planned. Here too, in the process of diagnosis, the religious and the biomedical can be tightly interwoven. The following narrative perfectly illustrates that kind of articulation between the two. Antonia,
a sixty-year-old housewife, is a devout Catholic who regularly attends both
charismatic prayer meetings and nocturnal adoration sessions in her parish.
A couple of years ago, she started suffering from serious back pains that left
her in a state of progressive paralysis. Her mobility was reduced to the point
that she could neither comb her hair nor eat by herself. She saw many doctors, but none of them was able to correctly diagnose the problem. When
her neighbour recommended a physician known for his expertise in back
paralysis, she quickly called for an appointment, but was unable to obtain
one due to his busy schedule. Meanwhile, her paralysis progressed and Antonia fell into despair. She told me that she was sitting on her bed one day,
crying to God that she could not bear the pain any more and did not want
to become disabled. Then, she had a vision of the biblical passage in which
Jesus calms a storm. She saw the storm, the little boat, and the disciples wak-
ing up Jesus, who was sleeping, and crying out to Him, 'Lord, save us! We're
going to drown!' He replied, 'You of little faith, why are you so afraid?' and
calmed the winds and waves.[8] After the vision, Antonia felt that she had to
go to a particular hospital in the city, but her husband objected because it
was not the one they were entitled to visit under the national health service,
and managing to have her attended to there would be difficult. However,
she insisted so strongly that they finally went, and the doctor who saw her
turned out to be the one they had been trying to reach without success.[9]
Needless to say, the doctor diagnosed the problem correctly, and Antonia
made a full recovery after brief medical treatment.

Antonia's vision is a sign of God's presence in her life. It is only after
this extraordinary experience that the healing process begins.

> The Lord took my hand and told me, 'Go there and you will find the solution'.
> When I realized that the doctor attending to me was the one I had tried so hard
> to reach, I started crying, I felt so emotional! For me, it's a miracle. If that had
> happened to you, you would have realized that it isn't normal, there are too many
> coincidences [...] But there are no coincidences, the Lord is always with us!

As in the case of situations in which a patient's improvement and the success of their medical treatment are attributed to God, the biomedical system takes full charge of Antonia's illness. However, God's intervention is crucial. When Antonia, like the disciples, was asking to be saved, God affirmed His presence by calming the storm, that is, by leading her to the doctor who would cure her back pains. Here, we can once again see how religious meaning encompasses medical treatment. Antonia's vision can be interpreted as a metaphor of what was going on in her life. She was concerned and suffering because she was unable to hit upon the right course of action: to see the doctor who would eventually cure her illness. Her vision is precisely what set her upon that course, in a rather unexpected way. In her view, there is a clear connection between the vision and going to the hospital where she found the doctor. God's action thus becomes the ultimate cause of her healing process, and medical treatment the proximate cause.[10]

As can be seen in the previous ethnographic accounts, God works closely with biomedicine in illness and healing processes. He is involved in such processes in a very direct, manifest way, leading charismatics to attribute healing to his intervention. Sometimes, however, accounts of illness limit the role of God to that of providing comfort. The articulation between the biomedical and the religious is somehow blurred when God stands close by, accompanying the patient and their family throughout the process of their illness, infusing them with peace and serenity. In such cases, charismatics do not claim that God has healed them, but insist that they feel comforted and accompanied by the Lord. This presence is very important for a religious movement that affirms that Jesus is alive and active in believers' everyday lives. Feeling God's calming presence allows Catholic charismatics to cope with suffering without falling into despair, and functions as confirmation of the divine presence in their daily lives.

Conclusions

Catholic charismatics' experiences of illness and healing constitute a prime area for the interaction of biomedicine and religion. Biomedical representations and practices and religious beliefs and rituals all come into play in charismatic healing. In order to understand how the articulation between those different approaches to illness and healing is established, I have analysed McCauley's work, in which he explores religious and scientific thought from both a cognitive and a cultural perspective. McCauley suggests that religious ideas and modes of thought are better suited to our natural cognition system than scientific thought is. Still, the dichotomy between science as a cognitively costly activity and naturally appealing religion does not suffice where our attempt to understand charismatic healing processes is concerned, and merits further examination. On one hand, biomedicine cannot be reduced to science, for the scientific knowledge it produces is then applied to human bodies through an array of tools and procedures. Biomedicine is not a search for truth for its own sake, so to speak, but has a predominantly practical aim, namely healing. Furthermore, biomedicine is embedded in a set of social relationships and connected to other social domains. Turning now to religious beliefs, the CCR has developed a complex system of representations and practices around illness and health. As we have seen, not all of those representations are equally attention grabbing.

Besides engaging in a number of religious rituals and narratives, Catholic charismatics do not refrain from seeking medical attention when they are sick. The relationship between biomedicine and religion is not seen as contradictory, and combining prayers with pills causes no conflict at all. The ethnographic examples provided reflect different possible articulations between biomedicine and religion, with medical treatment accommodating divine intervention that takes distinct forms and occurs at different stages of the healing process.

Nonetheless, biomedicine and religion do not have the same status. While God is credited with unlimited healing powers and religion is a source of meaning for addressing suffering and distress, biomedicine is reduced to a divine instrument for accomplishing His healing action. For charismatics, the value of biomedicine is essentially practical. It is the means to God's end, the way His activity manifests itself. In other words, biomedicine is viewed as a technology (in McCauley's sense) within a larger framework of religious beliefs that shape experiences of illness and give them meaning.

The above observations are consistent with McCauley's remarks on the unnaturalness of scientific explanations and religion's natural appeal. For Catholic charismatics, scientific explanations of illness and healing are rather irrelevant, in contrast to the importance of religious ideas and practices, in terms of fashioning a meaningful experience. It is not that they are seen as false or misguided, but they are clearly insufficient as explanations. This chapter has repeatedly made a point concerning the naturalness or unnaturalness of certain cultural ideas and the ways in which this affects their transmissibility. Whereas major cognitive investments are required to assimilate scientific ideas, religious precepts are much more attuned to the evolved characteristics of the human mind/brain. Not all religious ideas enjoy the same degree of transmissibility though. Following

Whitehouse's theory of modes of religiosity, we have seen how intuitive (or minimally counter-intuitive) beliefs, such as the idea that God is full of goodness and love, seem to profit from our hard-wired concepts of good health, happiness and joy. However, other ideas, such as different forms of miraculous healing, can only be assimilated by a combination of the doctrinal and imagistic modes of religiosity. Much the same could be argued concerning biomedicine. Taken as a world-view, it turns out to be as difficult to transmit as any other scientific idea. Regarded as a technology, on the other hand, it can be much more easily accommodated by our evolved cognitive architecture.

To conclude, Weber (1998) made the point that in a disenchanted world, meaning-infusing religious explanations would be replaced by the cold, meaningless rationality of science. From the Catholic charismatic perspective, it could be argued that he was partially right, in that science certainly does make the world meaningless by rendering it more rational and devoid of an overarching supreme moral intentionality. However, he was wrong in the sense that he did not envision the possibility that one of the most genuine products of modern science, biomedicine, could be seamlessly articulated with the enchantments of religious beliefs, as long as it is taken not as a world-view but as a technology that serves divine purposes.

Notes

1. Because I focus on the lived religion of common members and not the official doctrine of the CCR, I have not interviewed the movement's leaders, nor have I studied the charismatic movement's internal literature.
2. This includes intuitive physics, intuitive biology and intuitive psychology.
3. See Bowie (2003) for an account of religious experience in a contemporary Catholic movement.
4. Csordas provides a review of the movement's literature (Csordas 1994) and discusses the globalization of charismatic healing practices (Csordas 2011).
5. Besides those just outlined, healing can also occur through prayers of praise or through sacraments, such as the Eucharist.
6. See both Inglis and Melhuus (this volume) for other accounts of science and religion successfully accommodating one another.
7. During healing prayers, the leading priest receives 'words of science' from the Holy Spirit, which make him aware of how many people are being cured of a specific illness. It is common for charismatics to claim that healing has been accomplished and to thank God for that, even if the patient does not feel any extraordinary sensations or the healing is not medically certified. This is seen as proof of faith.

8. These quotations come from Matthew 8: 23–26: 'Then he got into the boat and his disciples followed him. Without warning, a furious storm came up on the lake, so that the waves swept over the boat. But Jesus was sleeping. The disciples went and woke him, saying, "Lord, save us! We're going to drown!" He replied, "You of little faith, why are you so afraid?" Then he got up and rebuked the winds and the waves, and it was completely calm'.

9. In Spain, doctors working in the public national health system can also have private practices. When her paralysis began, Antonia had asked for a private appointment. Thanks to her vision, she was treated by the same physician at a public hospital.

10. See Tanya Luhrmann's account of causality in witchcraft (Luhrmann 1989) and Evans-Pritchard's discussion of Zande causation (Evans-Pritchard 1976).

References

Boyer, P. 2001. *Religion Explained: The Evolutionary Origins of Religious Thought*. New York: Basic Books.

Bowie, F. 2003. 'An Anthropology of Religious Experience: Spirituality, Gender and Cultural Transmission in the Focolare Movement', *Ethnos* 68(1): 49–72.

Charuty, G. 1990. 'Les liturgies du malheur: le souci thérapeutique des chrétiens charismatiques', *Le Débat* 59(2): 68–89.

Csordas, T. 1994. *The Sacred Self: A Cultural Phenomenology of Charismatic Healing*. Berkeley: University of California Press.

——. 1997. *Language, Charisma, and Creativity: The Ritual Life of a Religious Movement*. Berkeley: University of California Press.

——. 2011, 'Catholic Charismatic Healing in Global Perspective: The Cases of India, Brazil, and Nigeria', in C.G. Brown (ed.), *Global Pentecostal and Charismatic Healing*. New York: Oxford University Press, pp.331–50.

Evans-Pritchard, E.E. 1976 [1937]. *Witchcraft, Oracles and Magic among the Azande*, abr. edn. Oxford: Oxford University Press.

Good, B.J. 1994. *Medicine, Rationality, and Experience: An Anthropological Perspective*. Cambridge: Cambridge University Press

Hébrard, M. 1991. *Les charismatiques*. Paris: Editions du Cerf.

Lindenbaum, S., and M. Lock (eds). 1993. *Knowledge, Power, and Practice: The Anthropology of Medicine and Everyday Life*. Berkeley: University of California Press.

Luhrmann, T.M. 1989. *Persuasions of the Witch's Craft: Ritual Magic in Modern Culture*. Cambridge, MA: Harvard University Press.

McCauley, R. 2011. *Why Religion Is Natural and Science Is Not*. New York: Oxford University Press.

McGuire, M. 1982. *Pentecostal Catholics*. Philadelphia: Temple University Press.

Robbins, J. 2004. 'The Globalization of Pentecostal and Charismatic Christianity', *Annual Review of Anthropology* 33: 117–41.

Taylor, C. 2007. *A Secular Age*. Cambridge, MA: Harvard University Press.

Weber, M. 1998 [1948]. 'Science as a Vocation', in H.H. Gerth and C. Wright Mills (eds), *From Max Weber: Essays in Sociology*. New York: Routledge.

Whitehouse, H. 2004. *Modes of Religiosity: A Cognitive Theory of Religious Transmission*. Walnut Creek, CA: AltaMira Press.

Part III

§§

Meaning Systems

Chapter Nine

On the Resilience of Superstition

João de Pina-Cabral

> Modernity, like modern science, could live with everything except an attenuated status and a limited, non-proselytizing social role for it.
>
> —Ashis Nandy, *The Intimate Enemy*

Anthropologists and philosophers have always taken very seriously the concept of 'belief' or *croyance*. Nevertheless, it has led to a long series of perplexities that do not seem to be fully resolved even today, nearly forty years after Rodney Needham published his fundamental essay on the topic (Needham 1972). On the other hand, the concept of 'superstition' as used by the fathers of anthropology (e.g. Frazer 1909) has simply been discarded as ethnocentric. The first has been pushed aside for its logical uncertainty, the second for its ethical uncertainty.

Yet the two concepts are surprisingly resilient, and they remain related by the fact that belief (as in 'the so-and-so believe this and that') is generally used to mean the knowledge of others to which the speaker does not adhere; that is, others' unfounded beliefs. As most commonly used, therefore, the category of belief implies the suppressed category of superstition, much like the common anthropological category 'the Other' – with capital 'o' – implies the suppressed category of the 'primitive'. Furthermore, this association is definitional: superstition is defined as 'unfounded belief', but the issue of the foundation of belief is at the centre of the anthropological and philosophical perplexities that have recently haunted epistemological thinking (see Toren and Pina-Cabral 2009; Fabian 2012: 444).

In this chapter, I will engage one of the oldest themes in anthropology: the efficacy of magic. As in previous essays, I will depend on Donald Davidson's epistemological views that amount to a type of minimalist realism and are essentially non-representationist (Davidson 2001: 138). I will use as examples two instances of magic: one taken from the early work of Joseph Conrad, the other from a news report concerning the common-law wife of the late writer Stieg Larsson.

Unwinding Participation

These examples fully evoke Lucien Lévy-Bruhl's notion of 'participation' as developed in his late personal notes, the *Carnets*, published posthumously in 1949 (Lévy-Bruhl 1998). For Lévy-Bruhl, the word describes the fact that 'the "primitive" frequently experiences participations between himself and this or that environing being or object, natural or supernatural, with which he is or comes to be in contact, and that, quite as frequently, he imagines similar participations between these beings and objects' (ibid.: 77–78).[1] He observes, 'individual beings or objects are only represented within a whole of which they are, if not the parts, at least integrating elements, composing elements (*les composants*), or reproductions' (ibid.: 22). Lévy-Bruhl's editor further clarifies by explaining that what Lévy-Bruhl had observed was that, 'the beings and objects which are associated in collective representations only reach representation on the basis of a link that makes them always already participating in one another, so that one can claim that this link is felt even before these objects have been represented and related to each other as represented objects' (Karsenti 1998: xxiv).

Now, many anthropologists today are highly sceptical of the appositeness of the notion of 'representation' (Toren 1999; Pina-Cabral 2010a). Davidson himself was a critic (Davidson 2001: 34), and the issue has been causing much debate of late (e.g. Clark 1996; Mandik and Clark 2002; Chemero 2009; Siegel 2011). Whatever the outcome of these discussions in light of any further scientific evidence that might surface concerning human mental functions, we can be certain that the way anthropologists have been using the notion of representation in the twentieth century (collective and individual) is today a major hindrance to anthropological theorizing.

In particular, notions like 'representation' and 'belief' operate a kind of silent compacting between personal dispositions (aspects of thought held in the mind of each one of us) and collective dispositions (statistical tendencies observed among the mental dispositions of members of a group). To presume that personal mental processes (representations) and collectively shared dispositions (collective representations) are somehow phenomena of the same nature is to presume that groups have minds of the same nature as persons – a supposition that we are hardly entitled to make. Our challenge, then, is to find a way of matching Lévy-Bruhl's profound insights concerning human thinking with contemporary epistemology, where the notion of representation as enshrined in the anthropological tradition is best avoided and where unstated isomorphisms between personal mental processes and collective tendencies are decidedly untenable.

I believe that we can do this by proposing that Lévy-Bruhl's notion of 'participation' synthesizes various aspects of the human condition that we would approach separately today. In this chapter, therefore, I will explore three major aspects of 'participation'.

The first aspect is mutuality of personhood – that is, in Marshall Sahlins's recent formulation (Sahlins 2011a, 2011b), the way in which persons are constituted multiply and relationally, all singularity being approximate and evanescent. Marilyn Strathern's concept of the 'dividual person' helps us understand how plurality is anterior to singularity, always reimposing itself (Strathern 1988; see also Mosko 2010; Pina-Cabral 2010b). Strathern's connected notion of 'partibility' describes objects and persons as mutually constituted and conceptually interconnected (Strathern 1984; cf. Pina-Cabral 2012). In fact, Strathern's thinking is deeply indebted to Maurice Leenhardt's work on Melanesia (Leenhardt 1971), which had similarly affected Lévy-Bruhl's late thinking on personhood.

For the second aspect, we will rely on Rodney Needham's contributions towards the better understanding of the epistemology of everyday life inspired by the late work of Wittgenstein – namely, an approach to category formation that emphasizes the way in which concepts in natural languages are not subject to the rules of non-contradiction and the excluded middle, rather relying on a notion of opposition that remains ever incomplete and approximate, and on unmediated notions of causality.[2] The way in which cognition is essentially embodied is an aspect of Needham's thought that has come to be fully confirmed, three decades later, by the work of neurophysiologists and philosophers of cognition, such as Clark and Chalmers (1995) and Chemero (2009), or of vision, such as Siegel (2011). In Needham words: 'the principle of opposition is reversible direction; and (directional) opposites are based on the spatial experience of the human body' (Needham 1987: 71–72). His argument concerning notions of causality similarly stresses the relationship between cognition and embodiment (Needham 1983: 66–92). Whilst many of the insights of Claude Lévi-Strauss in *The Savage Mind* (1966) concerning *bricolage* must be taken as an inspiration to all of these discussions, his general structuralist epistemology will have to be abandoned, as indeed Needham had come to realize by the time he wrote

Counterpoints (1987). In fact, category formation will be approached by us in much the same way that fuzzy logic does when it exploits the tolerance for imprecision in dealing with complex problems of engineering (Pina-Cabral 2010a; Ross 2010 [1995]).

The third aspect concerns the nature of human communication. We start from a realist posture that emphasizes the essentially veridical nature of belief: as Quine put it, 'to believe is to believe true' (Quine and Ullian 1970: 4). A necessary condition for successful interpretation, therefore, according to Davidson, is that 'the interpreter must so interpret as to make a speaker or agent largely correct about the world' (Davidson 2001: 152). However, whilst the constitution of belief is essentially veridical in that it depends formatively on people's assessment of what might be the case, one of its characteristics is the proneness to favour greater belief coherence. Here again, therefore, we are in a graded situation rather than one dominated by clear-cut binary opposites. Concerning belief, therefore, the rule of the excluded middle also makes no sense. Thus, ostensivity – that is, the association of heard words with things simultaneously observed – is indeed the boundary condition of belief, but it is often sidetracked by the need for belief coherence, giving rise to retentivity – that is, the tendency for beliefs to interconnect with each other, tending towards systematicity (without ever actually fully achieving it). As Quine puts it, 'We form habits of building beliefs such as we form our other habits; only in habits of building beliefs there is less room for idiosyncrasy' (Quine and Ullian 1970: 59). Retentivity consolidates over time in processes of collective coherence that, when identified by ethnographers, get called 'world-views'.

This is one of the conclusions reached by Gustav Jahoda in his extensive study of the category of superstition carried out nearly half a century ago (Jahoda 1970). The experience of meaning is relational and holistic – there is no such thing as an individual belief, as all beliefs are dependent on other beliefs. Humans are prone towards favouring the maximization of meaning, so retentivity and the constitution of world-views are instruments of that.

Now, the two examples that I will discuss are cases where the efficacy of the procedures was independent of what Lévy-Bruhl would have called *croyance* (belief). That is, if asked whether they 'believed in' the objective powers of the magic they are practising, most of the participants in these two cases would have denied it. Yet, they all experienced and reported the efficacy of the magic, and they were all emotionally affected by the events. We are, therefore, invited to rethink the category of 'belief', separating very clearly between, on the one hand, the propositional attitudes that were being entertained – that is, what Malcolm Ruel (2002 [1982]) would have called 'believing that'– and, on the other hand, the adherence to a collective world implied in the entertaining of such propositional attitudes – that is, 'believing in', or fideistic belief, to use Sabbatucci's favoured expression (Sabbatucci 2000; see also Pompa 2003).

Finally, in order to avoid challenging the Cartesian epistemology that ruled his day, Lévy-Bruhl had to harbour himself within the safe walls of the notion of the 'primitive'. Much as, later on in life, he added considerable nuance to his position in order to safeguard the essential unity of the human mind (e.g. Lévy-Bruhl 1998: 60), he remained bound by an 'us/them' polarity which meant he need not question the essential aspects of the Kantian status quo of his day.[4] Today, however, the notion that we might be examining some form of culturally specific or non-Western mode of thinking is totally beside the point. In fact, as I hope to show, the examples I have chosen are clear evidence of this. In short, we are led to abandon the primitivist disposition that continues to hide itself behind culturalist fashion in anthropology (Pina-Cabral and Lydell 2009). The phenomena of effectiveness that we observe in these charms have broadly universal reach.

In light of this, therefore, I will suggest below that we might usefully recover the much-maligned anthropological notion of 'superstition'. This would then be defined not as 'unfounded belief' but as the proneness of human beings anywhere to constitute their informal worlds in terms of mutuality of personhood, polythetic thinking and retentiveness of belief.

Conrad's Magic

Joseph Conrad's early fiction is situated around the coves and estuaries of the island-strewn coast of Sarawak in Malaysian Borneo (then known as the Eastern Archipelago: see Harrison 1970). It is a region he came to know very well during his maritime days, and for whose inhabitants he came to feel a distinct form of empathy. This is Conrad's 'East', a concept that plays a central part in his emotional economy during the contrastingly sedate days spent in Kent, writing vast quantities of fiction. It is equally important in the reception of his work by the numberless avid readers who, such as myself, find it hard to tear themselves away from Conrad's fiction. As he puts it vividly at the end of *Youth*: 'This was the East of the ancient navigators, so old, so mysterious, resplendent and sombre, living and unchanged, full of danger and promise' (Conrad 2011: 64).

The stories of the early books tend be mutually linked and, as we read on, we get a sense of meeting the same contexts and characters again and again: gun running against the Dutch; a relation between Europeans and locals that is a mixture of mutual fear and fascination; the tragic ambivalence of mixed people, mixed love and mixed friendship; the ups and downs of naval companionship; the marvels of British imperial power, and so on. One of the last pieces of Conrad's early period is a short story called 'Karain, A Memory' (Conrad 2012: 13–93), apparently related to a context with which he was very familiar and that, according to him, he repeated unwittingly in another story in the same collection, 'The Lagoon' (ibid.: 314–69). It is about a band of three gun-runners that strike up a friendship with a local potentate: a handsome man of fascinating presence, thoroughly respected in his small domain, whose back is permanently protected by an armed sorcerer. One day, the sorcerer dies of old age and the chieftain falls into terrible disarray. He is paralysed by fear of his ghostly enemies. He is at the point of losing the small kingdom he carved out for himself by means of sheer military prowess. His loving followers are stunned and bereft.

A tropical storm is upon the Europeans' boat, moored in the middle of the cove. They have not managed to see Karain, and this puzzles them, as they had struck up a genuine friendship with the fellow. Having carried out their business, they are preparing to leave but are held back by the brutality of the squall. To their surprise, out of the rain, the chieftain jumps into their boat. He is almost naked and carries nothing but his kris, having swum alone from the shore in cover of darkness. He is terrified and exhausted.

As the storm unfolds, he tells them his story: their family had sent him and his best friend on a revenge mission to kill a woman who had run away with a Dutch man, breaking a marriage agreement that had been agreed to by the elders, thus besmirching their ancestors' honour. Theirs was a long and arduous pilgrimage that took years until they found her. Finally, one morning, when the time had come to kill them, Karain spoiled the act of rightful vengeance by aiming his gun at his friend instead of at the woman's Dutch culprit. During the long and painful years of their search, without even being aware of it, Karain had fallen blindly in love with the image of her. He wanted nothing from her, but her death had become an impossibility for him.

Left alone and having no way back home, Karain is forced to confront the horror of his betrayal, but he finds protection in the magical powers of this sorcerer. Thus, he manages to direct his tremendous energy towards conquering a new home, his little seaside realm. Now that the sorcerer was dead, however, he was again at the mercy of his ghosts or, in any case, of his guilt. He begs to be taken to England, where the ghosts will not follow him as no one in England believes in them. But his European friends know only too well that this is hardly the case, that it will not bring solace; it will only postpone his self-destruction. One of them, called Hollis, suddenly, has an idea. He takes out of the boat's trunk his own personal box and opens it:

There were there a couple of reels of cotton, a packet of needles, a bit of silk ribbon, dark blue; a cabinet photograph, at which Hollis stole a glance before laying it on the table face downwards. A girl's portrait, I could see. There were, amongst a lot of various small objects, a bunch of flowers, a narrow white glove with many buttons, a slim packet of letters carefully tied up. Amulets of white men! Charms and talismans! Charms that keep them straight, that drive them crooked, that have the power to make a young man sigh, an old man smile. Potent things that procure dreams of joy, thoughts of regret; that soften hard hearts, and can temper a soft one to the hardness of steel. Gifts of heaven – things of earth. (ibid.: 79)

Then, as Hollis rummages through his box, Conrad lets us know:

All the ghosts driven out of the unbelieving West by men who pretend to be wise and alone and at peace – all the homeless ghosts of an unbelieving world – appeared suddenly round the figure of Hollis bending over the box ... [T]hey all seemed to come from the inhospitable regions of the earth to crowd into the gloomy cabin, as though it had been a refuge and, in all the unbelieving world, the only place of avenging belief ... It lasted a second – all disappeared. (ibid.)

Hollis picks up a gilt coin (a Jubilee sixpence) with a hole punched near the rim and shows it to Karain, saying: 'the image of the Great Queen [Victoria], and the most powerful thing the white men know', and he tells his companions, 'I shall make him a thing like those Italian peasants wear, you know' (ibid: 83). He cuts a bit of leather out of the narrow white glove that he had cherished for so long that the owner would no longer be waiting for his return; he sews it into a bag and ties it with the blue ribbon that the glove's owner had given him at his already distant departure from some English dock. Finally, he imposed it on Karain, crying out loud a spell: 'Forget, and be at peace!'

Later, as the sun is rising again and all is calm in the beautiful morning air, Karain realizes that he has been freed from the avenging ghost of his dead friend: 'He has departed again – forever!' he exclaims. And the narrator comments: 'The great thing was to impress him powerfully; to suggest absolute safety – the end of all trouble. We did our best; and I hope we affirmed our faith in the power of Hollis's charm efficiently enough to put the matter beyond the shadow of a doubt'.

Karain goes back among his people. 'He stood up in the boat, lifted up both his arms, then pointed to the infallible charm. We cheered again; and the Malays in the boats stared – very much puzzled and impressed. I wondered what they thought; what he thought; ... what the reader thinks?' (ibid.: 88). Now, precisely the matter of the reader's opinion concerning the power of the charm and of the ghosts seems to be the point of the story. What is, after all, the status of 'the homeless ghosts of an unbelieving world' that had crowded out around Hollis when he opened his box? How had belief avenged itself? The concluding paragraphs of the short story address this matter.

Many years later, the narrator meets by chance the third of his gun-runner companions in Piccadilly. They had not seen each other for more than a decade, and both had abandoned their naval nomadism. Soon after greeting each other, the now retired sailor asks the narrator (Conrad?):

> I wonder whether the charm worked – you remember Hollis' charm, of course. If it did ... Never was a sixpence wasted to better advantage! Poor devil! I wonder whether he got rid of that friend of his. Hope so ... Do you know, I sometimes think that [...] whether the thing was so, you know ... whether it really happened to him ... What do you think?' (ibid.: 91)

The narrator tries to distract his old partner's imagination by pointing to the palpable, modern carriage that is passing by them in all of its modern pomp in central London. The old sailor replies: 'Yes; I see it. [...] It is there; it pants, it runs, it rolls; it is strong and alive; it would smash you if you did not look out; but I'll be hanged if it is yet as real to me as ... as the other thing ... say, Karain's story' (ibid.: 93).

Conrad's conclusion – or is it only the narrator's conclusion? – is that the man 'had been too long away from home'. But the comment can only be ironic, never cynical, otherwise why would Conrad have told us this story at all? Further, note that what the old sailor doubts is not the charm's operational validity (indeed, 'Never was a sixpence wasted to better advantage!'), what he seems to doubt is 'Karain's story', 'whether it really happened to him'. That is, the part that puzzles the old sailor and brings out Conrad's ultimate message to his readers is the musing over the frighteningly deadly powers of Karain's childhood friend and their ancestors, who had been relying on the act of vengeance to clear their honour but were wronged.

Note that he tells us, when Hollis opens his box, that it contains the 'Amulets of white men! Charms and talismans! [...] Potent things that procure dreams of joy, thoughts of regret'. Confronted with the imperial breach – represented by the image of the Great Queen, 'the most powerful thing the white men know' – Conrad is enacting a scene of correspondence, a gesture of human universality in the face of human diversity (ibid.: 79).

Firstly, we are shown to be all equally subject to the mutuality of personhood – in Karain's case, he is subjected to his distant ghosts and he is also a plaything of love. The same, however, is the case with Hollis, his healer, whose ghosts too come to visit the boat in that stormy night, even if only momentarily, when he opens his case. Secondly, we are subject to overlapping modes of thinking. There is difference, all right; but there is sufficient overlap for communication to occur. Even if we are not too certain what goes on in Karain's mind, we too know how to operate with analogies by means of error assessment in modes which are akin to the systems of control based on fuzzy logic. Conrad plays on the way in which Karain's and Hollis's worlds overlap significantly, in all of their difference. But he is so certain of the proximity that he can even joke with the reader, knowing full well what the reader is feeling, thus challenging the reader's predictable surprise. Finally, even though we come from different backgrounds, we recognize the modes of 'participation' among the various parts of our mutual worlds, we can rely on retentivity to act upon us – even if, at the end, we feel obliged to leave behind a kind of ironic disclaimer.

Postmodern Charms

Stieg Larsson, the Danish author of the fabulously successful trilogy *Millennium* (Larsson 2010), died intestate of a sudden disease. Shortly after his death, it became clear that his novels would yield untold riches. His common-law wife, Eva Gabrielsson, who by all accounts had helped him write his novels, was left out of the inheritance, which was claimed exclusively by his father and brother with whom he had a distant relationship. Her anger and the public feeling of injustice led her to write a book about her travails that has been well received (2011). The *Herald Tribune* published an interview with her about the book where it is related that:

> Ms Gabrielsson ... talked forthrightly about the oddest passage in her book, a description of an elaborate Viking curse she delivered in New Year's Eve 2004 against all her and Larsson's enemies: the false friends, the cowards 'who let Stieg fight your battles while you raked in the salaries of your cushy jobs', the wearers of 'suits, ties, and wingtips', the evil ones 'who plotted, spied, and stirred up prejudice'. Traditionally such curses were accompanied by the sacrifice of a live horse, but instead Ms Gabrielsson broke a ceramic horse sculpture in two and tossed it into Stockholm's Lake Malaren. Nevertheless, it worked, she insisted. 'I felt immense relief and so did the others who were with me', she said, explaining, 'It's a ritual – we lack rituals for grief, for confusion, for rage; in my case, rage that Stieg's life was cut so short'. She added with satisfaction, that 'all the people who have profited from Stieg in his lifetime – they have not fared well. Bad things happen to them. I don't want to attribute that to the curse, but they are in trouble'.[5]

Again we meet with the same puzzlingly contradictory disclaim of belief – what would be the point of telling the story, if the curse had not been effective? Furthermore, one might be satisfied with the effect the curse had on those who made it, but we are told in no uncertain terms that it had broader and even dire effects. Ms Gabrielsson does not 'believe in' the curse, for her world-view would not have allowed her to claim that association, but she does 'believe that' the curse is operative since this curse is a central part of her own reconstruction of her world after bereavement.

In fact, the journalist (and, by implication, the *Herald Tribune*) joins her in this ambivalent disclaimer: 'the oddest passage in her book' turns out to be the major topic of the interview, the more 'newsworthy' aspect of her sorry saga. Again, as with Karain's story, we are presented with a mediating mechanism that allows distancing. There, it is 'Italian peasants', an ambiguous category of primitiveness; here, it is Viking rituals re-enacted in their original locus but at a distance of many centuries.

Again we find the same processes of 'participation' we found above. In her capacity to reconstitute herself and harm her enemies, there is creative imagination at work. It depends, firstly, on the partibility of those who, having depended on Stieg Larsson, can now be affected by the curse. Secondly, it uses processes of fuzzy logic that are synthetic and not analytical, and that rely on incomplete oppositions. Finally, it depends on the retentive aspects of belief that integrate contemporary Swedish notions of collective being by making use of the image of Vikings and of the urban lake.

Conclusion: On the Resilience of Superstition

Let us go further back to the origin of this discussion, as we will find that much more hangs on the notion of superstition than the emotional impact of a few quaint charms. In his book *Psyche's Task: A Discourse Concerning the Influence of Superstition on the Growth of Institutions* (1909), Sir James Frazer writes in defence of superstition: 'among certain races and at certain stages of evolution some social institutions which we all, or most of us, believe to be beneficial have partially rested on a bases of superstition' (Frazer 1909: 1). His argument is characteristic of his epoch: basically, for society to exist there has to be a lot of irrationality, and much good can come out of it. 'Among certain races and at certain stages of evolution' is a dreadfully ambiguous mode of characterizing this 'other' time, which suggests that, indeed, Frazer too, like Lévy-Bruhl, when confronted with the actual evidence, had great difficulty in precisely pinpointing the boundaries of primitiveness. But note how interesting are his chosen examples: government, property, marriage

and the respect for human life – the four basic pillars of bourgeois human-
ism. If these are essentially 'superstitions', then what is not?

Frazer was inspired by Westermarck's thoughts on superstition (ibid.:
27). The latter found that superstition is the very basis of morality, even in
modern society:

> in serving the cause of avarice and ambition[, superstition] subserved the cause
> of civilization, by fostering conceptions of the right of property and the sanctity
> of the marriage tie – conceptions which in time grew strong enough to stand
> by themselves and to fling away the crutch of superstition which in earlier days
> had been their sole support. For we shall scarcely err in believing that even in
> advanced societies the moral sentiments, in so far as they are merely sentiments
> and are not based on an induction from experience, derive much of their force
> from an original system of taboo. Thus on the taboo were grafted the golden
> fruits of law and morality, while the parent stem dwindled slowly into the sour
> crabs and empty husks of popular superstition on which the swine of modern
> society are still content to feed. (Westermarck 1908: 59)

Superstition, then, for these already distant ancestors, is unfounded belief – but unfounded in the sense of irrational and incoherent, not in the
sense of wrong or inadequate to live by. Their point is precisely that, whilst
they feel obliged to distance themselves from the thought processes that
characterized 'primitives', they cannot but recognize the universal validity
of the processes such 'wrong beliefs' produced.

Their notion of 'primitive' – that is, something that is elementary for
human life and, therefore, is simple and anterior – allowed them to contem-
plate the evidence that Lévy-Bruhl would later also confront: that human
behaviour could not satisfactorily be described by adhering to formal logic
and rational evidence as it was then seen. Today, we can no longer be satisfied with that strategy, however. We have discovered that we are all dividual
persons, whose unchecked processes of everyday thinking follow a kind of
fuzzy logic, and who are bound to stray away from strict ostensivity in our
judgements concerning truth. Moreover, the focus on the 'indeterminacy of
interpretation' (Davidson 2001) means that we cannot assume that anyone's
mental processes will be the same as anyone else's in more than an approximate way. The isomorphism between what the 'primitive' (personal) thinks
and what the 'primitive' (collective) thinks is no longer sustainable.

The implication of this conclusion is that we must abandon primitivism
decisively. If that is the case, then, the suppressed category of superstition
need no longer be taboo to anthropological mouths. What made it a dirty
word was the implication of primitiveness and human inferiority. Once this
is abandoned, it can satisfactorily be used to describe the quandaries con-

cerning belief that have not ceased to disturb us to this day. Just over a century ago, Conrad saw himself obliged to engage in irony to report the fact that the processes he was identifying in Karain's story were, in fact, fully applicable to his 'modern' world. Just the other day, Eva Gabrielsson found it useful again to take recourse to very similar processes for very similar reasons. If, instead of being seen as failings, these were seen as processes that permanently characterize our human condition, then we would not be obliged to engage in the sort of denial of belief that characterized both Conrad's and Eva Gabrielsson's narratives.

Finally, the evidence that Frazer and Westermarck unearthed that some of the central institutions of social living depend on processes that Lévy-Bruhl would call 'participation' need not be formulated in primitivist terms. If, then, we are willing to engage frontally with the mutuality of personhood, polythetic modes of thinking and retentivity in belief, we have no reason to avoid speaking of superstition to describe such modes of thinking, and to differentiate them from the modes of analytical thinking that have developed over the years for the purpose of the constitution of scientific and technical knowledge (and which we find almost impossible to apply thoroughly, try as we might, to our everyday engagement with things and people).

Having thoroughly examined the literature available in the mid twentieth century, Gustav Jahoda ends his essay on the psychology of superstition with a critique of those who continued to believe that education and the improvement of science will lead to a decrease in what was then called 'superstition'. He concluded, therefore, 'opinions of this kind are themselves irrational in nature', and 'the propensity can never be eradicated because, paradoxically, it is an integral part of mechanisms without which humanity would be unable to survive' (Jahoda 1970: 142, 147). Jahoda is not all that distant from Frazer and Westermarck, half a century before him, much like Sahlins's discussions concerning 'mutuality of being' are not all that distant from Lévy-Bruhl's 'participation', as Sahlins indeed acknowledges (Sahlins 2011a: 10).

The modes of thinking of scientific knowledge must not, then, be seen as the normal mode of human engagement with the world. Rather, they must be seen as the exception – mediated by a series of methodological technologies that have been developed precisely to help us sustain that exception. Superstition, on the contrary, must be seen as the more frequent mode of engaging our social worlds and constructing ourselves as persons.

Notes

1. All translations from non-English language texts cited in the bibliography are my own.
2. On polythetic categories and causality, see Needham (1983); on opposition, see Needham (1987).
3. Faced with this quote by Quine, readers often want to know why there might be less space for idiosyncrasy in belief than in other habits. I think that, when he wrote this, Quine was thinking of the holism of belief, that is, the way in which all beliefs are related to each other, but processually, not, of course, within a closed whole.
4. Here and there cracks appear in Lévy-Bruhl's argument, as when he notes that the argument concerning unmediated causality in the primitive's approach to the supernatural also applies to Christianity (Lévy-Bruhl 1998: 68–69). We can judge how difficult this issue continues to be for anthropology by the fact that Needham's argument in his essay 'Skulls and Causality' (Needham 1983: 66–92) is still hard reading today.
5. 'A Portrait of Stieg Larsson, By She Who Knew Him Best', *Herald Tribune*, 23 June 2011.

References

Chemero, A. 2009. *Radical Embodied Cognitive Science*. Cambridge, MA: MIT Press.

Clark, A. 1996. *Being There: Putting Brain, Body and World Together Again*. Cambridge, MA: MIT Press.

Clark, A., and D. Chalmers. 1995. 'The Extended Mind', Philosophy-Neuroscience-Psychology Research Report. St Louis, MO: Washington University.

Conrad, J. 2011 [1902]. *Youth, A Narrative*. UK: Create Space.

———. 2012 [1898]. *Tales of Unrest*. Cambridge: Cambridge University Press.

Davidson, D. 2001. *Subjective, Intersubjective, Objective*. Oxford: Oxford University Press.

Fabian, J. 2012. 'Cultural Anthropology and the Question of Knowledge', *Journal of the Royal Anthropological Institute* 18(2): 439–53.

Frazer, J.G. 1909. *Psyche's Task: A Discourse Concerning the Influence of Superstition on the Growth of Institutions*. London: Macmillan.

Gabrielsson, Eva. 2011. *Stieg and Me: Memories of My Life with Stieg Larsson*. London: Hachette.

Harrisson, T. 1970. *The Malays of South-West Sarawak before Malaysia: A Socio-ecological Survey*. London: Macmillan.

Jahoda, G. 1970. *The Psychology of Superstition*. Harmondsworth: Penguin.

Karsenti, B. 1998 [1949]. 'Présentation', in L. Lévy-Bruhl, *Les carnets*. Paris: Presses Universitaires de France.

Larsson, S. 2010. *Millennium Trilogy*. 3 vols. London: Quercus.

Leenhardt, M. 1971 [1947]. *Do kamo; la personne et le mythe dans le monde mélanésien*. Paris: Gallimard.

Lévi-Strauss, C. 1966. *The Savage Mind*. Chicago: University of Chicago Press.

Lévy-Bruhl, L. 1998 [1949]. *Les carnets*. Paris: Presses Universitaires de France.

Mandik, P., and A. Clark. 2002. 'Selective Representing and World-making', *Mind and Machines* 12(3): 383–95.

Mosko, M. 2010. 'Partible Penintents: Dividual Personhood and Christian Practice in Melanesia and the West', *Journal of the Royal Anthropological Institute* 16(2): 215–40.

Nandy, A. 1983. *The Intimate Enemy: Loss and Recovery of Self under Colonialism*. Delhi: Oxford University Press.

Needham, R. 1972. *Belief, Language, and Experience*. Oxford: Blackwell.

———. 1983. *Against the Tranquillity of Axioms*. Berkeley: University of California Press.

———. 1987. *Counterpoints*. Berkeley: University of California Press.

Pina-Cabral, J. 2010a. 'The Door in the Middle: Six Conditions for Anthropology', in D. James, E. Plaice and C. Toren (eds), *Culture Wars: Context, Models and Anthropologists' Accounts*. Oxford: Berghahn, pp.152–69.

———. 2010b. 'Xará: Namesakes in Southern Mozambique and Bahia (Brazil)', *Ethnos* 73(3): 323–45.

———. 2012. 'The Two Faces of Mutuality: Contemporary Themes in Anthropology', *Anthropological Quarterly* 86(1): 257–76.

Pina-Cabral, J. and J. Lydell. 2009. 'Larger Truths and Deeper Understandings', *Social Anthropology* 16(3): 346–54.

Pompa, C. 2003. *Religião como tradução: missionários, Tupi e Tapuia no Brasil colonial*. Bauru, SP: EDUSC.

Quine, W.V., and J.S. Ullian. 1970. *The Web of Belief*. New York: Random House.

Ross, T. 2010 [1995]. *Fuzzy Logic with Engineering Applications*. London: Wiley.

Ruel, M. 2002 [1982]. 'Christians as Believers', in M. Lambek (ed.), *A Reader in the Anthropology of Religion*. Oxford: Blackwell, pp.99–113.

Sabbatucci, D. 2000. *La prospettiva storico-religiosa*. Rome: Seam.

Sahlins, M. 2011a. 'What Kinship Is (Part One)', *Journal of the Royal Anthropological Institute* 17(1): 2–19.

———. 2011b. 'What Kinship Is (Part Two)', *Journal of the Royal Anthropological Institute* 17(2): 227–42.

Siegel, S. 2011. *The Contents of Visual Experience*. New York: Oxford University Press.

Strathern, M. 1984. 'Subject or Object? Women and the Circulation of Valuables in Highlands New Guinea', in R. Hirschon (ed.), *Women and Property, Women as Property*. London: Croom Helm, pp.158–75.

———. 1988. *The Gender of the Gift. Problems with Women and Problems with Society in Melanesia*. Berkeley: University of California Press.

Toren, C. 1999. *Mind, Materiality, and History: Explorations in Fijian Ethnography*. London: Routledge.

Toren, C., and J. Pina-Cabral. 2009. 'What's Happening to Epistemology?' *Social Analysis* 53(2): 1–18.

Westermarck, E. 1908. *The Origin and Development of Moral Ideas*. London: Macmillan.

Chapter Ten

Religion, Magic and Practical Reason

Meaning and Everyday Life
in Contemporary Ireland

Tom Inglis

Belief in a supernatural reality is not the same as the belief that the sun will rise in the morning. These two beliefs can, following Habermas (2004), be analytically conceptualized as belonging to different categories of knowledge that are directed by different interests. Knowledge of gods, saints, church teachings and so forth can be seen as belonging to the realm of religion and meaning; this knowledge emerges from an interest in bonding and belonging. The knowledge that the sun will rise belongs to the realm of science and technology, which emerges from an interest in mastering and controlling the environment. However, it is possible to identify another category of knowledge which falls between the realms of meaning and that of mastery and control. This knowledge involves ways of reading and interpreting signs and events. This knowledge emerges from an interest in trying to predict and control the uncertainties, vagaries, misfortunes, coincidences and inconsistencies of life: how and why it is that people suffer from good fortune or bad luck at different times? We can say that this knowledge and interest belongs to the realm of magic. People, then, develop a knowledge of magical beliefs, practices and objects, of charms, faith-healing practices, and of when, where and how to use them. Within Catholicism, the knowledge is of medals, relics, saints, prayers and devotional practices, and how they are employed to attain worldly ends.

However, conceptual analytical distinctions do not carry through to everyday life. In Catholic Ireland, the hard lines between scientific rationality, religion and magic are often blurred. But there is knowledge as to when, where, how and among whom this blurring can take place. In this chapter, using evidence from a qualitative study of the meaning of life in Ireland, I will show that people often resort to folk magic to manipulate and control their material circumstances. However, this folk magic sits easily beside, if not inside, their institutional Catholic life and their faith in scientific rationality (see Coma and Melhuus, this volume). There is, then, a logic to magical beliefs and practices. The task of the sociologist is to try discover and understand their logic for believers, and in doing so, as Bourdieu (2000) emphasized, not to confuse the logic of sociology, or the practice of logic, with the logic of practice, but rather to try to marry realist structural explanations with subjective meaning.

In this chapter, then, I explore the connections between religion, magic, science and everyday life. I begin by reviewing the contributions of Durkheim and Weber. I suggest that Durkheim was wrong to make a rigid distinction between religion and magic. As Collins points out, 'magic continues to exist within and alongside the world religions' (Collins 2008: 5). On the other hand, I argue that Weber was wrong to see magical thinking and practice gradually disappearing from religion and everyday life through increased rationalization. Magic is still endemic in everyday life in Western as much as non-Western societies. What is in doubt, however, is not so much the extent of magical thinking and practice, as to how much people believe in its efficacy. It may be better to see magical religion less as an attempt to master and control the material world, and more as part and parcel of creating and sustaining meaning. As Pina-Cabral (this volume) suggests, magical thinking is not superstitious or 'unfounded belief'; it is rather part and parcel of human beings sharing uncertainty, of believing in belief and that beliefs are polymorphous.

Durkheim and Weber

Durkheim recognized that religion and magic were similar, in that they both referred to a world where things were different from the ordinary, profane, material world (Durkheim 1976: 47). However, he was adamant that religion and magic were opposites. While there were some myths and dogmas in magic, these were elementary. Magic, he argued, is too oriented to utilitarian objectives to be concerned with developing a rationalized theology or belief system: magicians 'do not waste their time in pure speculation' (ibid.:

44). He agreed with Mauss that, 'magic is nothing more nor less than a crude industry based on incomplete science' (ibid.: 362). Thus, there is no church of magic, no systematized beliefs and practices that unite followers in a shared way of reading and understanding. There is no sustained collective consciousness. Indeed, magic 'takes a sort of professional pleasure in profaning holy things' (ibid.: 43).

Durkheim's differentiation between religion and magic is reflected in his different conceptions of priests and magicians. He sees the magician as a recluse, 'far from seeking society, he flees it' (ibid.: 45). He sees priests and churches as central to the religious field, and magicians as peripheral actors. A magician has a clientele rather than a church. Members of this clientele are often anonymous to each other, and visit the magician in the same way people visit their doctor or dentist.

The problem with this conceptualization is that it conflates magical thinking and action with magicians. There is more to magical thinking and action than magicians, in the same way that there is more to being religion than what is professed and propagated by priests, preachers and prophets. Yet Durkheim recognized that magic is 'always more or less general; it is very frequently diffused in large masses of the population' (ibid.: 45). He recognized that it is unlikely that 'there was ever a time when religion existed without magic', but, he argues, if there was, it was probably in the early formation of religion, 'when certain of its principles were extended to non-religious relations' (ibid.: 362).

Durkheim's differentiation does not help us understand contemporary religion. Many world religions are infused with magical thinking: supernatural forces can be invoked and manipulated to permeate and change the material world. When, where and how this occurs is defined, regulated and supervised by different churches, sects and groups. It is set out in institutional theologies and dogmas. Institutional religions struggle to maintain a monopoly on magical thinking. There is a constant danger that too much magical thinking could undermine what Collins (2008) refers to as the three forms of religion: membership of congregation, morality and mystical contact with the divine. The Catholic Church, like many other institutionalized religions, has to respond and accommodate to the magical interests, beliefs and practices of the laity. However, while it seeks to regulate and control magical beliefs and practices and to keep them within the institution, it does not succeed; there are too many other competing beliefs and practices propagated by disaffected members of the clergy and laity, folklorists, fortune tellers and faith healers.

Weber recognized that the elimination of magic was central to the creation of a rational, meaningful religious mood which, in turn, was the precursor to the creation of a systematic, rational way of life. As he noted:

> The intellectual seeks in various ways, the casuistry of which extends into infinity, to endow his life with pervasive meaning, and thus to find unity with himself, with his fellow men, and with the cosmos. It is the intellectual who conceives of the 'world' as a problem of meaning. As intellectualism suppresses belief in magic, the world's processes become disenchanted, lose their magical significance, and henceforth simply 'are' and 'happen' but no longer signify anything. As a consequence, there is a growing demand that the world and the total pattern of life be subject to an order that is significant and meaningful. (Weber 1978: 506)

However, Weber recognized that elements of magic still persist in many of the world's ethical salvationist religions, and that 'only ascetic Protestantism completely eliminated magic and the supernatural quest for salvation, of which the highest form was intellectualist, contemplative illumination'. He argued that magical elements were particularly prevalent in Catholicism, especially in what he referred to as its 'cult of masses and saints' (ibid.: 630, 518).

Weber tends to conflate magic with primitive attempts to attain charismatic leadership, and that when it becomes institutionalized, as sacraments in the Catholic Church, it only works for members who have 'become ethically purified in the sight of god' (ibid.: 241, 531). He pointed out that the Catholic belief in transubstantiation and Holy Communion, is magical: it is based on the belief that 'one may incorporate divine power into himself by the physical ingestion ... of some host that has been magically transformed into the body of a god' (ibid.: 559). He went on to argue that, because 'the Catholic priest continues to practice something of this magical power in executing the miracle of the mass', that Catholicism is different from Lutheranism and Judaism, in which there is a greater reliance on preaching. It is the reliance on magic that makes Catholicism closer to 'coercive religion' (making transformations take place), and the priest close to being a magician (ibid.: 422). Moreover, what reinforced the magical power of the priest was his ability to forgive sins in confession. This, for Weber, closely resembled people going to a magician or diviner when sickness or other blows of fate have led to the suspicion that some magical transgression is responsible, making it necessary to ascertain the means by which the aggrieved spirit, demon or god may be pacified (ibid.: 464). He recognized that, '[i]n practice, the viewpoint of the Catholic Church has oscillated between a relatively magical and a relatively ethical and soteriological orientation' (ibid.: 560). It may well be that Weber disparaged Catholicism because he saw it as condoning fleeing from this world through ecstasy. He saw ecstasy and orgy, or self-elimination through drugs, as a 'primordial form of religious association' (ibid.: 401). However, he never undertook a systematic description or analysis of how much magic is embedded in the teachings, discourse and habitus of the laity, and how it merges with religious and other interests.

But the permeation and impregnation of magical belief and practice in everyday life is not confined to Catholicism. Collins (2008: 6) argues that the most common forms of religion in East Asia are magical. Moreover, Chang (2007) has shown how business decision making among the Chinese is impregnated with supernatural beliefs and practices, many of which are magically oriented. What needs to be investigated, then, is the extent to which magical thinking still persists in everyday life in the West and, if so, where, when, in what ways and among whom. Is magical thinking confined to times of loss, suffering and tragedy when faith in rationality, science and technology is undermined? How does magical thinking manifest itself? Is it confined more to the private and personal? Is it more prevalent among the lower classes, particularly in rural areas, who seek compensation for their lack of worldly rewards (Stark and Bainbridge 1985, 1987)? And, most important of all, how do folk-traditional forms of magic operate with Church-sanctioned forms?

Stark (1968) argues that despite Weber's attempts at objectivity, when it came to the different attitudes to religion which he identified, he showed a preference for the creation of a systematic, methodical religious mood in which salvation was attained either through total immersion in the world (inner-worldly asceticism) or through total escape (as in the other-worldly mysticism of Buddhism). Weber, he argues, had less time for either inner-worldly mysticism – exemplified by mystics who remain in the world and perhaps use mystical behaviour as a means towards an earthly end (as in yoga) – or other-worldly asceticism, exemplified by early Christian monks (ibid.: 206–7). Whatever the accuracy of Stark's claim, Weber certainly wrote very little about Catholicism. It may well be that because he saw it as suffused with sacraments, a sacerdotal priesthood and magical-devotional practices, it inhibited rationality and reason.

When it comes to magical thinking, whether institutional or not, we can, following Weber's theory of action (Weber 1978: 64), develop a distinction between pure magical action and magically oriented action. With magical action people firmly believe that there is a formula, which if properly enacted, can cause material transformations in this life. This could involve ritual, prayer, sacraments, relics, holy water as well as charms, crystals, beads, stones and so forth. On the other hand, magically oriented action is when magical belief and practice is used not so much as a means to an end, but as a means for people to remind themselves about the arbitrariness and meaninglessness of life. Strange things do happen and, in the absence of a scientific rational explanation, people develop practical, reasonable explanations for their occurrence: they proclaim that 'it was pure magic' or 'it was a miracle'. In other words, magically oriented thinking, like emotions, can be seen as part of what Sayer calls practical reason (Sayer 2011: 61). For many people, magically oriented thinking becomes central to 'how we engage with the world, what we do and how we interact with others' (ibid.: 61). It may, Sayer argues, limit our understanding of the world, but it is not a barrier between us and the world. It is, rather, 'a fallible but invaluable resource for understanding and coping with it' (ibid.: 62). Practical reason is different from discursive reason. It does not have the same 'elevated social position of pure mental labour – the sheer luxury of unrestrained reflection' (ibid.: 63). It does not attempt to be detached from everyday material, social pressures. Rather it is embodied and intuitive, rooted in the practical necessity of making sense of the world, communicating with, and relating to others. In Weber's insistence that a systematic methodical religion was the basis for a systematic methodical way of life, he overlooked how magic serves as a release mechanism. Even for rational intellectuals, shared meaning can be easily threatened or undermined, particularly in times of illness, tragedy and death. It is in such times that people have recourse to religious and magical beliefs and practices.

Weber and Durkheim seem to have suffered from a malaise of modernity – the belief that an increase in scientific rational thought gradually reduces and eventually eliminates magical thinking. However, magical beliefs and practices can be central not just to producing feelings of trust, hope, comfort and consolation, but to creating and maintaining meaning. People may seek to be enlightened, they may commit to freeing themselves from ignorance and superstition, they may believe that they can be guided solely by the light of reason and experience, but they also seek to develop a shared understanding of the vagaries and arbitrariness of life (Becker 1932: 102). As Blume (this volume) argues, knowledge is 'multi-dimensional', and it includes different forms which 'are able to enrich, but not replace each other'. The reality is that, when it comes to human beings trying to explain the misfortunes, tragedies, coincidences and vagaries of life, they do not confine themselves to any one form of cultural knowledge. They use whatever is useful, whatever makes sense and brings meaning, solace and comfort.

The Permeation of Magical Thought

What needs to be done, then, is to identify, describe and analyse how magical beliefs and practices permeate religious action, and then, ask when, where, how and with whom both of these permeate rational scientific thought and action. The field of magico-religious thought has its own habitus, its own predispositions, its own ways of seeing and understanding the world, some of which are more oriented towards creating and sustaining meaning, and some towards trying to master and control the material world. The two realms can and do overlap. We can identify a realm of pure magical religious thought and action in which rational scientific ideas and practices are systematically eliminated. We can also identify a realm of pure rational scientific being in which magico-religious ideas and practices are systematically eliminated. However, in everyday life the two will often elide. What is then required is a mapping of when, where, how and among whom this elision takes place. Is this elision subject to a normative order? For example, people may firmly believe in medical science in terms of attempts to master and control illness. However, they may also believe in magico-religious interventions. The ways in which this elision takes place may be subject to a normative order which structures what is acceptable, when and where. In other words, there is a proper time and place for both magico-religious thinking and rational scientific thinking, and each should be in its proper time and place.

Within the field of Irish Catholicism, there have been regular struggles between what the institutional Church declares as bona fide interventions of God and the saints in this world, and what members of the laity claim to be interventions (Toibín 1985; Taylor 1995; Inglis 1998). The Church hierarchy in Rome investigates the miraculous interventions that are generally necessary for the titles 'Blessed' and 'Saint' to be bestowed. The struggle to maintain this monopoly of control often necessitates ignoring, dismissing or repudiating claims of miraculous interventions by members of the laity or disaffected members of the clergy or religious orders. Following Bourdieu (1990: 132–34), we can see this regulation and control by the institutional Church of the definition and means to being miraculous as a form of symbolic violence.

Magical devotional beliefs and practices have been central to Irish Catholicism (Turner and Turner 1978; Taylor 1995; Inglis 1998; Allen 2000; Salazar 2006). For generations, they have been – following Bourdieu and Wacquant's (1992: 127) conceptualization – part of the cultural air Catholics have breathed. Without these cultural beliefs and practices, they would have been like fish out of water. Magical devotional beliefs and practices were part of a habitus that was reaffirmed in everyday life in homes, schools and myriads of other spaces over which the Church presided. It was a world of regular petitions and requests to God, Jesus Christ, Our Lady and a whole host of different saints. There is a practical logic to the field of Catholic devotion. Some saints are known for special requests. Catholics know and understand why someone might pray to Saint Agatha if they had breast cancer, Saint Christopher if they were embarking on a journey, and Saint Joseph if they had lost something. Or, on the other hand, if they had become hopeless, lost in drink, grief or depression, they might pray to Saint Jude. Having grown up in a Catholic world, having been immersed from a young age in a field of God, Jesus and the saints, they are able to make fine distinctions between them, and know to whom they should turn when they have a particular need. It is a world with its own language, symbols, rituals and logic, full of devotional practices, novenas, pilgrimages and prayers, and of sacred objects such as relics, holy water and medals, of statues and holy pictures (Taylor 1995; Inglis 1998, 2003). As Sørensen (this volume) suggests – following Stark and Bainbridge (1987) – the Catholic world of magico-devotional religion delivers a different product to that of the world of rational, systematic theology: magic offers goods that provide more immediate, palpable effects; religion tends to offer more long-term, non-palpable effects such as salvation.

But how are we to analytically distinguish this Catholic world of magical devotional religion with the world of faith healing, fairies, cures, lucky charms, horoscopes and superstitions? There are many devoted Catholics in Ireland who believe that illnesses can be cured by the seventh son of a seventh son. There are others who believe that some people have been given special curative powers for ailments such as burns, ringworm, thrush and so forth. And there are others who believe it is a sign of impinging sorrow to see a single magpie. However, in the Catholic world of meaning, it would seem that there is a time and a place for Catholic magico-devotional religion, and a time and a place for non-Catholic magical beliefs and practices such as faith healing, fairies, superstitions, lucky charms and so forth. It is as if there is a non-material, spiritual world that can be entered into, and there are Catholic and non-Catholic ways of being in this world. Adept players have learnt that superstitions and lucky charms do not have a place in a Catholic space. In this sense, following Salazar (this volume), we can say that while both magic and religion have to do with violations of a natural reality or ordinary reality, what distinguishes them is the nature of the violations and when, how, where and by whom they occur. However, as in Brazil (Sansi-Roca, this volume), the history of the Catholic Church in Ireland can be seen as an attempt to develop a monopoly over when, where and how violations of ordinary reality occur and, as much as possible, to suppress popular cultural expressions and practices, making sure that the proper time and place for magic is only within the institution.

I will try to show how magical thinking is still endemic in Ireland. However, I will argue that, like religious belief and practice generally, it is becoming less public and more personal and private. Magical thinking manifests itself in three main ways: in superstitions and non-institutional forms of popular culture; in the form of devotional Catholicism, particularly in terms of religious experiences and seeking divine intervention through God and the saints; and in non-institutional forms such as faith-healing beliefs and practices.

This study provides a more in-depth ethnographic insight into findings from the International Social Survey Project (ISSP) in the Irish Republic in 2008. That survey of 2049 respondents revealed high levels of belief in God, of God's intervention in this world, and in miracles. The majority of the respondents said they believed in God (81 per cent) – 44 per cent indicated they had no doubts about his existence. Two-thirds said they believed that God concerns himself with human beings, and two-thirds said that they believed in miracles.

The number of respondents who believed in non-institutional forms of magic was smaller but still significant. Four in ten agreed that it was probably true that good luck charms do bring good luck, but only 8 per cent said that it was definitely true. There was a similar pattern with regard to fortune telling: four in ten agreed that it was probably true that fortune tellers can see the future, but only 7 per cent said it was definitely true. The study also explored the relation between religion and magic: six in ten of respondents agreed that it was probably true that faith healers have God-given healing powers.

The Study

The study was carried out in five different areas around Ireland, with twenty respondents interviewed in each area. The aim was to interview a cross section of people in each location with as large a range as possible of males and females, young, middle aged and elderly, and the different social classes representative of Irish society. I also sought out respondents who were migrants, non-Catholics, members of the travelling community and so forth. I relied on a gatekeeper in each area to introduce me to respondents. Although I knew the gatekeepers, I did not know any of the respondents. While I was successful in getting a good cross-section of respondents, there were some biases as a result of the gatekeeper and the areas chosen. Nevertheless, there was a good distribution across gender, age and social class. In what follows, all place names and personal names are pseudonyms.

Mayfarm is a well-established working-class area of Dublin; respondents were recruited through a local community activist. Falderry is a middle-class area of Dublin, and here I conducted most of my interviews with students, lecturers and administrators in tertiary education. Hillbrook is a midland town; my gatekeeper here lived on the outskirts of the town and is involved in women's groups. Castlebay is a rural area in the west of Ireland; here my gatekeeper was an artist. Finally, Greyrock is a village in the east of Ireland which has grown rapidly in recent years due to its proximity (forty miles) from Dublin; my gatekeeper here was the principal of a local primary school.

I conducted all the interviews myself, most of them in people's homes, but many in other locations. They were semi-structured and centred on discovering what was important and meaningful in people's lives. The first set of questions revolved around getting respondents to talk about themselves, where they had grown up, their family of origin, and the main events in their lives. The second set of questions focused on what was important to them, what gave them pleasure and satisfaction, work and leisure, the stresses and strains of everyday life, any disappointments and losses they had encountered and what they understood as a good life. Towards the end of the interview, respondents were asked about their religious beliefs and practices.

Magical Objects and Practices

Very few participants firmly believed in magical practices, charms, fortune tellers or horoscopes. Some, like Linda Grey, said they found it difficult not to believe in some magical practices. She is not religious in any traditional sense: she believes that God is a force of energy. But she has had a couple of experiences with fortune tellers who have told her things about people and events that were 'frightening', 'ridiculously dead on', 'things that I have done in my life that nobody knows and would have no way of knowing it'.

Like religion and other forms of culture, people are socialized into magical thinking, belief and practice. Most of those who said they engaged in magical practices, such as reading their horoscope or using magical objects such as charms or crystal balls, were critically reflective about their participating in the illusion of the field of magic and embodying a magical habitus (Bourdieu and Wacquant 1992: 98, 116). Hilary Maher is a 44-year-old Canadian who married and Irishman and lives with him and their three children. 'I have a book of horoscopes that I read every night before I go to bed ... and

I have these balls in my window that are supposed to attract evil spirits ... but I don't take any of it too seriously'. Danielle Burton echoed this. She says she used to be much more superstitious. However, even though she does not believe in them, there are times when she gets the newspaper that 'the first page I'd probably be reading when things aren't good ... is a horoscope, and an awful lot of stuff like that'. However, like Hilary Maher, she sees through it: 'I know it's all kind of hairy fairy'.

Some participants took a practical attitude and mentioned not walking under a ladder, and thought that breaking a mirror or seeing an injured bird was a sign of bad luck. Jim O'Brien said he does not really believe in fairies. But he said, 'I certainly wouldn't do anything to annoy them [laughs]'. And when it comes a lone hawthorn tree in the middle of a field: 'I certainly wouldn't pull one of those or break it or do anything like that with it'.

Some superstitious beliefs seem to take hold more than others. Seven participants mentioned their concerns when they saw a lone magpie. The folk belief is that seeing one magpie is a sign for sorrow, two is for joy, three for a girl, four for a boy. This system goes up to ten, but most people only know of the first four signs. Like two other participants, Angela Doyle knew that if she saw just one magpie, the trick was to salute or greet it, as this would cancel any bad luck it might bring.

The most common form of magical belief and practice was in faith healing and cures. There were sixteen participants who believed that there was a variety of illnesses – including whooping cough, eczema, colic, ring worm, thrush, warts and burns – which could be successfully treated by faith healers or people who 'had the cure'. There were a number of different treatments, including spitting, burying coins or beads and licking the stomach of a mankeeper (a small lizard). Danny O'Brien lives in the west of Ireland in Castlebay. He told me that he had the ability to cure burns, and that he got it from a mandkeeper (a small Irish lizard). He told me: 'They're very small ... You find them on the mountain ... And eh, if you catch one and you lick its stomach you get the cure of the burn ... apparently ... My father caught one one time, when I was young I licked its belly. But if I got a burn now on the hand and I licked it ... I don't know if it's my own mind or if it's actually true, but it wouldn't be sore after'.

Among the hundred participants in this study, twenty-five believed in miracles. This varied from a firm belief for some, to a vague and fragile belief for others. There were a few people like Bernie Young who had personal experience of a miracle. Bernie had scoliosis as a child. Her mother had to take her to the hospital every week for a check-up. Then her mother took her to Knock, the biggest pilgrimage site in Ireland: 'I got the blessing of the sick and then when I went back to the hospital ... for another check-up. They couldn't find anything. They said ... it was like I never had it'.

Fergal Heuston is a dedicated Catholic. He goes regularly on retreats and pilgrimages. Once, he went to Lough Derg, a penitential pilgrimage site. A relation of his wife had just given birth to twins who were blind. 'I really, really prayed strong to heaven for them, and it turned out it was very, very severe glaucoma ... I believe that that was a miracle'. However, sometimes participants talked about miracles more in terms of a vague sense of good luck. Stephen Young drives everywhere as part of his job. He believes in miracles and thinks it is a miracle that he has not been in a car accident. 'Now I have a little Mary. I have had four vans in the time I've been driving and she comes with me in every van, and she's been with me and I think, yeah, but she's been protecting me on the road, and I think then sometimes it might be a miracle'. However, most participants who believed in miracles had not witnessed or experienced a miracle themselves.

It would seem that for many of the people I interviewed, there was no strong demarcating line between the realm of institutional religion and the world of cures and faith healing. It is not that they elide, but rather that they have their own time and place. Brian Doheny is a Catholic priest. When I asked him if he believed in magic, charms or horoscopes, he said, 'I don't feel very strongly about them one way or another'. However, he said he did believe in cures and faith healing: 'I have experienced that ... Some of them really work, so then you've got to have faith in some of them'. When I asked him how they worked, he said: 'I just don't know. I believe that it's some qualities or gifts or herbal remedies that are passed on down through generations and some of them [work] incredibly ... '. When I asked him if it was related to God, he said, 'whether it's God or Jesus, I don't know'. As Sørensen (this volume) points out, in popular religious culture, in which there is no attempt to develop a systemic, rational, coherent theology, it is quite easy for contradictory beliefs about reincarnation and faith healing to sit side by side with Catholic beliefs about God, heaven and hell and salvation.

A Catholic World of Fine Difference

Sarah Gilsenan came across as a devoted Catholic. She is sixty-eight years old and lives in the inner suburbs of Dublin in the same apartment in which she lived with her parents. She never married. She worked for most of her life in a factory and lived with her mother who died seven years ago. She was very devoted to her mother, who also was a devout Catholic. In her apartment, she has pictures and statues of her favourite saints and others including the Holy Face, the Child of Prague and Our Lady of Fatima. She talks to God every day. She feels his presence. For her, talking to God is mainly saying traditional Catholic prayers, every morning and night. But there are others, guardian angels and saints, to whom she prays as well. 'I say my prayers every morning. I say them every night. If I have any problem or if I'm in the car I'll ask my guardian angel to get me parking, things like that'. When she prays, it is usually to one of her three favourite saints: the Mother of Good Counsel, Padre Pio or Francis Xavier.

Sarah became devoted to Padre Pio through a woman at work. 'He was alive at the time and she used to write to the convent [where Padre Pio lived] and it was her who told us'. Her devotion to the Mother of Good Counsel was simply because it was the name of the local parish church. The devotion to Saint Francis came about because 'we always did the novena of grace, always, all my friends and myself ... That was a big thing, every March'. Again, when she refers to 'the' novena, she assumes that people will know that she is referring to the nine-day solemn novena. The lack of immediate recognition is a reflection of how attendance at novenas has changed. 'It's not the same. Like years ago you wouldn't even get into the church ... They'd be out in the car park and in the school'. Sarah grew up in a world of churches, masses, saints and novenas. In those days, priests were celebrities. Sarah lives out her life in a web of meaning that was developed in and through her mother, but sustained by a myriad of Catholic friends and fellow workers who populated her everyday life. The world of saints and their differences creates a shared understanding and way of adapting to the mysteries, miseries and misfortunes of life.

Sarah's mother was very religious: she was devoted to Saint Rita, the patron saint of the impossible. Sarah, then, grew up in a world of fine Catholic differences in which people adopted different saints. It was mostly her mother who had all the medals, statues and holy pictures. Sarah inherited them. They have become part of Sarah's habitus, an unquestioned orthodoxy. When I asked her if they gave her a sense of peace and calm, she said: 'I inherited a lot of them I suppose, and then you feel guilty if you throw them out. ... You would just find it hard ... when they're religious pictures to just discard them'. The prayers she says, the statues and pictures, are all part of her everyday religious life. 'I don't know how people survive without their faith, cos I couldn't'.

Evelyn Hutchinson is in her early fifties. She was adamant that she did not believe in 'God and Jesus and all this stuff'. But she was brought up a Catholic and she likes the idea of miracles. 'Like I do get little miracles. When I was with my dad and we'd be going into town, and I'd say "Now Dad, pray for a miracle", and he'd say "What miracle is this?" And I'd say

"A parking space outside the bookshop"'. These prayers for little miracles can be seen as an attempt to give meaning to life chances and coincidences, to the arbitrariness of events, to the inability to predict, master and control what happens in everyday life. What Evelyn's description reveals is how she embraced, perhaps as part of her role as a caring daughter, the same habitus, way of thinking and talking as her father. It helped create and sustain a sense of bonding and belonging. But, as Bourdieu (2000: 11–12) suggests, following Pascal, the more Evelyn talked like this the more she believed. She may not have the same degree of conviction as her father, but in talking and invoking the same spirits, she created meaning and a sense of belonging with him. She obviously did this quite often. Often enough that she says she believes in little miracles. She was sharing feelings about the arbitrariness of life with her father, and in doing so made the world sensible and created meaning. It is not a question of whether she believes it or not. It is a question of whether she engaged in this magical thinking with other people, or was it something special between herself and her father? And, now that he is dead, believing in little miracles is a way of remembering him.

Mixing and Matching

There are, then, Catholic and non-Catholic forms of magical belief and practice. The question is if they interact and, if they do, when, where and how this occurs. More importantly perhaps is how they interact with rational scientific knowledge and practice. We can get some insight into this from George Flynn. George is a practical man. He works a small family farm in Castlebay and, at the same time, runs a small motor repair company. He takes delight in taking on challenges, in fixing things that people think cannot be fixed. He takes pleasure in doing a good job. He is what would traditionally have been called 'a good Catholic'. He has been on pilgrimages to Lourdes and Medjugorje with his wife, who is a devout Catholic. He has had a vision of Our Lady: 'And I'm positive, certain, sure I had a vision one night up in the local grotto. A good few of us had the same vision, so we all couldn't have seen the one thing wrong'. Some years previously, he had an operation on his appendix that did not work. He was certain he was going to die. His lungs had collapsed, his whole body had swelled up. They could not control his bleeding. His body was unable to heat the blood that he was being given. His family was told that he did not have much time. He tells the story:

And then my cousin came in to say goodbye to me, and he asked me why they couldn't cure me in the hospital. And I said I was bleeding, and they couldn't stop it ... And he said there was no problem there ... I was in intensive care at the time ... He said, 'Sure John Adams in the north, he's able to stop any blood', he says. He went on with rigmarole ... some cow cut her jugular and John Adams cured it ... So he rang John Adams and [his cousin told him] he was going to do the cure at six [o'clock] ... The Angelus bell rang, and that was six o'clock, and so I blessed myself and I happened to release wind, and it was the first wind I had released ... I think I was nine weeks in intensive care at that stage ... It was the first wind I released.

George was convinced that it was the intervention of John Adams that saved him. When I asked him if Adams was the seventh son of a seventh son, he said he did not know as he had never met him. 'But I do owe my life to him', he said. He was not sure of the provenance of the cure but, when I asked him if he thought it was Christian, he said: 'I'm sure it was. I wouldn't have it done if I thought it wasn't Christian'.

It would seem, then, that instead of being rationally differentiated from each other, magic, religion and medical science are easily enmeshed in the everyday life of George Flynn. He insists that it was not his prayers nor Our Lady, but the faith healer John Adams that cured him. However, what we do not know is to what extent George Flynn would have accepted being in a hospital in which doctors, nurses and surgeons engaged in faith healing and magical beliefs and practices. It may be that George Flynn tells this story as part of his role in creating and maintaining myths which he sees as central to understanding life, as an attempt to bring some meaning to the arbitrariness of life chances, and to building and cementing the bonds that bind his family and friends together. Belief in faith healing is embodied belief embedded in social relations, not in abstract general thinking (see Coleman, this volume). Consequently, if we accept the distinction between maturational thought which belongs to the realm of magic and religion, and the 'unnatural cognition' of science (McCauley, this volume), the task, following Coma's (this volume) description of the way Charismatic Catholics integrate religion into science, is to investigate when, where and how they become conflated, particularly within the highly defined, well-marshalled fields of science.

Conclusion

When the people I interviewed talked of saints, cures, faith healers and divine interventions, it was within the shared context of the mystery and meaning of life, and how they witnessed being part of some miraculous or magical event. The reason why magical beliefs and practices have declined is because, compared to science, it is difficult to make verifiable, reliable statements about cause and effect. People can believe that a transformation was caused by God's intervention, faith healing or the manipulation of spirits, but it is very difficult to prove it. Secondly, the acceptance of saying that a miracle and magical transformation happened depends on people living within a community (which can extend to wider society) who believe in miracles and magical transformations. People have as much interest in creating and sustaining communication and meaning as they do in mastering and controlling their environment and social relations. They are happy to believe in God, magic and the power of faith healing, and to believe in the scientifically verifiable proposition that the sun will rise in the morning (Ruel 2002; Pina-Cabral, this volume).The problem is that these two interests are often incompatible. The rationalization of the life-world has led to a greater expectation that when people speak that they do so sincerely (and not to deceive), that it is within a shared context of meaning, and that what they say is verifiable (Habermas 1984: 307).

There are two related problems. It may be, for whatever reason, that belief in miracles and magical transformations becomes central to the way in which people communicate and make meaning. If this happens, then empirical verification of miracles and magical transformation becomes less of an issue. If it is taken to an extreme – and religious and magical belief penetrates not just the religious field but other social fields – then the validity of scientific statements may be challenged. However, it seems from the way that the participants in this study spoke that not only do scientific rational thought and magical thought peacefully coexist, but there is a recognition that there is a time and place for both. In considering the relation between religious and rational scientific thought, it would be wrong to think that they are immiscible and that, with modernity and rationalization, religion and magic will eventually be replaced by science. But given that the meaning of life will never be resolved, and that religion revolves around creating and sustaining shared meaning, there will always be ideas, concepts, beliefs and practices that create and maintain an explanation for life chances and, in doing so, provide participants with comfort and consolation. In Ireland, people have grown up in webs of meaning that have been spun over generations. For most Irish people, for most of modernity, the religious was predominantly Catholic but interwoven with beliefs about fairies, spirits and magical cures.

The question is to what extent magical thinking and practice is interwoven not just with religion but with other aspects of social life, particularly those that have become highly rationalized and scientific. While there were regular references to beliefs in miraculous events and divine interventions among the people I interviewed, there was never any sense that they were the dominant way of thinking and acting, or that such thinking played a significant role in people's lives. There was no evidence that everyday life revolved around the constant hope and expectation of magical transformations. It is as if magical thinking is a parallel realm of thought that can and does become interwoven with people's greater reliance and dependence on science and technology, but this interweaving does not take place in any regulated way.

People may pray for a miraculous recovery from an illness, but they do not pray for a leg to reappear after it has been amputated. People may pray to God to help them find a parking space, or for their car to start, but they do not pray that the shattered windscreen will be made whole. In this sense, Weber was correct: the possibility of leading a systematic, predictable, methodical and, more importantly, an ethical religious life becomes difficult if someone constantly resorts to magical beliefs and practices (Kalberg 1990: 60). So, following Weber, we can see that the history of Irish society, like the history of the West, has involved the rationalization of religious belief, the demise of a world of spirits and demons, of good and dark supernatural forces and, as a consequence, an increasing disenchantment of everyday life.

But, again, we can see that the Catholic Church, responding to the interests of the laity, and balancing the need to develop a rational, consistent religious mood through its theology and, at the same time, trying to provide comfort and consolation for its members, operates within parallel realms of thought, between rationalized teaching and beliefs and practices based on magical thought and practice. The sacraments, which involve magical transformations, are a core element of Catholic teaching. However, there is a proper time and place for sacraments, and magical belief and practice, and the Church is rational and methodical in policing these. Similarly, in everyday life, people are supervised and controlled in relation to how much they invoke and rely on superstitions and non-Catholic forms of magic. Following Weber (1978: 415–16), we can say, then, that it is not a question of magical thinking being eliminated, but rather that for each individual, as well as the Church, there are impetuses to engage in magical beliefs and practices. As much as in the Church itself, there are outbreaks of magical thinking in people's everyday lives, but this does not mean that their overall rational methodical life is undermined. It may well be that magical thinking functions as an important escape valve when faith in rational religious and scientific thinking has been weakened and found not to be fulfilling, rewarding or meaningful. It may well be that people who engage in magical practices do not believe in their efficacy, validity and reliability in the same way that they belief in gravity, but they are enacted as part of maintaining shared meaning and communication. Faced with potential breakdown in the plausibility of religion or science, magical thinking does not threaten these realms of knowledge, but by revealing their inadequacy in explaining chaos, tragedy, illness, loss and death, it provides an important form of bonding and belonging.

The language and practices of those who believe in Catholic saints, miracles and divine interventions, and those who believe in faith healing and the power of the cure, can be seen as lingering legacies of traditional Ireland which, with progressive rationalization, will slowly fade away. But the legacies of myth and meaning-making are embedded in the present. It is difficult to imagine a society in which meaning is based solely on rational causation and statements that can be validly and reliably tested. And while we may strive to live in an enlightened world based on rational communication, we also have to realize that there are many forms of thinking and practice in everyday life that have a different reason and logic.

References

Allen, M. 2000. 'From Ecstasy to Power: Marian Apparitions in Contemporary Irish Catholicism', *Anthropological Journal on European Cultures* 9(1): 11–35.

Becker, C. 1932. *The Heavenly City of the Eighteenth-century Philosophers*. New Haven: Yale University Press.

Bourdieu, P. 1990. *The Logic of Practice*. Cambridge: Polity Press.

———. 2000. *Pascalian Meditations*. Cambridge: Polity Press.

Bourdieu, P., and L. Wacquant. 1992. 'The Purpose of Reflexive Sociology (The Chicago Workshop)', in P. Bourdieu and L. Wacquant, *An Invitation to Reflexive Sociology*, Oxford: Polity Press, pp.98–140.

Chang, W.L. 2007. 'A Preliminary Exploration of the Impact of Supernatural Beliefs in Chinese Business Decision-making', *Hong Kong Journal of Social Science* 33: 1–40.

Collins, R. 2008. 'The Four Ms of Religion: Magic, Membership, Morality and Mysticism', *Review of Religious Research* 50(1): 5–15.

Durkheim, E. 1976 [1915]. *The Elementary Forms of the Religious Life*. London: Allen and Unwin.

Habermas, J. 1984. *The Theory of Communicative Action*, vol. 1: *Reason and the Rationalization of Society*. Boston: Beacon Press.

———. 2004. *Knowledge and Human Interests*. Cambridge: Polity Press.

Inglis, T. 1998. *Moral Monopoly: The Rise and Fall of the Catholic Church in Modern Ireland*. Dublin: University College Dublin Press.

——. 2003. 'Catholic Church, Religious Capital and Symbolic Domination', in M. Böss and E. Maher (eds), *Engaging Modernity: Readings of Irish Politics, Culture and Literature at the Turn of the Century*. Dublin: Veritas, pp.43–70.

Kalberg, S. 1990. 'The Rationalization of Action in Max Weber's Sociology of Religion', *Sociological Theory* 8(1): 56–84.

Ruel, M. 2002. 'Christians as Believers', in M. Lambek (ed.), *A Reader in the Anthropology of Religion*. Oxford: Blackwell, pp.99–113.

Salazar, C. 2006. *Anthropology and Sexual Morality: A Theoretical Investigation*. New York: Berghahn.

Sayer, A. 2011. *Why Things Matter to People: Social Sciences, Values and Ethical Life*. Cambridge: Cambridge University Press.

Stark, W. 1968. 'The Place of Catholicism in Max Weber's Sociology of Religion', *Sociological Analysis* 29(4): 202–10.

Stark, R., and W.S. Bainbridge 1985. *The Future of Religion*. Berkeley: University of California Press.

——. 1987. *A Theory of Religion*. New York: Peter Lang.

Taylor, L. 1995. *Occasions of Faith: An Anthropology of Irish Catholics*. Dublin: Lilliput Press.

Toibín, C. 1985. *Seeing is Believing: Moving Statues in Ireland*. Mountrath: Pilgrim Press.

Turner, V., and E. Turner. 1978. *Image and Place in Christian Culture: Anthropological Perspectives*. Oxford: Blackwell.

Weber, M. 1978. *Economy and Society*. Berkeley: University of California Press.

Chapter Eleven

Can the Dead Suffer Trauma?

Religion and Science after the Vietnam War

Heonik Kwon

ॐॐ

Interest in how modern warfare can cause destructive effects on the human mind and soul, as well as the human body, have long been part of modern anthropology. Above all, the work of W.H.R. Rivers comes to mind. Rivers was a pioneer of comparative method in kinship studies but, during the First World War, he also worked at the Craiglockhart War Hospital for Officers near Edinburgh as a psychopathologist. His encounter with the renowned poet Siegfried Sassoon at the hospital is widely known thanks to Pat Barker's gripping novels, the *Regeneration* trilogy. It was partly through Rivers's clinical engagement with Sassoon and other British officers who were troubled by their experiences of trench warfare that the idea of shell shock later became widely recognized and accepted. Rivers considered shell shock as a real illness, and believed that the driving force behind this war neurosis was the instinct of self-preservation, thus departing considerably from the then prevalent theory of neurosis that emphasized early sexual experience and sexual instincts (see Young 1993).

The history of the Vietnam War also looms large in the history of war neurosis. According to Allan Young (1995), it was after the Vietnam War that the phenomenon we now call post-traumatic stress disorder (PTSD) came to occupy a firm place in social knowledge and institutional practice, first in the United States and later much more broadly. Initially, according to Young (ibid.: 113), conditions referred to as PTSD were identified primarily with the lives of American veterans of the Vietnam War, whose combat experience in a foreign war was presumed to constitute the etiological event for post-traumatic symptoms after the war. Indeed, American accounts of the Vietnam War abound with stories of painful personal wounds – wounds that continued to trouble the bodies and souls of those who experienced the brutal and protracted war long after it was over. This is evidently the case in the memoirs written by former US veterans of the Vietnam War in fictional or biographical form. In Philip Caputo's autobiographical account, *The Rumour of War*, the veteran is haunted by the deaths of his fellow soldiers and his Vietnamese acquaintances (Caputo 1977). Some of these accounts show that the Vietnam War left deep scars not only in individual bodies but also in the collective body – thus, the idea of the Vietnam syndrome that refers to the Vietnam War's enduring, haunting effects on the American collective consciousness and its body politic.

The Vietnam War was a turbulent and agonizing experience for many in the United States, but it was surely a much more destructive and violent event for people in Vietnam. In Vietnam, however, there was no rise of what Allan Young (1995) calls psychiatric culture and technology after the devastating war. On the contrary, the political authority of the newly unified Vietnam made enormous administrative and political efforts to shield the society from dwelling on war-induced personal and communal wounds. Since the beginning of the 1990s, by contrast, there has been a sudden eruption of powerful communal interest in these long-held wounds of war across the country, and this involved the recognition that the violence of war can cause enduring wounds to the human soul. Interestingly, the wounds of war revealed in this process typically, although not exclusively, concerned the suffering that is believed to be endured by the dead rather than troubles that continue to haunt the survivors of the war.

This chapter explores the particular idea of war wounds revealed in this recent development, and how to situate this idea in proper historical and cultural context. I will then expand the discussion and ask whether it is possible to explain the two separate ways that war-generated wounds to human beings are to be found in postwar Vietnamese and American societies.

Revolutionary Optimism

Postwar Vietnamese society was strongly mobilized to focus its attention on the forward-looking revolutionary vision for a prosperous political community and a collective optimism based on 'revolutionary sentiment' and 'love of labour'. Crucial to this process was the empowerment of a heroic memory of war and a related civic morality of commemoration. This process materialized in the form of numerous cemeteries of revolutionary war martyrs and memorials dedicated to their memory, erected in the immediate postwar years at the centre of the communal public spaces throughout the central and southern regions of Vietnam.

This postwar revolutionary optimism is concretized in public war memorials. Many of these adopt the form known as 'bird' to Vietnamese memorial artists, consisting of a pointed neo-Gothic tower and two wings unfolding from the lower level of the tower. A traditional incense burner and an altar are typically placed between the two wings and in front of the tower, on the surface of which is inscribed the classical dictum of official Vietnamese commemorative war art, 'Your ancestral land remembers your merit'. In one typical example, found in the hamlet Thuy Bo, Quang Nam province, a sculpture above the inscription shows a family of three, including a man in uniform holding the flag of Vietnam. A small boy stands beside the man, also holding the flagpole, and, behind him, a woman rests her arm on the boy's shoulder while holding a gun with another arm. The self-sacrifice of this revolutionary nuclear family constitutes the radical symbolic transition between the imagery depicted by the two lower wings. The wing on the left paints a historical picture of the wartime village, mixing elements of village history with those of national history, showing soldiers in combat gear as well as a legendary local war heroine who is known to have stood against advancing enemy tanks. Moving to the opposite wing, the landscape changes radically, now depicting a peaceful, prosperous view of postwar village life. Children walk to school, women become schoolteachers and mothers, men sit on tractors, and they are surrounded by lush forest and expansive farmland. These installations solidify the memory of heroic death as the threshold through which the violent past of war transforms into the prosperous communal life of the future. The villagers' self-sacrifice for the ancestral land enables this transformation. The nuclear family at the top of the Thuy Bo memorial signifies the transformation of the military command, 'All Forward!', into a forward movement in economic development; this motif of regeneration is dominant in Vietnamese monumental art.

The state-instituted centrality of the heroic memory of war in postwar Vietnamese society has also changed domestic space. The political campaigns focused on substituting the commemoration of heroic war dead for the traditional cult of ancestors, first in the north after independence in 1945, and then in the southern and central regions after the unification of the country in 1975. The memorabilia of war martyrs and revolutionary leaders have replaced ancestral tablets in the domestic space; the communal ancestral temples and other religious sites were closed down, and these gave way to the people's assembly hall. In the latter, ordinary citizens and their administrative leaders discussed community affairs and production quotas surrounded by the vestiges of the revolutionary war in a structurally similar way to how peasants and village notables earlier talked about rents and the ritual calendar in the village's communal house surrounded by the relics of the village's founding ancestors.

Changes in the 1990s

Recent accounts from prominent Vietnamese writers show how this construction of heroic national memory contributed to excluding and stigmatizing the wounds and expressions of pain from the postwar era, not only in the public realm, but also in the intimate spheres of communal life. The stories told by such celebrated writers as Bao Ninh, Duong Thu Huong and Le Minh Hue commonly take issue with the inability to express publicly the grief about the destructive past and the losses incurred in postwar Vietnamese society – without the right to be sad, as one observer says (Templer 1998: 3). They all make a break with the conventional, official narrative of war based on the paradigm of the heroic revolutionary struggle of a unified nation against the intervention of a foreign power. The protagonist in Bao Ninh's *The Sorrow of War* (1993), a survivor of a battle that killed all of his close comrades, finds it impossible to readjust to life after the war is over. He finds it hard 'to remember a time when his whole personality and character had been intact, a time before the cruelty and the destruction of war had warped his soul'. He is haunted by the memories of the dead and the death he was responsible for, and his own solace is to recover in writing the lost and the killed, known or unknown. Bao Ninh's novel was published in Hanoi in 1991 and banned immediately after release, although the act of censorship made his work even more popular in Vietnam and beyond. The works by the two other writers mentioned above all appeared in the early 1990s and experienced a similar fate to *The Sorrow of War*. Their appearance represented the momentous change that engulfed Vietnamese society at the time.

In the early 1990s, while rumours concerning the above writers circulated in towns, Vietnamese rural communities also began to forcefully assert their liberty to express and attend to their war-induced wounds, although in different ways and using different means of expression. Their acts involved, most prominently, the revival of traditional commemorative rituals and the related change in death commemoration from a conventional postwar practice focused exclusively on the category of heroic sacrifice, to a more inclusive practice that is open to other diverse casualties of war. In the material culture of commemoration, the change was manifested in the form of rebuilding new domestic ancestral shrines, family ancestral temples and community ancestral halls, all of which mushroomed across Vietnam throughout the 1990s. In many areas, particularly in the central region of the country, this development, referred to as 'commemorative fever' by some observers (Tai 2001: 1), included revival of rituals on the categorically opposite side of ancestor worship in Vietnamese religious tradition, which is the milieu of the spirits of the dead unrelated to the commemorator in ties of kinship. As a result of this development, the structure of contemporary Vietnamese domestic commemorative ritual, in Quang Nam and Quang Ngai provinces where I studied the local history of war in the second half of the 1990s, situates the ritual actor in between two separate modes of after-life and milieus of memory. On the one hand lies the household ancestral shrine, or the equivalent in the community ancestral temple, which keeps the vestiges of family ancestors and household deities. The other side is ori-ented towards what Michael Taussig calls 'the open space of death', which is the imagined life-world of the tragic, non-ancestral, unsettled and unre-lated spirits of the dead (Taussig 1987: 7). The ritual tradition in the central region represents this open space of death in the form of a small external shrine, popularly called *khom* in Quang Ngai and Quang Nam provinces, which is usually placed at the boundary between the domestic garden and the street. Within this dual concentric spatial organization, the typical ritual action in this region engages with both the interior and exterior milieus of memory through a simple movement of the body. The most habitual act of commemoration consists of kowtowing and offering incense to the ancestors of the house, and turning the body in the opposite direction to repeat the action towards the street-wandering ghosts. This two-directional act may be accompanied by a single beat of a gong followed by three or four beats of a drum.

The Grievous Dead

The communal development described above arises in central Vietnam against the enduring wounds of war felt in communal lives as well as against the background of the postwar politics of memory, mentioned earlier, fo-cused on the heritage of heroic war deaths. These persisting wounds are forcefully expressed in stories of the apparition of grievous ghosts of war popular in rural Vietnam. In the part of Quang Ngai province that the in-ternational community came to know as My Lai during the Vietnam War, after a tragic mass killing of civilians in March 1968, the residents told me many stories of the spirits of the dead in pain. Some of them vividly recalled the lamentations of ghosts in the villages, cries which they had heard coming from the killing sites. Residents in one particular settlement claimed that they had seen the ghosts of old women sucking the arms and legs of the ghosts of small children; they interpreted this as an effort by the elderly victims to ease the wounded children's pain. Some people in another settlement graphically described the ghosts of young women, each walking with a small child in their arms and lamenting the child's lifeless body. These ghosts were grieving, the villagers explained, for their dead children. One family living along the dirt road that leads to the seashore claimed that they had seen a group of ghosts of children trailing faithfully behind a group of ghosts of young mothers. According to this family, this happened a night or two before the massacre's anniversary. On this occasion, they could hear the ghosts conversing jovially among themselves.

According to the old village undertaker I often spoke with, the village's 'invisible neighbours', as he often referred to these ghosts, would lament their own physical pain or feel pain when their loved ones suffered pain; they might have grievous feelings about their own tragic, unjust death or cry over their children's deaths as if they, themselves, were not yet dead. Their moods and sentiments, and even their form, fluctuated with the circumstances. The child ghosts appeared dead in their grieving mother's arms on a moonless night during a rainy season; these same children could be seen playfully running after their mothers on a pleasant evening before the day of the massacre's anniversary. It appeared to me that My Lai's ghosts led lives with their own ups and downs, and that the fluctuations in their lives were intertwined with the rhythms of life among their neighbours.

The My Lai villagers regularly held modest rituals at home and outside them on behalf of their 'invisible neighbours' – offering them incense, food and sometimes votive money notes to the *khom*, the sites of apparitions or elsewhere – and they explained the condition of these invisible neighbours' lives with the concept of 'grievous death' or 'unjust death' (*chet oan*). The concept entails that the agony of a violent, unjust death and the memory of its terror entrap the soul in negative conditions of afterlife. The human soul in this condition of post-mortem incarceration does not remember the terror as we, the living, normally would; rather, they are believed to relive the violent event, perpetually re-experiencing the agony of violent death. The memory of death for the tragically dead, in other words, is a living memory in its most brutal sense.

The idea that the dead can feel physical pain has a long history in Vietnamese mortuary and religious tradition, and it relates to the notion that the human soul is a duplex entity. It has the spiritual part, *hon*, as well as the bodily, material part of *via* – a model which may be considered in the light of spiritus and its opposite, *anima*, in the European philosophical tradition. The material soul senses and feels, whereas the spiritual soul thinks and imagines. In a 'good' death (which Vietnamese call *chet nha*, meaning 'death at home', as opposed to *chet duong*, 'death in the street'), occurring at home under peaceful circumstances, surrounded by loved ones, after enjoying longevity, the material soul eventually perishes together with the decomposing body. Only the spiritual soul survives a good death (although in case the deceased's body is buried in an inappropriate place for entombment, this material soul is reawakened and may feel the discomfort and pain of improper burial). It is believed that the ritually appropriated pure spirit travels across the imaginary threshold between the world of the living (*duong*) and the world of the dead (*am*) to eventually join the pure domain of ancestor worship. The soul of one who experiences a bad death (that is, violent death away from home, *chet duong*), however, remains largely intact and keeps its pre-death dual formation because of the absence of ritual separation. The material soul is believed to linger near the place of death and the place where its decomposing body is buried. It feels the discomfort of improper burial and awakens the spiritual soul to the embodied memory of the violent death. The material soul's bodily pain and the spiritual soul's painful memory communicate with one another, and this communication between the two kinds of soul can generate the perilous condition, mentioned above, that the Vietnamese call *chet oan*, or 'grievous death'. The mass deaths such as those suffered at My Lai, although they took place 'at home' and therefore may not be strictly speaking classed as 'death in the street', nevertheless constitute *chet duong* and *chet oan*. In this case, the intensity of violence changed the idea of home, turning it inside out, and resulted in mass graves where people unrelated in kinship terms were enmeshed together.

Being captivated by the memory of the violent death event, the soul experiencing 'grievous death' is unable to depart to the other world until the situation is corrected by the intervention of an external power. This perpetual re-experiencing is conveyed by the idea of 'incarceration' (*nguc*) within the mortal historical drama. The grievance of *oan* and the self-imprisonment of *nguc* describe the same phenomenon: grievance creates the imaginary prison, whereas the prison arrests the grievance and augments its intensity.

One man in a village of Quang Nam province, the village's specialist in death and Taoist rituals, suggested a road accident when he kindly tried to explain the meaning of 'grievous death'. He said that all accidental deaths on the road are tragic, but only some of them result in grievous death, *chet oan*. If a man is driving his scooter at a speed that is not permissible, he is doing it in the knowledge that his action could lead to a fatal accident. If he crashes into a tree trunk and dies on the way to the hospital, his death is not necessarily a grievous one, according to the Taoist master. This man did not intend to die, but he helped to create the circumstances of a possible death. Hence, the death that is circumstantially expected circumvents the cultural category of unjust and grievous death. The road accident of a prudent schoolgirl on her bicycle is, on the contrary, clearly a grievous death. She is not responsible, the master explained, for the tiredness of the overworked truck driver who crashed into her bicycle from behind. She neither created the circumstances of the road accident, nor expected any such tragedy on her usual way back from school. Accidental death in these circumstances was not part of the person's self-awareness, and it therefore induces grievous feelings in the spirit of the dead.

The same logic applies to the condition of war. Whereas soldiers fought the war with a certain awareness of the risk of their activity, villagers supported their fighting without, in principle, having to risk their lives for doing so. The death of armed soldiers was anticipated, whereas the unarmed villagers were expected only to till the soil, raise the pigs and children, and protect their families and village. For these two groups, war death takes on different meanings, and civilian death becomes ritually more complicated to deal with than a soldier's death because of its added meaning of unjustified, grievance-causing death. A large-scale civilian killing in a confined place, such as occurred in My Lai in 1968, is clearly a tragic, unjust event, but its injustice has added meanings relating to a specific cultural understanding of the ethics of war and the morality of memory. This understanding resonates with the legal concept of non-combatant immunity in the theory of justified war, but the 'injustice' of death in Vietnamese conception relates further to the morality and ethics of commemoration.

The My Lai villagers mentioned names of certain old villagers as the most grievous victims of the 1968 massacre, and these names belonged to families whose genealogy was decimated by the violence. A decimated family genealogy provoked the strongest sense of injustice and moral indignation in other communities affected by civilian massacres. A grievous death in this context involves not only the destruction of innocent lives, but also a crisis in the social foundation of commemoration, and the idea of justice implied in the category points to the right to be commemorated and accounted for. According to this culturally specific conception of human rights, the right of the dead to be liberated from the violent history of death is inalienable, and the protection of this right depends on the secular institutions of commemoration.

The concept of 'grievous death' signifies a state of imprisonment within the vexing and mortifying memory of experiencing a violent, unjust event, but it also has a progressive connotation that points to concrete measures against captivity. In Vietnamese conception, the liberation from the incarceration of grievous memory is referred to as 'disentangling the grievance' (*giai oan*) or 'breaking the prison' (*giai nguc*). The work against grievance involves the appropriate intervention of sympathetic others; family or village-based death commemorations and the provision of ritual offerings to the 'invisible neighbours' are two prominent forms of this moral intervention. The commitment to this work of memory, and its demonstration in communal ritual activities was, as mentioned earlier, one of the most prominent changes in Vietnamese villages in the 1990s.

The work of memory is also a collaborative project. It ought to involve not only acts of outside intervention in the form of death commemoration, but also the fateful inmate's strong will for freedom from history. Apparitions such as those of ghosts of mothers and children mentioned earlier are commonly understood as a sign of the growth of self-consciousness and self-determination on the part of the sufferers of grievous historical memory. That the souls of the dead can suffer from the enduring effects of a traumatic historical experience is an established, legitimate idea in Vietnamese moral and cultural tradition. In addition, this idea is firmly present in the eruption of 'commemorative fever', and in the related, forceful ritual revival. The idea is bound up with everyday Vietnamese ritual commemorative practices, which paint the world as a place that the living must share with the dead. In this milieu of interaction with the past, the apparitions in My Lai are more than history's ruins or uncanny traces. Rather, these ghosts are vital historical witnesses, testifying to the war's unjust destruction of human life, with broken lives but unbreakable spirits. The suffering endured by My Lai's ghosts are not the same as those we gloss over as traumatic memory. However, we can imagine that their collective existence is a reflection of the historical trauma the community as a whole suffered.

The political authorities in postwar Vietnam sought to come to terms with the destruction of war with a forward-looking spirit and mobilized the heroism of patriotic and revolutionary sacrifice for that purpose. In recent years, the focus of commemoration in Vietnamese society has shifted from the centrality of heroic memory to the plurality of historical memory. The latter, and its manifestation in recent revivals of ancestral and other commemorative rituals, is based on the notion that the spirits of the dead can suffer from traumatic memories, and the related awareness that the living have an ethical responsibility to help free them from their confinement in a historical trauma. What we learn from this development is, first, that the constitution of political reality is intimately related to the trauma of war, that is, to the question of whether and how the historical trauma is publicly recognized. To understand this relationship, moreover, it is important to recognize that the trauma of war may have different loci and different ways of being dealt with.

The Reality Question

Allan Young notes, with reference to the reality of PTSD in post-Vietnam War American society, that he intends 'not to deny its reality but to explain how it and its traumatic memory have been *made* real' (A. Young 1995: 5–6, original emphasis). Just as Ian Hacking does in his gripping account of the history of multiple personality disorder partly in relation to modern culture's obsession with repressed memories (Hacking 1995: 16), Young disavows interest in the 'reality question' of the object of his investigation. He also makes the plea, however, that his research did not entail 'trivializing the acts of violence and the terrible losses that stand behind many traumatic memories' (A. Young 1995: 6). His primary interest is instead to show how the reality of post-trauma was 'achieved' and 'to describe the mechanisms through which these phenomena penetrate people's life worlds, acquire facticity, and the self-knowledge of patients, clinicians, and researchers' (ibid.). In this light, Young highlights the DSM-III 'revolution' that began in 1974 – the entry of PTSD into the third edition of the *Diagnostic Statistical Manual*, the psychiatric profession's bible. He also details how this stamp of approval was 'inextricably connected with the lives of American veterans of the Vietnam War, with their experiences as combatants and, later, as patients of the Veterans Administration Medical System' (ibid.: 108). If PTSD is partly a 'disease of time', as Young maintains (ibid.), how was the rise of this phenomenon related to the experience and memory of the Vietnam War?

Young considers the above relationship mainly in the institutional settings of veteran care and in terms of the interaction between this institutional establishment and the existing broad psychiatric profession. We may broaden the setting, however. The Vietnam War is commonly referred to as having been a 'traumatic' experience for American society as a whole. According to one commentator, 'The Vietnam War was traumatic not only for those who fought in it but also for those who were strongly opposed to it' (Neal 2005: 79). Americans, Marilyn Young observes, indeed remember the Vietnam War mainly as conflicts among Americans: 'The Vietnam war, in short, was a civil war, but – and this may puzzle Vietnamese, who are currently discovering the extent to which it was a civil war for them – it was an *American* civil war' (M. Young 1995: 516, original emphasis). The radical division of a nation as to the objective and the conduct of a war that it was compelled to fight had a lot to do with how the memory of this war turned into a 'traumatic' memory, and the war's prolific violence against innocent civilians such as the tragedy of My Lai played a major part in provoking and deepening this division. Marilyn Young writes: 'More divisive than any conflict Americans have engaged in since the Civil War, the Vietnam War raised questions about the nation's identity. These questions have not been settled. The battle over interpreting the Vietnam War is a battle over interpreting America and it continues to the present day' (ibid.). It is a widely held view among observers of the post-Vietnam War period in the US that conflicts within society as to the war's purpose and related interpretive battles over the nation's identity were intimately tied to the personal alienation that many American veterans of the Vietnam War experienced on their return home. Furthermore, it is argued that this widespread alienation was partly responsible for the way in which their war experience turned to the etiological event for post-traumatic symptoms (Figley and Leventman 1990). Hence, we may say that the Vietnam War was a traumatic event for many Americans in literal as well as metaphoric senses, in personal as well as collective terms, and that these two separate senses of the term were interconnected in making the event a traumatic memory.

Allan Young's book, *The Harmony of Illusions*, includes an ethnographic description of the institutional setting mentioned above, featuring detailed accounts of the troubling flashbacks and nightmares that torment veterans diagnosed as PTSD patients. In their accounts, social alienation indeed appears to be a major issue. Moreover, Young was surprised to discover also that veterans' troubled memories of the combat experience were not always related to combat. In the case of Brian Murray, whose PTSD diagnosis Young introduces (A. Young 1995: 149–53), the veteran testifies that he could not readjust to society after he left the service and that he experienced a host of troubles with his family and at his job after returning home. He said:

> I had a lot of contact with Vietnamese people as a result of my job [in the military police], and I thought of them as being a very interesting culture. When I came back to the U.S., everything was silly bullshit. Everybody I came into contact with seemed so childish ... The geography looked the same as before, but the people were all clones. (ibid.: 152)

Murray's nightmares return to the place that he had to patrol as a military policeman, a place where captured Vietnamese prisoners and civilians were being interrogated. Murray was later ordered to assist with the interrogations, and this is 'where he has his traumatic experience' (ibid.: 150). In a compelling narrative, Young introduces stories of these complicated lives, told in the treatment unit where the anguish of the veterans is re-enacted in the presence of the treatment staff. The anguish is often of the tortuous mixture of being both a victim and a perpetrator of violence, of the horrors simultaneously experienced and perpetrated by these men.

Young says that his history of the PTSD is not to prove or disprove the truth of the phenomenon – similar phenomena have long been known since the time of the Great War as testified by the career of W.H.R Rivers – but rather to detail how the phenomenon was made publicly truthful in particular historical circumstances, within which he highlights the aftermath of the Vietnam War, and against a particular cultural historical background. This background has been, according to Hacking (1995: 5), part of the development in Western medicine to 'scientize the soul' since the late nineteenth century. Young's ethnography of the development of PTSD is not meant to challenge or trivialize the reality of post-traumatic sufferings; he says emphatically, 'The suffering is real; PTSD is real' (A. Young 1995: 10). In my understanding, Young is referring to the reality of post-trauma as it is experienced by individual veterans and patients – a reality that should not be confused with PTSD as a reality and truth in clinical medicine and diagnostic science. It is the latter, and this alone, that Young makes an object of ethnographic and historical investigation, that is, as a contested reality of truth and as a historically constituted phenomenon.

Conclusion

Young's analytic strategy can be applied to the grievous spirits of war dead in Vietnam. My intention in introducing the accounts of grievous war death is not to prove or disprove the reality of the phenomenon that the souls of the dead can suffer from trauma. Nor is it to use these accounts to make a statement, as do several anthropologists today, about the plural nature of human ontological reality. I have no means to know whether human souls survive the event of death, not to mention if the agony of re-experiencing violent events of the past can torment these souls of the dead. What I do know is simply that this idea, the trauma of the dead, has helped shape the momentous changes that Vietnamese society underwent after the Vietnam War. The idea of 'grievous death' is a deep-rooted cultural category in Vietnam, and the contemporary manifestation of this idea is a product of history, inseparable from the violent history of a long war and rising against the postwar historical background in which people were not able to publicly engage, under the revolutionary politics of memory, with the multitude of broken human lives and their vital historical traces that did not possess the credentials of the category of heroic death.

The concept of trauma that emerged in postwar Vietnamese society is evidently not the same thing as that which developed in post-Vietnam War American society. It is not possible to put the trauma suffered by living bodies and those endured by the souls of the dead in the same category. Beyond the plurality of forms and even the categorical incompatibility between the concepts of trauma discussed in this essay, however, I am not inclined to think that the traumas of war in Vietnam and those in America are entirely unrelated. I believe it is possible to think of these radically diverging forms of human trauma in relational terms, without diminishing the authenticity of each of these forms. The traumatic memories of the Vietnam War among the American survivors of this war, and the memories of violent death among the Vietnamese victims of the war: these two radically different manifestations of trauma have their origins in a common tragedy of human suffering. It is true that they arose from variant historical circumstances and cultural backgrounds. Yet, it is also true that these divergent ways to express what Hacking calls 'a wound to the soul' (Hacking 1995: 4) have a shared origin of destruction that created these wounds in the first place. Perhaps it is this question of common historical origin that our concerns about the trauma of war, including those about their plural nature, ultimately point to. For it is in the process of eliciting the common origin that we come to realize it necessary to contextualize the trauma of war in its proper historical context and, accordingly, to recognize the plurality of human culture to express traumatic memories of war.

The real difference between the two forms of war trauma discussed here is not the disparity between a universally valid scientific culture and a locally meaningful religious culture. It is rather the parochial character of the former versus an orientation towards universalism manifested in the local religious form. The Vietnamese idea of grievous death applies to all souls of the dead, irrespective of their variant origins in terms of national, racial or political belonging. This is how the popular ritual acts addressed to these unfortunate souls do not discriminate the spirits of fallen revolutionary soldiers against the spirits of those who died on the opposite side of the political divide. Furthermore, the inclusive morality and aesthetics of these rituals, as I show elsewhere (Kwon 2006: 172–74), do not discriminate the spirits of the Vietnamese dead against those of foreign combatants. The idea of PTSD is, by contrast, very much parochial in its application. As mentioned at the outset, the genesis of this idea is strictly limited to predicaments and troubles experienced by a particular group of combatants, and by a particular national community. As such, it seldom has shown interest in the sufferings endured by other communities and by individuals standing on the other side of the political divide. The real difference between the two forms of war trauma and between the related two traditions of knowledge is, therefore, the fact that one of them is truthful to the common, shared historical origin of suffering, whereas the other is blind to this truism. The latter is part of what we call the modern clinical scientific tradition.

Acknowledgement

The research for this article has received a generous support from the Academy of Korean Studies (AKS-2010-DZZ-3104).

References

Bao Ninh. 1993. *The Sorrow of War*. London: Secker and Warburg.
Caputo, P. 1977. *A Rumour of War*. London: Macmillan.
Figley, C.R., and S. Leventman (eds). 1990. *Strangers at Home: Vietnam Veterans since the War*. New York: Routledge.
Hacking, I. 1995. *Rewriting the Soul: Multiple Personality and the Sciences of Memory*. Princeton: Princeton University Press.
Kwon, H. 2006. *After the Massacre: Commemoration and Consolation in Ha My and My Lai*. Berkeley: University of California Press.
——. 2008. *Ghosts of War in Vietnam*. Cambridge: Cambridge University Press.
Neal, A.G. 2005. *National Trauma and Collective Memory: Extraordinary Events in the American Experience*. New York: M.E. Sharpe.
Tai, H.-T.H. (ed.). 2001. *The Country of Memory: Remaking the Past in Late Socialist Vietnam*. Berkeley: University of California Press.
Taussig, M. 1987. *Shamanism, Colonialism, and the Wild Man: A Study in Terror and Healing*. Chicago: University of Chicago Press.
Templer, R. 1998. *Shadows and Wind: A View of Modern Vietnam*. London: Abacus.
Young, A. 1993. 'W.H.R. Rivers and the Anthropology of Psychiatry', *Social Science and Medicine* 36: ii–vii.
——. 1995. *The Harmony of Illusions: Inventing Post-traumatic Stress Disorder*. Princeton: Princeton University Press.
Young, M.B. 1995. 'The Vietnam War in American Memory', in M.E. Gettleman, J. Franklin, M.B. Young and H.B. Franklin (eds), *Vietnam and America: A Documented History*. New York: Grove Press, pp.515–22.

Notes on Contributors

Joan Bestard is Professor of Social Anthropology and director of the research centre on Kinship and Family at the University of Barcelona. His research interests include kinship and religion, and he is currently engaged on a research project concerning religion in south-east Poland. Among his recent publications is *Familias* (2012).

Michael Blume currently lectures in religious studies at Cologne University. His research has focused on theories of religion in the brain sciences (the so-called 'neurotheologies'). His current work is concerned with the evolutionary potentials of religiosity, looking at the complex workings of religious communities augmenting birth and survival rates (and thus evolutionary success) in comparison to their (more) secular neighbours.

Simon Coleman is Chancellor Jackman Professor in the Department for the Study of Religion, University of Toronto. He has carried out fieldwork on charismatics in Sweden, England and Nigeria, on creationists around England, and on pilgrims to the English shrine of Walsingham. He has previously been editor of the *Journal of the Royal Anthropological Institute*, and he is currently co-editor of *Religion and Society: Progress in Research*.

Maria Coma trained at the Department of Cultural Anthropology of the University of Barcelona and at the Ecole des Hautes Etudes en Sciences Sociales in Paris, and is currently based at the University of Barcelona. She has done fieldwork in Nepal and India among Tibetan immigrants and in a Catholic charismatic church of Barcelona.

Tom Inglis is Associate Professor of Sociology at University College Dublin. He has written extensively about Irish culture, particularly in relation to religion, sexuality, the media, globalisation, love and the meaning of life.

He has published numerous articles and books in these areas, including *Moral Monopoly: The Catholic Church in Modern Irish Society* (1987), *Lessons in Irish Sexuality* (1998), *Truth, Power and Lies: Modern Irish Society and the Case of the Kerry Babies* (2003), *Global Ireland: Same Difference* (2008), *Making Love: A Memoir* (2012) and *Love* (2013). He is also the co-editor of Religion and Politics (2000).

Timothy Jenkins is Reader in Anthropology and Religion at the University of Cambridge. He was trained at the Oxford Institute of Social Anthropology and has carried out fieldwork in Britain and France. His interests include theoretical approaches in the social sciences, European ethnography, especially concerning politics and language, and the study of religion, particularly moral uses of scientific discoveries. He is the author of *Religion in English Everyday Life* (1999), *The Life of Property* (2010), and, most recently, *Of Flying Saucers and Social Scientists* (2013).

Heonik Kwon is Professorial Senior Research Fellow in Social Anthropology at Trinity College, University of Cambridge, and author of *Ghosts of War in Vietnam* (2008) and *The Other Cold War* (2010).

Robert N. McCauley is a philosopher of cognitive science and a cognitive scientist of religion. He is the author of *Why Religion Is Natural and Science Is Not* (2011) and co-author (with E. Thomas Lawson) of *Rethinking Religion* (1990) and *Bringing Ritual to Mind* (2002). He is also the editor of *The Churchlands and Their Critics* (1996) and (with Harvey Whitehouse) of *Mind and Religion* (2005). He has been the president of the Society for Philosophy and Psychology (1997–98) and the International Association for the Cognitive Science of Religion (2010–2012).

Marit Melhuus is Professor of Social Anthropology at the University of Oslo. Her most recent book, *Problems of Conception: Issues of Law, Biotechnology, Individuals and Kinship* (2012) explores the incorporation of reproductive technologies in contemporary Norwegian society, addressing such fundamental questions as the relation between individual and society, meanings of kinship, and the role of science, religion and ethics in state policies. She has previously worked in Argentina and Mexico, focusing on economic anthropology, gender and morality. Her earlier publications include the co-edited volumes *Machos, Mistresses, Madonnas* (1996) and *Holding Worlds Together* (2007).

João de Pina-Cabral is Professor of Anthropology and head of the School of Anthropology and Conservation at the University of Kent, Canterbury. He has been academic director of the Institute of Social Sciences of the University of Lisbon (Portugal), president of the Portuguese Association of Anthropology and president of the European Association of Social Anthropologists. He has published extensively on matters related to the house and family, personhood, ethnicity in postcolonial contexts and anthropological theory. He has carried out fieldwork on the Alto Minho (Portugal), Macau (China) and Bahia (Brazil).

Carles Salazar is Professor of Social and Cultural Anthropology at the University of Lleida. He received his PhD from the University of Cambridge and has carried out ethnographic fieldwork in Ireland and Catalonia on cooperation, religion and kinship. He is interested in the cognitive and evolutionary approach to the study of culture from an interdisciplinary point of view, which includes perspectives from the natural sciences and the humanities. His recent publications include *Anthropology and Sexual Morality: A Theoretical Investigation* (2006) and the co-edited volume *European Kinship in the Age of Biotechnology* (2009).

Roger Sansi is Ramon y Cajal Senior Researcher at the University of Barcelona. He has worked extensively on Afro-Brazilian culture and religion. His publications include *Fetishes and Monuments: Afro-Brazilian Art and Culture in the Twentieth Century* (2007) and co-edited *Sorcery in the Black Atlantic* (2011).

Jesper Sørensen is MIND*Lab* Associate Professor in the Department of Culture and Society, Aarhus University. He is the author of *A Cognitive Theory of Magic* (2007) and he has published numerous articles on the cognitive science of religion, in particular on magic, ritual and conceptual transmission, as well as more general papers pertaining to theoretical issues within the scientific study of religion. Formerly an International Fellow at the Institute of Cognition and Culture, Queen's University Belfast, Sørensen is currently involved in a number of experimental research projects investigating the effects of ritualized behaviour on human cognitive processes.

Index

❦